OAKWOOD LIBRARY OF RAILWAY HISTORY

Isle of Portland Railways

Volume Two
The Weymouth & Portland Railway
The Easton & Church Hope Railway

B.L. Jackson

THE OAKWOOD PRESS

© Oakwood Press & B.L. Jackson 2000

British Library Cataloguing in Publication Data
A Record for this book is available from the British Library
ISBN 0 85361 551 9

Typeset by Oakwood Graphics.
Repro by Ford Graphics, Ringwood, Hants.
Printed by Cambrian Printers, Aberystwyth, Dyfed.

A notice board from the branch. A wooden notice from the foot crossing near Melcombe Regis station, shown here on display in Clapham Transport Museum.

Front cover: Easton station, a painting by N. Keith Lock based on photographs of the branch scene towards the end of the passenger service.

Rear cover, top: GWR pannier tank No. 4624 shunts at Easton on 30th September, 1961. The remains of the engine shed are behind the engine, the water tower survives to supply the engine of the daily goods train. Now almost 40 years later the background is worthy of note, in Station Road, a genuine red telephone box, a Morris 1000 delivery van, and the corner shop. In the background the petrol pumps of Fancy's Garage, pre-war the home of the Portland Express Buses, now like the railway, the shop, van and garage are items of Portland's history. *C.L. Caddy*

Rear cover, bottom: Saturday 27th March, 1965, fireman Dennis Turner takes a last look at the remains of Rodwell station as Ivatt class '2' 2-6-2 No. 41324 heads towards Portland with the last special passenger train to use the branch. *C.L. Caddy*

Published by The Oakwood Press, P.O. Box 13, Usk, Mon., NP15 1YS.
E-mail: oakwood-press@dial.pipex.com
Website: http://ds.dial.pipex.com/oakwood-press

Contents

A GW & LSWR notice at Melcombe Regis.

The collection of fossils that for many years stood on the platform of Easton station.

J.H. Lucking Collection

'O2' class No. 213 descending around the East side of the island with a Weymouth-bound train. The first coach in the formation is one of the former 'H13' type steam railmotors. The second vehicle is former 'H12' class steam railmotor No. 1, as coach No. 740, the rear two coaches being of the type originally hauled by 'C14' class locomotives.   *Author's Collection*

Acknowledgements

To assemble a work of this nature reference has been made to a great many documents, books, newspapers and other sources. The surviving Minute books of both the Weymouth & Portland Railway and the Easton & Church Hope Railway companies, together with other railway documents at the Public Record Office have been consulted, as have the three principal local newspapers, the *Southern Times*, *Dorset County Chronicle* and *Dorset Evening Echo*. Various transport magazines including the *Railway Magazine*, *Trains Illustrated*, *LSWR Gazette*, and the Great Western Railway staff magazine have also proved valuable.

Previous published works include, *Railways of Dorset*, J.H. Lucking (RCTS), *The Great Western at Weymouth*, J.H. Lucking (David & Charles), *Weymouth Harbour Tramway*, J.H. Lucking (OPC), *The Royal Navy at Portland*, G. Carter, (Maritime Books), *LSWR Carriages, Vol. 1*, G.R. Weddell (Wild Swan), *Locomotives of the LSWR, Vols 1 & 2*, D.L. Bradley, (RCTS).

The assistance of the following organisations is gratefully acknowledged; British Railways Public Relations Departments at both Paddington and Waterloo, Dorset County Archives Department, Dorset County Library Service, Dorset County Museum, Weymouth & Portland Museum services, The Public Record Office (Kew), The Great Western Museum (Swindon), Swindon Public Library, the National Railway Museum, and the Signalling Record Society.

The Local Studies Department of Weymouth library has been of great assistance, in particular Mrs Maureen Attwooll, whose vast knowledge of local history is invaluable. Railway staff, both serving and retired, at Weymouth have been most helpful over the years, as have many Portlanders, including Messrs Edward Andrews, Stuart Morris, and the late Peter Trim, all experts on the Island's history.

Thanks are also due to George Pryer for his work on the track and signalling diagrams and his expert assistance on railway matters. Michael Tattershall also deserves special thanks for much hard work on the manuscript in the early stages. A general index will be available in Volume Three.

I am also grateful to the following for their particular assistance with the work, D.E.H. Box, C.L. Caddy, R.S. Carpenter, E.D.K. Coombe, D. Cullum, R. Diment, P.A. Fry, D.M. Habgood, M. King, F. Larcombe, W. Macey, S.C. Nash, W. Newman, K. Nichols, G. Pritchard, R.C. Riley, P. Short, J. Smith, B. Thirlwall, M. Thresh, R.H. Tunstall, A. Vaughan, G.R. Weddell, J.A.C. West and G. White.

Over the many years occupied by the research for this book it is regretted that K. Bakes, John Blackburn, G.H. Jenvey, Dick Gossling, John Lucking, Eric Latcham, A.B. McLeod, A.J. Pike, S.C. Townroe, Peter Trim, A.E. West and other enthusiasts have taken their final journey without seeing it completed. Therefore this work is dedicated to them, and to all railwaymen involved with the Portland branch.

Finally I should like to thank my wife, herself a Portlander, for her encouragement and help whilst this work was being written.

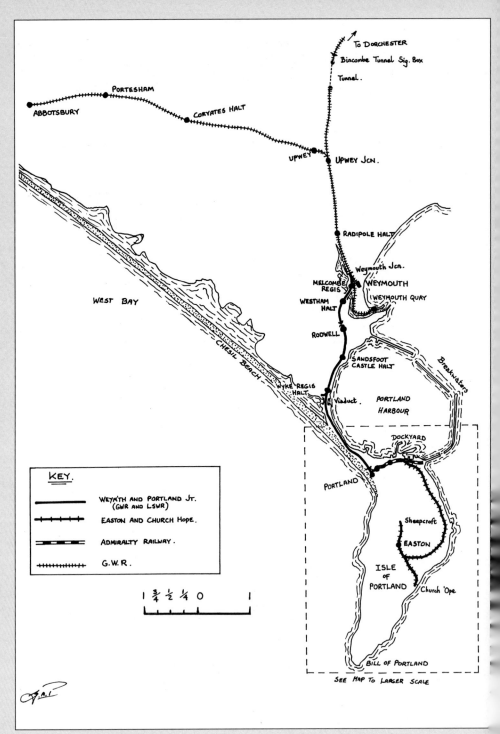

General arrangement map of the railways in the Weymouth & Portland area.

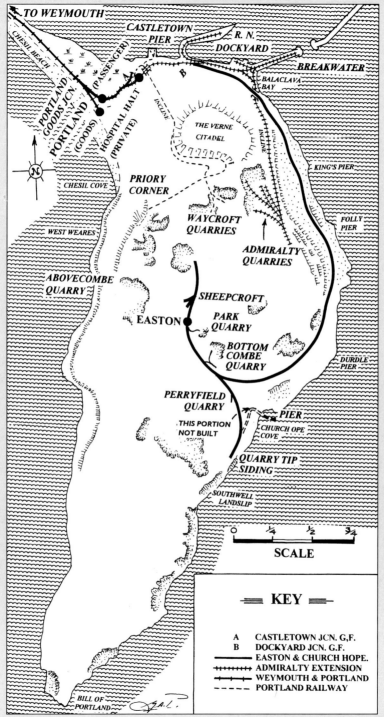

Map showing the general layout of the principal standard gauge railways on the Isle of Portland.

Introduction

This, the second volume of the history of the Railways of Portland, covers the branch from Weymouth of the Weymouth & Portland Railway Company, and the extension to the top of the island constructed for the Easton & Church Hope Railway Company.

The various quarry railways and the Admiralty railways, all of which played an important part in the island's transport history, are covered in Volume One which also includes a brief history of the island and the stone industry (Oakwood Press, 1999).

The Portland Branch linked Weymouth with Portland, and a later extension finally took it to the centre of the Island at Easton. The line was built by two separate companies but was operated jointly as a single unit by the Great Western and the London & South Western Railways, the latter eventually becoming the Southern Railway. The Weymouth & Portland and the Easton & Church Hope companies are each dealt with separately until the latter was completed to form one continuous line, although they retained their separate identities until nationalisation in 1948.

Magazine articles covering the branch have appeared over the years, some trying to cover the entire history in a few pages, some of limited scope and others containing misleading information. The author does not claim this work to be the Alpha and Omega, but research on the material has taken over 30 years, and the author has been dependent on access to such documents as survive supplemented by the memories of those people concerned with the lines. As the years go by the likelihood of new information coming to light becomes ever more slight, and the time has therefore come to close the files and go to print with what is known. It is hoped that this book will meet the requirements of those who seek a general history of the railways and transportation systems of the Isle of Portland.

B.L. Jackson
Weymouth
1999

A postcard on sale at the time the Easton line opened to passenger traffic.

Author's Collection

8

Chapter One

Historical Background
and Early Railway Schemes

Weymouth stands on low land at the mouth of the River Wey and along the shoreline of a bay facing east. There was an encampment at Weymouth during the Bronze Age. The present Borough originated as two separate towns, Weymouth itself on the south side of the harbour and Melcombe Regis on the north side. In 1280 King Edward 1 settled Melcombe Regis on his Queen and granted the Burgesses a Charter of Incorporation which gave the inhabitants the same liberties as those enjoyed by the citizens of London. In the reign of Edward II both towns were granted a market and fair, and during 1571 Queen Elizabeth 1 granted a Charter of Union to the two towns.

Shortly afterwards the first bridge was built across the harbour. There was no bridge before the Union, and there had been constant brawling between the inhabitants of the two Boroughs - mainly over their respective share of the harbour dues. In those days Weymouth was a very busy sea-port, and it is reputed that the Black Death entered the Country through its harbour, brought in aboard a foreign ship.

It was in 1789 that King George III, Queen Charlotte, and the three Princesses came to Weymouth. They liked the place and stayed for three months, returning for varying periods over many years. This gave the town the status of a Royal watering place, and it soon became a fashionable resort.

The arrival of the railway and regular shipping service to the Channel Islands opened the town to the outside world, but holidays remained solely for the privileged classes until late in the 19th century.

Paddle steamer excursions were available after 1848, and until the railway reached Dorchester in 1847 steamers had provided a service between Weymouth and Southampton. A regular steamer service was also operated to Portland before the arrival of the railway and for many years afterwards.

With the introduction of set holidays in industry the residences on the sea front, once owned by Gentlemen, were converted into hotels. In the years between the wars Weymouth became an established holiday resort, and today, during the summer months, the town is packed with visitors. The harbour trade has declined severely, at the time of writing a Summer-only high speed catamaran service to the Channel Islands operates. Most of the mooring space in Weymouth Harbour is now occupied by private yachts.

Much has changed over the years. When the Portland branch was opened Westham hardly existed, Rodwell was the south edge of the town, and only gentlemen's residences occupied the roads to Wyke Regis where the village clustered around the church. The branch passed through open land all along the route, but by 1952 development ran alongside the line all the way to Ferrybridge.

Likewise Portland has also developed, the history of the Island being fully described in Volume One of this work. Cut off from neighbouring Weymouth prior to the opening of a bridge (known as Ferrybridge) in 1839, the only way to reach it was by boat from Weymouth or by way of the ferry provided at Wyke Regis.

9

The Industrial Revolution came to Portland very suddenly with the construction of the breakwater, the convict prison, the railway, and the use of steam power (which advanced the methods of quarrying), coupled with the influx of labour that came with this new technology. The arrival of the ships of the Royal Navy which followed the construction of the breakwater caused great changes in the local way of life.

By the turn of the century the population had reached 15,199, of which 6,587 were either Naval, Military, or prison personnel, and instead of the breakwater forming a shelter for sailing ships, it became a port where the mighty steamships came to collect fuel.

Further changes have taken place in the 20th century. The stone industry has receded in recent years, whilst the dockyard was altered to suit the needs of a changing defence policy, finally closing in 1996. The closure of the Naval air station early in 1999 finally removed a Service link dating back over 150 years, whilst the prison service which arrived to assist with the construction of the breakwater now has three establishments on the island and is the major employer.

* * * * * * * * * * * *

Dorset joined the fast growing railway system on 1st June, 1847 when the Southampton & Dorchester Railway opened to traffic. In 1839 the London & South Western Railway (LSWR) had opened its main line from London to Southampton, the Great Western following with its London-Bristol line in June 1841, and the Bristol & Exeter Railway Company extending this line westwards via Bridgwater and Taunton to Exeter in May 1844. With these lines in place a vast tract of countryside was left ripe for railway development.

As early as 1836 there had been a scheme for a line leaving the Great Western Railway (GWR) at Bath to reach Weymouth via Wincanton, Cerne Abbas, and Dorchester. In 1844 a Salisbury-Dorchester-Weymouth Railway (via Wimborne) was proposed, as was a Bristol & Exeter Company branch from Durston, (just north of Taunton) via Yeovil to Weymouth. The Wilts, Somerset & Weymouth Company, supported by the Great Western, planned to build a line from just west of Chippenham to head towards Weymouth via Frome, Yeovil, and Dorchester, and the Bristol & Exeter therefore decided to terminate its line at Yeovil. The main aim of all these schemes was to reach Weymouth, where a port for the Channel Islands trade could be established.

At the same time a Wimborne solicitor, Charles Castleman, prepared a scheme to construct a line commencing at a junction with the existing London line at Southampton and proceeding westwards via Totton, Lyndhurst, and Brockenhurst, before swinging inland to serve the once-important market towns of Ringwood and Wimborne. Thereafter it curved south to the present site of Hamworthy Junction before proceeding via Wareham, Wool and Moreton to terminate at Dorchester. At that time Bournemouth did not exist and the port of Poole was to be served by a branch from 'Poole Junction' (now Hamworthy Junction) to Hamworthy on the south side of Poole Harbour. This enterprise was known as the Southampton & Dorchester Railway.

Moorsom, the Engineer of the Southampton & Dorchester, considered the hills between Dorchester and Weymouth would create too steep a gradient for a normal railway, and plans were deposited in November 1846 for a branch railway to Weymouth. This would leave the main line at Moreton and proceed along the west side of the present main road via Warmwell, through a 1,200 yds-long tunnel near Poxwell, passing close to Osmington and taking the natural fold of the hills through Sutton Poyntz and Preston, finally crossing Lodmoor to a terminus just below St John's Church, Weymouth, with a short spur for goods traffic linking it to the proposed Great Western station. Although receiving its Act of Parliament no work ever started on this project, which was estimated to cost £190,000.

During that period the Government was keen to have a continuous line of railway along the South Coast between Dover and Plymouth, principally as a means of moving troops quickly in the event of invasion, so Castleman had a hidden agenda to extend the line west of Dorchester to Exeter via Bridport and Axminster. However railway policy and political events, together with the opening of the Wilts, Somerset & Weymouth line directly across his path at Dorchester, finally sealed the fate of Castleman's scheme.

Of the various schemes for a railway to reach Dorchester only two survived the Parliamentary process - the Wilts Somerset & Weymouth, and the Southampton & Dorchester, receiving their Acts of Parliament on 30th June and 21st July, 1845 respectively. Both Acts provided for a junction between the lines at Dorchester. Work on the Southampton & Dorchester proceeded well, all being complete by 11th May, 1847. Following inspection by the Board of Trade on 20th/21st May, the line opened to public traffic on 1st June, 1847.

Meanwhile there was tardy progress on the Wilts, Somerset & Weymouth line, where lack of funds delayed construction. Throughout the counties of Wilts, Somerset and Dorset there were partly completed earthworks. Following the 'Railway Mania' confidence in investment in railway schemes was severely shaken. The Wilts, Somerset & Weymouth managed to complete its line to Westbury in September 1848, by which time the financial circumstances of the company were at breaking point, and construction work virtually came to a stand. On 14th March, 1850, the Great Western took over the assets and commitments of the Wilts, Somerset & Weymouth, Frome was reached in October 1850, and the Salisbury branch opened to Warminster on 1st September, 1851.

Powers to construct branches to Sherborne, Bridport and Weymouth Quay were quietly allowed to slip away, but the lines to Salisbury and Weymouth were seen as a necessary evil to defend broad gauge territory against the LSWR. Eventually Yeovil was reached in September 1856, and finally the line opened to Weymouth on 20th January, 1857.

The actual opening of the railway at Weymouth failed to cause great excitement in the town. Tuesday 20th January, 1857 was a typical dismal January day. The weather was indifferent, and there were no celebrations or civic send off for the first train which departed at 6.15 am hauled by 'Victoria' class 2-4-0 *Otho*. The following GWR train departed at 8.30 am, whilst the first LSWR departure was not until 11.55 am!

WEYMOUTH (1857)

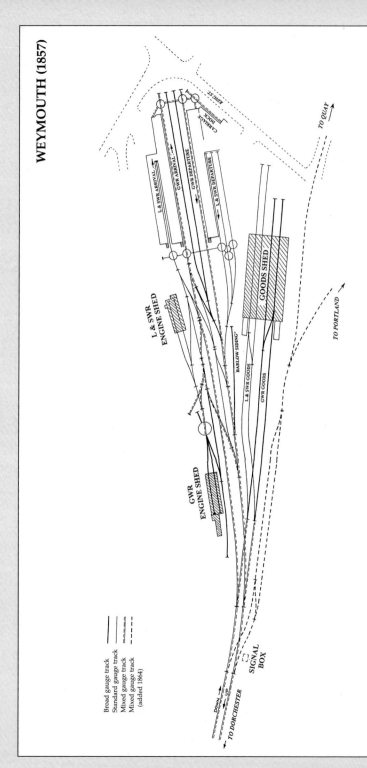

The complex track arrangements at Weymouth as a mixed layout, with the mixed gauge Weymouth & Portland Railway added at the bottom of the diagram.

The *Dorset County Chronicle* commented: 'No salvo of artillery, no band with joyous music announced the fact that Weymouth at last had a railway, and may now be said literally to have entered the path of prosperity'. The *Chronicle* blamed the railway company for the short notice given for the opening of the line. The celebrations to mark the opening actually took place a week later - on 27th January - when there were the usual processions, speeches, and dinners, and a public holiday was declared. For the lucky ones there was a free return trip to Yeovil, 300 complimentary tickets being handed out by the GWR.

The *Western Gazette* remarked:

> It is usual to have such rejoicings on the day of opening, but the railway was so long about, so many rumours were raised that it would be opened next week - the week after, for certain - positively on the 1st proximo, &c. that it is excusable that Weymouth took a whole week to convince itself that the railway was really opened and in operation.

A spur from the LSWR station at Dorchester joined the Great Western line at Dorchester Junction, enabling LSWR trains to run over the GWR into Weymouth. The GWR line was of course constructed to the 7 ft 'broad gauge', necessitating mixed gauge track between Dorchester Junction and the GWR terminus at Weymouth to accommodate the LSWR trains, which were of the 'standard gauge' of 4ft 8½ in. Weymouth station layout consisted of mixed gauge, broad gauge and standard gauge tracks, with all the complications of working for both companies, a situation that was to prevail until the elimination of the broad gauge from the area in June 1874.

Weymouth station was an imposing timber structure built in the Brunel tradition, a glazed roof spanning all tracks into the terminus. The entire structure rested on piles driven into the ground, as much of the railway was constructed on reclaimed marsh land alongside the Backwater. The entire works, including the goods shed and engine shed, cost over £44,000. Apart from the construction of a new engine shed in 1885 on a site well north of the station, the rebuilding of the goods shed, the lengthening of the platforms, and the erection of various signal boxes during the 1876-1890 period, the station changed very little until the removal of the overall roof in 1951.

With the opening of the railway Weymouth prospered and became a cross-Channel port and an expanding holiday resort. London was 169 miles (via Swindon) by the GWR line, whilst the LSWR route via Wimborne and Ringwood was only 145 miles. It also prompted action for a steamship service to the Channel Islands, as Weymouth offered the shortest crossing. Although several short-lived services had operated earlier, the added attraction of the railway connection paved the way for a regular service. Both the LSWR and the Weymouth & Channel Islands Steam Packet Company Limited (acting for the GWR) immediately made plans to commence such a service, the LSWR commencing on 13th April, 1857 and the Weymouth & Channel Islands Steam Packet Company on the 17th.

Following the loss of the PS *Express* in August 1859 the LSWR withdrew from the service at the end of the year , leaving the Weymouth-Channel Islands route entirely to the Packet Company, and later the GWR.

The cross-Channel service established, the next move was for the construction of a railway to the harbour, this opening in October 1865 as part of the Weymouth & Portland Railway, the main subject of this book.

At that time there were demands for the erection of a station in the Upwey area. On 21st June, 1871 a small station was opened on the north side of the railway bridge in what is now known as Old Station Road. With the opening of the Abbotsbury branch in November 1885 a replacement station was constructed at Upwey Junction, opening in April 1886. The original Upwey station then closed and faded into history.

To put the remainder of the county's railways into perspective, the following major developments took place after the opening of the two main lines. In November 1857 the Maiden Newton-Bridport branch opened, and the Dorset Central from Wimborne to Blandford followed in 1860, this later becoming part of the legendary Somerset & Dorset Railway. The Salisbury & Dorset followed in 1864. The West Bay extension to the Bridport branch opened in 1884 and the Swanage branch in 1885. The rapid development of Bournemouth brought more railway development to the area, and the final section of a direct route from Brockenhurst, the Holes Bay Curve, was completed in 1893, putting Weymouth within 142 miles of London.

Likewise in 1900 the opening of the 'Stert cut-off' between Patney & Chirton and Westbury to make the 'Berks & Hants line' a direct route reduced the Weymouth-Paddington mileage to 155. Of the two routes it was very much a case of personal choice, but the LSWR to Waterloo was the fastest. By the early 1900s several daily fast trains reached Waterloo in around 3 h. 10 min. It also gave good connections with the naval ports of Portsmouth and Chatham - a matter of importance to many Portland passengers. On the other hand the GWR provided connections to the West of England, Bristol, South Wales, and the Midlands, and came into its own during the Summer when many visitors made Weymouth their holiday choice. It was also the freight route to the Midlands and the North. This pattern remained until the 'Beeching era' and the closure of most of Dorset's other railways - all well after the closure of the Portland branch.

Today the railway map of Dorset is almost back to where it was in 1847. The eastern and western sections of the Southampton & Dorchester form the principal route to London, and the former Wilts, Somerset & Weymouth line (albeit a shadow of its former self) remains, together with Dorset's first branch line to Hamworthy.

Apart from that portion of the former LSWR main line to the West which skirts through the north of the county, these are now the sole survivors, with 150 years of history behind them.

Chapter Two

The Weymouth & Portland Railway
1861-1865

Stone was a valuable export from the Island. Although two railways existed on the Island - the 'Merchants' and the 'Admiralty' - they were both internal systems designed to transport stone from the top of the Island to the water's edge. There was no way of exporting large blocks of stone other than by sea. It was a heavy and difficult cargo to handle, and the old saying 'To sink like a stone' became an awful truth, for such was the fate of many a good vessel that met bad weather conditions whilst plying the stone trade.

In January 1857 the main line reached Weymouth, and in the same year the first scheme for the construction of a railway to Portland was drawn up. It was to have been 4 miles 2 furlongs and 2¾ chains in length. The proposed route was to leave the main line just outside Weymouth station and run along the Backwater and harbour by means of a massive timber viaduct 1,110 yds long which would have been built slightly to the west of Weymouth's present Commercial Road. At that time Melcombe Regis Gardens and some other quayside buildings did not exist, these being constructed on reclaimed land at a later date. The viaduct was to have curved across the harbour west of the Town Bridge, and having reached the old town side the line was to proceed through the Chapelhay area to Wyke Regis. From there it was to cross the Fleet to the island by means of a second 300 yds-long viaduct, to terminate on the north side of Victoria Square, Portland. On 30th November, 1857 these plans were deposited with the Clerk of the Peace for the County of Dorset at his office in Sherborne.

In a December issue of the *Southern Times* Weymouth Corporation stated that they wished to remain neutral over the proposed Weymouth and Portland Railway, while at the same time reserving themselves a right to oppose the same at any time. The scheme could best be described as a non-starter, and receiving little support, was consequently dropped. The next mention of a railway to Portland was in 1861, when two schemes were put forward. One, promoted by a local company, was for a line 5 miles 9 chains in length. It was to take the route of the line that was eventually built, except that the Fleet was to be crossed to the west side of Ferrybridge, and the toll road crossed on the level before Portland was reached. This line would have terminated at the works of the breakwater at Portland.

The second scheme was for a railway 3 miles 6 furlongs 4½ chains long from a point just north of Weymouth station to Portland Victoria Square, with a 34-chain tramway to connect up with the 'Merchants' Railway' incline at Castletown. A tramway was also proposed to the toll house at Weymouth pier, a length of 1 mile 3½ chains.

Interest was shown by James Aldridge Devenish, of the family of well-known Weymouth brewers. In March of the same year he had written to the Great Western Railway outlining what he called, 'A well digested scheme for a tramway', and he proposed to form a company to construct a tramway between

Weymouth station and the harbour. Mr Devenish, a Director of the Weymouth & Channel Islands Steam Packet Company Ltd who had been operating steamers since 1857, was now striving to obtain much-needed direct communication between ship and railway. His scheme did not materialise, but the proposers joined forces with the proposers of the Weymouth & Portland Railway, and a meeting was held at the Royal Hotel, Weymouth, on Monday 7th October, 1861. The chair was taken by Captain Prowse RN, the Mayor of Weymouth, and during the meeting he called upon Mr Ward, Chief Engineer of the Great Western Railway, to produce the plans of the two lines' railways and give a full account of both.

Scheme 'A' envisaged a line leaving Weymouth Railway terminus to pass straight along the Backwater, crossing the harbour just above the Town Bridge at 'Ferry's Corner'. Scheme 'B' was to cross the Backwater above Arthur's Bridge. Mr Ward personally favoured the first plan, but made it clear that if the inhabitants of the area differed from his opinion, he would not object to the latter.

After much discussion it was finally proposed by W. Thompson Esq.,

> That it is highly desirable to extend the existing railway system from Weymouth to Portland, and the line explained by Mr Ward, crossing the Backwater above Arthur's Bridge, combining a tramway to the Quay to near the Weymouth Customs House, appears to this meeting worthy of support.

The proposal was seconded by Captain Barrington Browne, and carried unanimously. The Reverend Hogarth of Portland made a proposal which was seconded by Mr Richard Reynolds, 'That a deputation wait upon the Directors of the Great Western Railway with a view to obtaining their assistance and co-operation in carrying out the undertaking'.

With the growing importance of Portland as a place of refuge for shipping as a result of the construction of the breakwater, and the need for a quick method of transporting stone from the Island, one would have thought that all would have been in favour of the scheme, but this was not so. In the *Weymouth, Portland and Dorchester Telegram* dated Thursday 28th November, 1861, there appeared a letter from a gentleman who complained bitterly about the interest shown by certain members of the Weymouth Council in the proposed railway scheme. He wished to remind readers of the enormous debt of £18,000 still owing on the harbour, the £12,700 spent on the pier and the £5,000 debt on the bridge, and was worried that the steamers would suffer. He claimed that they carried all the required traffic to and from the Island. The letter concluded, 'Does the town want a railroad to such a place as Portland?'

At a meeting of the Town Council held on 30th December, Alderman Devenish told everybody that a tramway was needed to the harbour, the lack of rail connection causing a serious loss of trade. The GWR was highly favourable to such a scheme, and in fact the late I.K. Brunel had included a tramway in his original plan. Councillor Drew supported the construction of a tramway to the harbour, but considered that a railway to Portland 'would be a decided injury to the town', leading to the development of Portland Harbour as a competitive port. He was not happy to find that both railways had been embodied in the same scheme, but offered every support to a tramway to the harbour provided it was not linked to a Portland project.

It was indeed a clear case of self interest, and explains why the plans were not very well reported in the local paper! Mr Joseph Drew JP founded the *Southern Times* newspaper at Weymouth in 1851, and the following year joined Captain Joseph Cosens as part owner in a small fleet of paddle steamers that operated to Portland. Drew later became Chairman of Cosens & Company.

There is little doubt that the local enthusiasm for the tramway greatly assisted the Portland railway scheme on its way. The Council were very willing to accept the tramway without causing too many problems; in fact, so keen were they that many safeguards one would have expected a local authority to have insisted on being incorporated into the Act of Parliament were not included! After all, the Mayor, Captain Prowse RN, was a Director of the Steam Packet Company, as was Alderman Devenish, whilst Councillor Maunders was the Secretary of the Packet Company. It therefore seemed that the principal Directors of the new Company were mainly interested in the tramway, the Portland branch being a means to an end!

Enthusiasm for the scheme was so great that little time was lost in giving the various legal matters attention. The Board of Trade approved of the Weymouth & Portland Railway Bill, on condition that the line was laid with mixed gauge track. As it stood, the situation was a rather complex one. The GWR line to Weymouth was broad gauge (7 ft) and the LSWR line from Southampton standard gauge (4 ft 8½ in.). The line between Dorchester Junction and Weymouth was of mixed gauge, therefore the construction of the Portland railway as a mixed gauge line would facilitate the movement of both the Great Western and the London & South Western railways' traffic and allow continuous communication throughout both systems.

On 17th March, 1862 the preamble to the Act of Parliament for the railway was passed by the Committee of the House of Commons. There was only one petition against the Bill, this being on behalf of the local steamer company who feared the breaking of their virtual monopoly of traffic between Weymouth and Portland, but this was soon withdrawn and the Weymouth & Portland Railway Act received the Royal Assent on 30th June, 1862. The passing of the Act itself was a landmark in local railway history, for during the same session of Parliament both the GWR and LSWR were fighting a battle in which each endeavoured to reach their rival's principal towns of Bristol and Southampton. Yet at Portland both agreed from the start that it should be a joint mixed gauge line!

The Act itself ran into 16 pages and was very detailed. It contained the usual sections covering the legal aspects of the Company Clauses Consolidation Act, and the Railway Clauses Consolidation Act of 1845, and also sections of the agreement between the GWR and the LSWR as to the working of the line. The company was authorised to raise capital of £75,000 divided into 7,500 shares of £10 each, with borrowing powers of £25,000 once the initial capital of £75,000 had been fully subscribed. It was clearly laid down in the Act that the line had to be constructed to mixed gauge and a junction formed with the Wilts, Somerset & Weymouth branch of the GWR with both broad and narrow gauge rails. It stated, 'The Railway shall not be opened for public traffic unless, and until, the junction is made with both these sets of rails'. A lodge had to be erected at each point where the line crossed the road on the level, and plans of the viaducts across both the Backwater and the Fleet had to be deposited at the Admiralty office for the attention of the Lord High Admiral of the United Kingdom. During the construction of the viaducts a lamp was to be placed to warn vessels of the obstruction, and after completion, a lamp for the guidance of vessels was to be maintained near the centre of each viaduct at the expense of the company. The lamps were to be lit from sunset to sunrise.

With the Act passed, the company was in a position to proceed with the construction of the line, (or 'Railways' as the Act stated), the system being in four sections as follows:

1. The line from the viaduct over the Backwater to Portland Victoria Square.
2. A short section of line between the Backwater and a junction to be formed with the GWR north of Weymouth station.
3. The Harbour Tramway.
4. A short branch from Portland Victoria Square to the foot of the 'Merchants' Railway' incline.

Except for section three (the Harbour Tramway), the other sections were to be operated as one line. However, the Harbour Tramway - although legally part of the Weymouth & Portland Railway - will only be mentioned hereafter when its story coincides with that of the Portland line proper, as it was always worked as a separate unit, and any attempt to go into detail would only add confusion to an already complicated story. (The history of the Harbour Tramway is well documented in the book of that name by J.H. Lucking.)

The first Board meeting of the company was held at No. 6 Victoria Street, Westminster, London on 30th July, 1862. Mr J.A. Devenish was appointed Chairman and Mr A.T.P. Barlow Vice Chairman, whilst Joseph Maunders, Secretary of the Weymouth & Channel Island Steam Packet Company, also become Secretary of the new railway company at a salary of £100 per annum. The first Directors were named as James Aldridge Devenish, John William Barrington Browne, William Henry Purcell Weston, and Thomas Pratt Barlow.

It was agreed at the meeting to give the contract for the construction of the line to John Aird & Son, contractors for public works, of Belvedere Road, London, at an agreed price of £90,000, this sum to include the purchase of the land and other expenses.

Other domestic matters finalised at the meeting included the appointment of Messrs Glyn Mills of London and Messrs Eliot, Pearce, Eliot and Eliot as company bankers. John Fowler and Mr R.J.Ward were appointed as joint Engineers, and Messrs Baxter Rose Norton & Company of London and Richard Hare of Weymouth, joint solicitors to the company.

A notice of intention to hold the first Ordinary General Meeting of the company was placed in the *Southern Times* and several other newspapers, the venue being No. 6 Victoria Street, Westminster, at 4 pm on Monday 29th September, 1862. The appointed time arrived - but the shareholders did not! The statutory hour elapsed, but nobody turned up and the meeting was adjourned until the following day. The next day the story was the same; the shareholders did not appear and the meeting was cancelled. Despite this lack of enthusiasm to attend the company meetings by those who had invested their money in the project, work on the line commenced in the December, sufficient land being purchased to allow the doubling of the line at a future date if required, Rodwell tunnel being constructed wide enough for two tracks.

Mr Crickmay, who owned a brickworks and kilns near the workhouse (later Portwey Hospital) in Wyke Road, Weymouth, brought a case against the company in the County Court. He had been in possession of the works since 1849 at an annual rent of £30, and now the railway was to run right through the middle of the property. The result of the case was that the railway would be built as planned, Crickmay being awarded the sum of £288 8s. 8d. with £10 costs for the loss of the site.

Early in January 1863 the *Southern Times* reported on the building of a bridge over the Chickerell Road, and stated that a locomotive had arrived to assist with the construction work. On 22nd January it reported, 'Strenuous efforts will be made to complete the line by January next, and the contractors are sanguine enough to believe that they will accomplish it by that period'.

The land required for the line across the Marsh at Weymouth had not been purchased by the contractor by February 1863, and the company solicitors were still at loggerheads with the Town Council over the purchase price. Despite the delay this was causing work was being pushed ahead elsewhere along the line towards Wyke Regis, and work had commenced on the Backwater viaduct. The *Dorset County Chronicle* for 5th March reported, 'soon the entire length of the line will be marked by fencing'.

The second Ordinary General Meeting of shareholders was arranged for Thursday 12th March, 1863, again at Victoria Street, Westminster, but, as with those during the previous year, the meeting was postponed to the following day due to lack of support. As before, nobody turned up and the meeting was cancelled. Two days prior to the meeting, the keystone of the bridge crossing the Chickerell Road had been ceremoniously placed in position by Mr Maunder, the company Secretary. As it was also the wedding day of the Prince of Wales - later to become Edward VII - the keystone had been carved with the Prince of Wales feathers as a momentum of the occasion. After the ceremony the usual celebrations took place for the remainder of the day.

The *Dorset County Chronicle* for 7th May reported, 'Piles are being driven in near Ferrybridge, and the work is being carried out at night by the aid of gas lights'. Two months earlier (in March) work had started on driving piles into the Backwater at Weymouth for the construction of the viaduct, but in July certain members of the Town Council had a change of mind and came out in favour of an embankment across the Backwater instead of a viaduct. Two months of discussions on the subject followed, and in September it was agreed to continue with the viaduct.

Meanwhile work was rapidly being pushed ahead on other parts of the line, and by the end of August a considerable amount of track had been laid. The shareholders must have been well pleased with the progress made - although they failed to show it, for the third Ordinary General Meeting of shareholders called for 30th September was again abandoned owing to lack of support.

The keystone at the east end of the bridge over Chickerell Road clearly showing the Prince of Wales Feathers.   *Author*

A report from the Engineers, Messrs Fowler and Ward, stated,

Since December 1862, 193,000 cubic yards of excavation has been completed out of 419,000 cubic yards, the viaduct over the Backwater is nearly complete, and the one over the Fleet at Ferrybridge is half built. It is anticipated that the line will be open for traffic next April or May.

At Portland work was also progressing well. By early October the bridge under Castletown Road was under construction, this being on the section of line that was to meet the foot of the Merchants' Incline, and at the same time it was reported that a local company was building a gasworks on a site adjacent to Portland station.

The *Dorset County Chronicle* for 29th October, 1863 reported, 'The tunnel under the Wyke Road is nearly complete and the temporary bridge used by vehicles and pedestrians will soon be taken away'. It would appear that the construction of the tunnel had been a 'cut and cover' operation, there being only a shallow covering of ground above it. The excavation of the cutting through the Lansdowne Estate, later the site of Rodwell station, had been difficult, requiring several blasting operations. The material removed helped to build up the Marsh embankment.

As the name implies, the Marsh embankment was being constructed on ground that was very swampy by nature, having once been an inlet of the harbour, and it therefore required a great amount of tipping to obtain a solid footing. The embankment, which is 700 yards long and over 50 ft high at one point, is on a rising gradient towards Wyke Road. During November work was progressing day and night to complete it. Landslips were frequent, and a foundation some 15 to 20 feet below the surface of the Marsh had to be created to form a stable base.

Despite the statement made by the contractors the previous January on the completion date, January 1864 saw the line far from complete, although during the first week of the new year a locomotive was reported to be taking materials from Portland to Ferrybridge.

An Extraordinary Meeting of the shareholders was held at the Royal Hotel, Weymouth on Friday 8th January, with Mr J.A. Devenish in the chair. Other persons present included Mr A. Barlow, Captain Barrington Browne, Richard Hare, Phillip Rose, Robert Barter, and Messrs John Aird (both father and son) the contractors.

At last the shareholders were taking a long hard look at the affairs of the company, and after much deliberation, it was resolved that the borrowing powers incorporated in the Act of Parliament should be put to use at once. Later the same day at a Directors' meeting it was agreed to issue bonds at 4½ per cent per annum to the sum of £25,000.

Mid-February saw the station buildings at Portland under construction. The difficulties with the Marsh embankment had been overcome and it was now completed up to the bridge over Newstead Road. The whole of the bank was completed by the end of the month, and it was possible for a locomotive to travel from Portland to the tunnel under the Wyke Road. Work on the three-arched bridge that carried Buxton Road over the line was also nearing

WEYMOUTH & PORTLAND RAILWAY

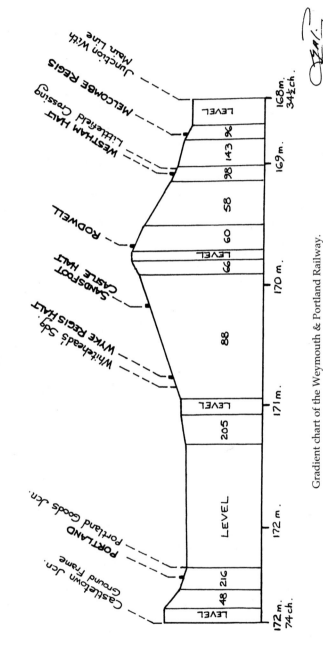

Gradient chart of the Weymouth & Portland Railway.

completion. Despite the successful Extraordinary Meeting held at Weymouth in January, the fourth Ordinary General Meeting called for 31st March at Victoria Street, Westminster,was again cancelled due to lack of support.

On Saturday 5th May, 1864 a train was run over the entire length of the railway, a broad gauge engine with a train of standard gauge wagons travelling from Weymouth to Portland and back in the early evening. The train conveyed Mr Stannard, the contractor's agent, the Weymouth station master, Mr Maunders the company Secretary, and a few friends. With the exception of several small jobs - such as the erection of the telegraph wires - which were completed the following week, the main branch was now ready for inspection by the Board of Trade.

The inspection was carried out on 19th May by Col Yolland, RE., and owing to the line being of mixed gauge, two locomotives were used for the purpose. The GWR provided a broad gauge Gooch 0-6-0 standard goods engine named *Clyde*, complete with carriage, brake van, and horse box. The LSWR supplied a 2-4-0 Beattie well tank named *Hood* and a carriage. Distinguished persons at the inspection included R.J. Ward (Engineer to the Weymouth & Portland Railway), Mr Lane (GWR Engineer), Mr Strapp (LSWR Engineer), Mr Graham (GWR manager), Mr Mears (district superintendent LSWR), Mr Tanner (GWR district manager), Mr Maunders (Secretary to the Weymouth & Portland Railway), Mr John Aird Jnr the contractor, and several other railway company officers.

The Inspector's report was not as enthusiastic as the shareholders had hoped. In general the small bridges along the line were to his satisfaction, but both the Backwater and Fleet viaducts came in for fierce criticism. He stated:

The viaducts are entirely of wood with openings mostly of 20 to 22 feet, and they are both very unsatisfactory structures. The usual beams for these openings are two whole beams placed one above each other, and bolted together. In these viaducts a baulk has been sawn in two parts, and then laid one over each other, with bolts through them. The calculated bearing weight of one of these beams is about 11½ tons, but it is very uncertain what weight one of these half baulks fixed over the other, as now done in these viaducts, would carry. It is quite certain that they are much too weak, that the workmanship is not good, and that sufficient care has not been exercised and defective pieces of timber have been made use of. It is very doubtful whether the viaducts will not require to be entirely reconstructed, as it is not clear whether the piles do not give under the weight of an engine.

The Inspector was also concerned that other beams and tie rods were missing from the structure. Of equal concern was the shunting and signalling arrangements at Portland Junction. In fact, it would appear that no arrangements had been made, and the old adage 'It will be alright on the night' was going to be the order of the day! Col Yolland insisted that the existing signalling required alteration, and to be brought together at a properly covered 'stage' at the Junction and properly interlocked. The distance of 600 yards between the Junction and Weymouth station was far in excess of that considered safe to reverse a passenger train, and that matter required attention.

At Portland the Inspector was not satisfied with various aspects of the work,

. . . some of the sidings leaving the main line are only constructed for the broad gauge and others only for the narrow. In all cases the mixed gauge should be completed to avoid danger by the presentation of the narrow gauge facing points to a broad gauge train and converse.

Adequate accommodation is not provided at Portland station for two companies to work traffic independently of each other. It is quite possible that enough has been done to enable one company to work the local traffic between Portland and Weymouth, but the GWR and the LSWR companies will probably both propose to work their regular trains, and also excursion trains on to Portland within a short interval of time of each other. A covered platform for each company will eventually be required of a greater length than the existing platform, and also additional sidings for the reception of carriages.

If however it is intended by these companies to make Portland their terminal station instead of Weymouth it is very questionable whether they should bear a portion if not the whole of the cost of adapting this station for a terminal station, and in that case an engine turntable would be required.

It is clear from the foregoing comments that Colonel Yolland was either not fully informed of the operational set-up planned by the joint companies or he suspected that, as at other places where both companies came into contact, there could be problems. Separate accommodation for both companies was never provided and neither was the turntable, and other improvements were slow to appear over the years. Furthermore, following the opening of the line the relationship between the two operating companies was good considering the cut and thrust of competition and the sharing of accounts!

As with all good Board of Trade reports, an excellent description of the line's construction is given.

The width of the line at formation level is 10 feet; it is constructed of the mixed gauge, and the space between the main line and the sidings is 6 foot. It is laid with flat bottomed rails weighing 62 lbs per linear yard in lengths of 18, 21 and 24 feet. No chairs are used as the rails are placed directly on transverse sleepers, 1 ft 9 in. apart at the joints and from 2 ft 8½ in. to 2 ft 9½ in. apart between intermediate sleepers. The rails are secured to the sleepers by two fang bolts through the sleepers near the joints, and by fang bolts and screws to the intermediate sleepers. The joints of the rails are fished with a plate on each side of the rail and by four bolts with screw nuts. The sleepers are of Baltic timber, not creosoted, 10 ft 11 in. long by 10 in. by 5 in. rectangular. The ballast is partly broken stone and partly shingle and sand said to be 1 foot deep below the undersides of the sleepers.

Following his findings the Inspector refused to sanction the opening of the line until work was duly carried out on the viaducts and some of the other points he had raised, and a second inspection took place on 6th August, 1864, when he found that some strengthening of the viaducts by the addition of extra piles and timbers had been carried out, but few of the other defects had received much attention. The fencing he had requested on the seaward side of the line across the causeway had only been erected in places, and the additional fang bolts had not been fitted to the track, and most important of all, the signalling at Portland Junction was still incomplete! It would appear that the railway companies had not yet come up with a satisfactory method of working trains between the Junction and the station, and two suggestions were made by the Inspector; to remodel Weymouth station and change over the positions of the passenger station and goods yard, or alternatively station accommodation should be constructed for Portland trains to the west of the goods yard, but he admitted that either would be very inconvenient and expensive.

By now the whole affair was becoming a farce. A shareholders' meeting held on Friday 30th September was a failure, as once again few people put in an appearance - despite the fact there were several important issues overshadowing the future of the railway. It had become an accepted fact of life for this company that the shareholders simply left the Board of Directors to act without their authority or backing, but it could be argued that London was not the ideal location for the meetings of a local company. There was a train service between Weymouth and the Capital, but it was not the easy, quick and comfortable journey it is today.

On 1st October a special train conveying Captain Mangles, Chairman of the LSWR Board of Directors, and other officials, travelled over the line, but no trains were run for the general public. A month went by, and the local population was getting a little frustrated by the delay, the *Dorset County Chronicle* commenting 'No information can be gleaned as to when this line is to be opened. The public think sufficient time has elapsed for the two companies to arrange a service for the line'. A public meeting was held, attended by about 200 persons, the object being to discuss the best course of action to adopt in order to secure a speedy opening of the line.

The half-yearly report of the LSWR offered an explanation for the delay:

The Directors regret that they are unable to announce the opening of the Weymouth & Portland line, in consequence of fresh difficulties having arisen between the promoters and the GWR as to the Weymouth station, the line having to be worked jointly by the GWR and the LSWR. It will be seen at once that the action of the one company has been impeded by the inability of the other to commence traffic.

The reason for the delay in opening the line was now obvious. A disagreement had occurred over accommodation for Portland trains at Weymouth station, the dispute being over the interpretation of the Act of Parliament regarding the arrangements made in March 1862 between the GWR the LSWR - an agreement confirmed by the Act.

It had been agreed that the line be maintained, managed, and worked jointly by both companies on a perpetual lease from the Weymouth & Portland company, who retained ownership of the line. Now a situation had arisen where all three parties were in disagreement as to its operation.

The Weymouth & Portland considered it was not obliged to provide a separate station at Weymouth, and considered that the existing Great Western station was suitable for the accommodation of Portland traffic. This was contested by both the GWR and the LSWR, the latter stating that the local company should provide its own station. Demands by the GWR that payment should be made for the use of existing facilities were also resisted.

Owing to the disagreement between the GWR and the LSWR, the Directors of the Weymouth & Portland desperately approached the Board of Trade with a novel suggestion for permission to open the line if the Great Western would give an undertaking to operate the broad gauge only. This was refused, on the grounds that, the line being mixed gauge, sanction could only be given for the working of the entire line! For a whole year the dispute over arrangements at Weymouth station continued, the line lying disused.

The argument eventually went to arbitration, which was presided over by Capt. Galton. His ruling was that the Weymouth & Portland company could use Weymouth station and pay the GWR £2,600 for the accommodation provided. It was also to pay £3,175 for land and works carried out by the GWR where the Portland branch joined the main line.

This ruling did not, however, bring about a prompt opening of the line, as now all three companies argued over the exact details of the arrangements. Throughout this time of waiting and argument the Harbour Tramway had been completed and was ready for the operation of horse-drawn traffic, but it had to remain out of use by virtue of its legal position as part of the Weymouth & Portland Railway, no working being allowed until the Portland branch itself was open.

The dispute was eventually settled in September 1865, and early in October the Board of Trade agreed to the working arrangements. Goods traffic commenced on 9th October and timetables were issued giving notice of an impending passenger service of 11 trains each way on weekdays and six on Sundays. The single fares were to be 6*d*. first class, 4*d*. second class, and 3*d*. third class, with return fares of 9*d*., 6*d*. and 5*d*. respectively.

Monday 16th October, 1865 saw the long awaited railway in full operation. The first passenger train departed from Weymouth at 7.30 am, with Beattie 2-4-0WT *Nile* hauling six 4-wheeled coaches. Apart from railway officials and a Borough Police sergeant, few took advantage of this first train, although later trains were well filled, and many people went to the lineside to watch the trains pass by.

The opening did not cause the great excitement that had heralded the opening of many railways. The committee formed the previous year to attend to the celebrations had doubtless given up in despair, and even the local papers were not over-enthusiastic about the event. The *Dorset County Chronicle* reported, 'After many vexatious delays, the Weymouth and Portland Railway was opened on Monday last'. It then carried three columns which outlined the history of the line to date. The *Weymouth, Portland and Dorchester Telegram* stated,

It has been truly said that all earthly things must have an end, and such is at last happily the case with the doubts respecting the Weymouth and Portland Railway. The opening of the line for passenger traffic is now an event of the past, the doubts and surmises respecting it being finally settled on Monday morning by the 7.30 train from Weymouth drawn by the good engine *Nile* conveying the first freight of living souls to Portland.

Neither the shunting required at Portland Junction to get a train onto the branch, which occupied 10 minutes and became the curse of the line for the next 44 years, nor the delay in opening for traffic escaped the attention of the press, the *Weymouth Journal* adding:

The long delayed opening of this line of railway is *un fait accompli*. Yes, verily, we have seen it with our own eyes, and therefore we can assure our readers of the fact. For months and months past this line has been laying unused, and it has been going to be opened so many times that people declared they would not believe it would be, without seeing it themselves.

Chapter Three

The Weymouth & Portland Railway
1865 to 1902

The Weymouth & Portland Railway was now, after many trials and tribulations, in operation. To celebrate the opening a public dinner was held at the Royal Victoria Lodge Hotel, Portland, on Tuesday 26th November, 1865. The service offered to the public from the opening was 11 trains each way on weekdays and four on Sundays. After a few weeks of operation the company assessed the traffic situation, and this resulted in the withdrawal of three of the weekday and one of the Sunday trains from the timetable, the management having obviously over-estimated the numbers expected to use the line.

The railway soon had its first Royal visitor. On Monday 28th November, 1865 Prince Alfred arrived at Portland Harbour on board the *Racoon* and stayed the night at the Breakwater Hotel. The next morning he travelled on the new line to Weymouth for a shopping expedition and visited the Royal Hotel, returning to Portland by train later the same day. Within a few weeks the railway was to receive a less welcome visitor, when a severe gale forced sea water over Chesil Beach, severely flooding the railway at the Portland end. This was a recurring problem that inconvenienced the railway for its entire life.

The railway was running smoothly and Portland - an expanding community - was greatly helped by a regular service to the mainland. The company finances were sound, and the agreed rent of £4,500 had been duly received from the Great Western and the London & South Western companies who were jointly operating the line. But the shareholders were still not taking an active interest. A meeting convened on 9th March, 1866 was cancelled owing to lack of support, and a local meeting held at the offices of the Weymouth & Channel Islands Steam Packet Company, South Quay, Weymouth, failed to attract the required number of shareholders, the same being the case at both another London meeting in March 1867, and one at Weymouth in May.

It would appear that apathy had set in, the operating companies having difficulties in getting various important matters resolved. The original facilities at Castletown for the transfer of stone from the 'Merchants' Railway' were found to be unsuitable within weeks of the branch opening, extra siding and crane capacity being required. The same applied at Portland station where the lack of facilities was also causing problems. Added to this the premature deterioration of several buildings was a problem; for example, it was stated that 'The pointsman's hut is already unfit for further use'.

Two years later in November 1867 little had been done. No improvements had taken place at Castletown, and Portland station still required a heavy crane for stone loading. Added to these problems was the fact that the line between the station to Castletown was at that time worked as a horse-drawn tramway, contractors being hired to carry out the loading and unloading and haulage over this section. There had also been much dissatisfaction, and several changes of contractor. At the end of 1867 the Portland Stone Company tendered to supply 10,000 tons of stone for the reconstruction of St Thomas' Hospital,

A very early view of Portland station taken in the late 1860s; standing at the buffer stops is 2-4-0 well tank No. 143 *Nelson*.   *R.C. Riley Collection*

A view of Littlefield crossing taken pre-1880, the gates and crossing keeper's cottage appear in the centre of the photograph, in the foreground is the old wooden toll bridge crossing the Backwater. A double-arm signal can be seen through the lifting section of the bridge. At that time Westham like most of the land to the west of the Backwater was still open country.

Weymouth & Portland Museum Services

London, to be transported at the rate of 9s. per ton, this making the need for improvements more pressing!

Despite the evident lack of support for past meetings, one was successfully held in London during March 1868, and this resulted in several changes in the management of the company. Mr J.A. Devenish retired as Director and Chairman, the chair being taken by J.T. Mills, of Watton, Norfolk. Mr Maunders retired as company Secretary, his place being taken by William Fresher of Westminster at a salary of £40 per annum. The company offices were also moved to 26 George Street, Westminster. This was the end of local involvement in the management of the company; the Steam Packet shareholders had their tramway. The previous year John Aird (Jun.) had been appointed as a Director - after all his family had paid for 75 per cent of the railway! A year after the opening of the line a petition was received from the public asking for a station to be built at Rodwell for the convenience of the people living on the Weymouth side of the harbour. The matter rested until July 1869, when the site of the proposed station was visited by engineers. Early in December the Weymouth Town Council corresponded with the GWR requesting that a date be fixed for the commencement of the building of the new station, to which the GWR replied that construction would start at once. In fact work was actually started in January 1870 by the appointed contractor E.C. Leaman.

The platform was 100 ft long with a booking office and other facilities, access to the station being by means of a footpath from Wyke Road. As the station was built in a deep cutting, no goods yard could be provided due to lack of space and the difficulty of providing road access.

The new Rodwell station opened on Wednesday 1st June, 1870, 14 passengers boarding the 7.35 am - the first train to call bound for Portland. It was a wet day, and on the return journey the train overshot the platform and had to shunt back to unload. There was no official opening ceremony, although several of the company's officials were present to ensure smooth working of the new facilities. With the opening of the new station the ticket platform at Portland Junction (the original name of Weymouth Junction signal box) was taken out of service, as tickets could now be checked at Rodwell.

A minor mishap occurred at Portland during October, when the early train from Weymouth collided with the stop blocks. Little damage was done, and the official explanation was given thus, 'On account of the violent wind and the slippery state of the metals, the driver was unable to bring the train to a standstill at the station'.

It became a regular habit with local people to use the railway line as a footpath, and later the same month (October) a man was killed one evening by a passing train near Ferrybridge. This was by no means the first fatal accident or 'near miss' caused by people walking on the track, and the local paper commented that this was

... one more to add to the list of fatal accidents that have occurred on the Weymouth & Portland Railway through the reckless manner in which persons persist in using the line as a public highway in spite of the sad warnings that have been given on previous occasions.

Rodwell Station

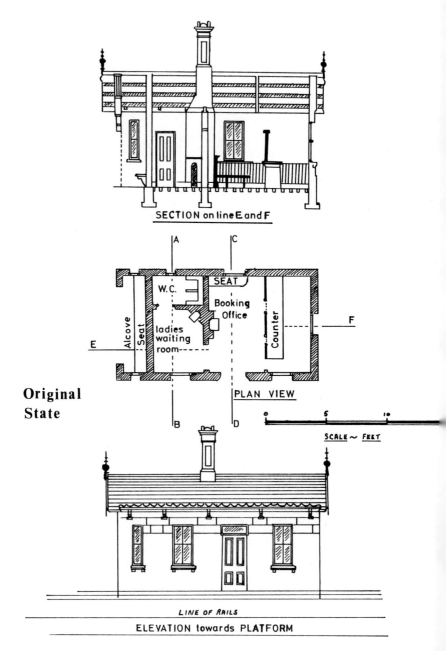

SECTION on line E and F

Original State

A   C

W.C.

SEAT

Booking Office

ladies waiting room

Alcove   Seat

Counter

E

F

PLAN VIEW

B   D

SCALE ~ FEET

0   5   10

LINE OF RAILS

ELEVATION towards PLATFORM

Rodwell. Plans for station as constructed in 1870.

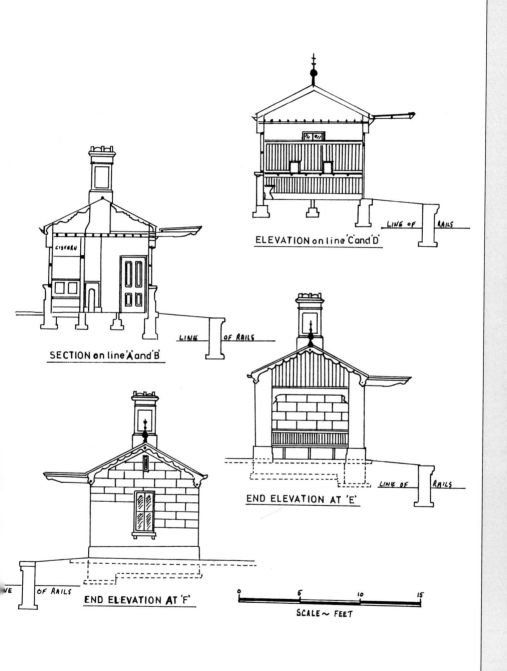

ELEVATION on line 'C' and 'D'

LINE OF RAILS

CISTERN

SECTION on line 'A' and 'B'

LINE OF RAILS

END ELEVATION AT 'E'

LINE OF RAILS

END ELEVATION AT 'F'

OF RAILS

0   5   10   15

SCALE ~ FEET

In fact the railway was ill-fated with accidents in its early days. In 1868 a drunken fisherman had fallen between the engine and carriages, the following year a man committed suicide on the line, and in 1870 a sailor who was walking along the line was struck by a train and received fatal injuries.

On 4th January, 1871 James Aldridge Devenish, first Chairman of the Weymouth & Portland Railway Company, died after an illness lasting many months. His passing at the age of 63 years robbed Weymouth of a personality who had done much good for the town. His family had purchased a local brewery in 1824, and by 1843 James had been admitted as a partner. His election as a Town Councillor for Weymouth followed in 1846. He became an Alderman in 1850 and Mayor in 1852, an office to which he was re-elected for 1853/54. He resigned as Alderman in 1866, and two years later severed his ties with the Weymouth & Portland Railway. He had also been a Director of the Weymouth & Channel Islands Steam Packet Company, and by his own personal efforts and his involvement in local affairs had assisted in getting the Harbour Tramway and the railway to Portland. These projects must have taken their toll on him in later life with failing health.

The close proximity of the line to the sea south of Sandsfoot Castle caused problems on several occasions, and at times resulted in the employment of lookout men and speed restrictions. In January 1872 sixty yards of permanent way sank 12 ft as the result of coast erosion, services being suspended whilst repair work was carried out.

The use of horses on the Weymouth & Portland Railway (except possibly for the movement of wagons in the goods yard) is never mentioned except for the following report of an accident on Wednesday 12th March, 1873, the *Weymouth, Portland & Dorchester Telegram* stating thus:

> On Wednesday night a packer on the Portland Railway, William Harvey, met his death between Rodwell station and the Wyke Road viaduct. Some trucks loaded with wood had been drawn up the incline from Weymouth by horses, and they were to be run down the line on the decline towards Portland. At this point the deceased fell under the moving trucks and was crushed.

From the account it would appear the horse was being used in conjunction with maintenance work on the line.

The eventual fate of the broad gauge on the GWR had become a foregone conclusion even at the time the Portland branch was opened. The conversion of the entire Wilts, Somerset & Weymouth line including branches to standard gauge took place between 18th-22nd June, 1874. This involved alteration to 131 miles of railway excluding sidings.

A great deal has been written concerning the gauge change in general so only the local events require explanation. The majority of broad gauge stock had already been removed from the area by Thursday 18th June, the remainder departing that evening at 11 pm.

The last broad gauge engine then left Weymouth, and with it went the certificates from the station masters at Portland and Weymouth stating that all broad gauge stock was clear of their stations and district. As both the branch and the main line to Dorchester were laid with mixed gauge track there was not the complete disruption to traffic that other areas had experienced, the broad gauge rails on both the branch and the Harbour Tramway being removed more or less at leisure.

As fully documented in Volume One, an agreement was concluded between the Admiralty, the GWR and the LSWR for the construction of a line to join the Weymouth & Portland Railway with the breakwater. This was to add great importance to the Portland branch, for the new line would give direct access to the breakwater for all railway traffic.

Wet weather during 1874 caused an engineering problem on the branch, a slip occurring in the cutting near Ferrybridge. A section of the embankment had fallen in and pushed the line out of position, but fortunately it was noticed by men on their way to work, and the alarm was given before the first train arrived.

There had been many problems with the various cartage agents employed over the years at Portland station, and as with the Castletown Tramway, various contractors had been employed. The cartage matter came to a head in January 1876, when Mr Hodder stated that 'two horses and two men had been constantly employed, and that the work could not be done with less in consequence of the hilly character of the roads'. In consequence a revised cartage rate was agreed, although this was to become an ongoing dispute!

On Wednesday 13th September, 1876 a collision occurred at Portland which could well have had more disastrous results. The 6.45 pm from Weymouth, which on that occasion was not only heavily loaded with passengers, but also had several cattle wagons coupled between the engine and the carriages, was approaching the station when the driver, Henry Tildesley, applied the brakes and found they would not hold, so he repeatedly sounded the whistle. Before any other action could be taken the engine had smashed into the buffer stops with great force. Cabmen and others waiting for the arrival of the train took refuge, afraid that the boiler would burst. Although great confusion was caused there were no serious casualties, mainly cuts and bruises. The engine driver had a lucky escape, suffering only three broken ribs. The first class carriage took the brunt of the collision and was the most severely damaged. Amongst the passengers travelling in the carriage were three doctors, Dr Rae, Dr Barnard, and Dr Parsons, who were getting ready to vacate the train when the collision occurred. Dr Parsons had just adjusted his high-crown Lincoln top hat upon his head when the crash came, knocking him completely off balance. He was thrown head first towards the front of the carriage, the top of his hat striking the wall like a battering ram! The hat crumpled like a concertina and forced the brim down over his eyes, but fortunately he was not injured. After undergoing the indignity of having his hat pulled from his head, and with his vision restored, he assisted his colleagues - who had suffered only minor cuts from falling glass - to render medical aid to the other passengers. The Reverend Ottley left the train in such a hurry, that he forgot to pick up his purse which contained £10 - the proceeds of a church bazaar he had just attended! But all ended well, for it was later returned to him via Mr Puntis, the station clerk, to whom it had been handed for safe custody. At 9 pm a special train was sent to collect passengers who wished to return to Weymouth.

An inquiry into the accident was held in the superintendent's office at Portland on Tuesday 4th November. Those present included Mr G.F. Parsons, Portland station master, Captain Tyler of the Board of Trade, Mr Verrinder, superintendent, LSWR, Mr Graham, Bristol district superintendent, GWR, the driver and guard of the train, and other employees at the station on duty at the time of the collision. The brake system employed on the railway came in for a great deal of criticism. The local press had already offered their views as to the cause, the *Southern Times* reporting directly after the accident:

We believe it will be found the brake power was not sufficient considering the train was heavy, and it is to be hoped for the future cattle trucks will not be allowed on passenger trains. Had they not been connected on Wednesday, the accident would not have happened, for the stoker would have been able to reach another brake, and there would have been more power to stop the train.

A regular passenger wrote with a contrary opinion:

Had the cattle trucks which were on the train between the engine and the brake van not been there I feel convinced that the poor old patched, battered and shaky carriages, which are habitually used on the Weymouth and Portland line would have fared much worse than they did, and, consequently, the passengers as well.

Later a case against the LSWR was brought to Court by a Miss Cozens. This lady had been a passenger on the train, and had been thrown about by the force of the collision. She claimed that there was no transport at the station after the accident, and she had been obliged to walk the ¼ mile to her home although she was bruised and shaken. Medical evidence was given to show that the plaintiff was suffering from concussion of the spine, and it was uncertain when she would recover. Miss Cozens assisted her mother and sister in the running of a boarding school for young ladies at Portland, and her incapacity had made it necessary for them to employ extra staff. The medical expenses and the cost of employing assistance in the school were being sought from the railway company, who criticised several items on the grounds that the claim was exaggerated. However, Mr Justice Hawkins awarded the plaintiff £325.

The shareholders' half-yearly General Meeting was held at Great George Street, Westminster in August 1877, and the following statement of accounts was published.

	£	s.	d.
Total amount of capital created	75,000	0	0
Rent received from the GWR and			
LSWR for the total length of five miles of line	221	17	6
Available balance to be paid as dividend	1,184	3	10
The Board recommend that a dividend of	4	7	8
per cent per annum for the half-year be declared.			

The cost of the dividend would amount to a total of £1,640 12s. 6d. which left a balance of £243 11s. 4d. to be carried forward to the next half year.

A second serious case of brake failure occurred at Portland station on Sunday

23rd December, 1877, when the 9.30 am train from Weymouth failed to stop and ran into an empty coach already standing in the platform, causing damage to vehicles and minor injuries to eight passengers. Curiously, few details of this incident were reported in the local press at the time.

This time it was a Great Western train at fault. Following the previous accident a form of continuous brake known as 'modified Fay's Brake' had been fitted to the stock in use since September.

The brake involved in this accident was mechanically operated by revolving rods under the coaches, a universal coupling and bar joining each vehicle. The guard, by turning his brake wheel, applied brakes to all vehicles fitted. Slackness in the joints made the system somewhat imperfect, and it had the basic weakness of relying on action by the guard as soon as the driver blew his whistle.

The train at Portland consisted of a set of five coaches all fitted with the brake and with a brake van each end, but unfortunately two extra coaches not so fitted were placed between the engine and the remainder of the train. Therefore the term 'continuous brake' must not be confused with the vacuum brake which become common during the 1880s and provided a brake controlled from the locomotive and operative on all vehicles. After hearing evidence from all concerned in the accident and other interested parties, the Board of Trade Inspector Colonel W.Yolland could find no fault with the rolling stock. The driver, Charles A. Acourt, received some of the blame for approaching the station at too great a speed, but guard Benjamin Mantell was also condemned for failing to apply the continuous brakes with which the train was fitted.

The modified 'Fay's' brake did not escape criticism. This system was operated by a wheel put into gear by the guard in the rear brake van before the start of the journey, the guard having first to put the wheel in the van at the other end of the train out of gear. If the guard forgot to carry out this procedure he could turn the wheel many times before discovering it was not in gear, as it took about 20 turns to operate the brakes.

The report also mentioned that part of the brake mechanism was found on the railway the following day some 1½ miles from the station. It concluded,

This gives rise to a suspicion, which almost amounts to a certainty, that it must have been carried there for the purpose of supporting the statement that the continuous brakes had become defective and failed to operate when required to do so.

On 1st February, 1878 the LSWR took over the running of the service, the *Southern Times* reporting that 'a new train had commenced running on the line and has two brakes at each end!'

Although by that time Weymouth had become an established cross-Channel port, the GWR was in negotiation over the use of the new Admiralty breakwater at Portland for its shipping services as opposed to Weymouth Harbour. At the time an Act of Parliament for the GWR to operate its own steamship services was being progressed, and it received the Royal Assent on 13th July, 1871. This empowered the GWR to 'own and operate steamers between Weymouth and/or Portland, the Channel Islands, Cherbourg and St Malo, and between Milford Haven, Cork and Waterford'.

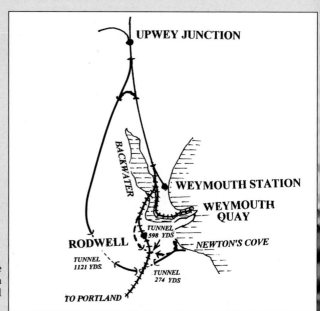

Plans for branches to serve the proposed dock schemes, within the vicinity of the Portland branch.

UPWEY JUNCTION

BACKWATER

WEYMOUTH STATION

WEYMOUTH QUAY

TUNNEL 598 YDS.

RODWELL

NEWTON'S COVE

TUNNEL 1121 YDS.

TUNNEL 274 YDS.

TO PORTLAND

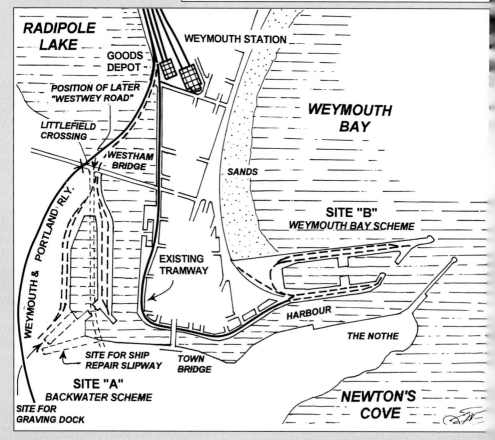

RADIPOLE LAKE

WEYMOUTH STATION

GOODS DEPOT

POSITION OF LATER "WESTWEY ROAD"

LITTLEFIELD CROSSING

WESTHAM BRIDGE

WEYMOUTH & PORTLAND RLY.

WEYMOUTH BAY

SANDS

SITE "B"
WEYMOUTH BAY SCHEME

EXISTING TRAMWAY

HARBOUR

THE NOTHE

SITE FOR SHIP REPAIR SLIPWAY

TOWN BRIDGE

SITE "A"
BACKWATER SCHEME

SITE FOR GRAVING DOCK

NEWTON'S COVE

In the event, affairs at Milford took precedence, and the Portland scheme was left in abeyance until 1875 when the GWR approached the LSWR (who had been involved in the 1871 discussions), with the suggestion of a joint service between Portland the Channel Islands and France. This time the LSWR declined.

During the late 1870s facilities at Weymouth Harbour had improved, but the lack of space had given rise to many problems, and in January 1883 Captain T.S. Leckey, the Great Western marine superintendent, made known his disapproval of the situation. In his opinion Portland was the answer to his problems, there being sufficient space there to develop the facilities required. In a report drawn up shortly after he took office, he suggested an 'L' shaped pier running out into the harbour from the existing Admiralty coal depot, and as a railway already connected the Portland branch with the breakwater, he saw little difficulty in adapting the line to carry passenger traffic. Captain Lecky estimated the entire cost of this project to be around £30,000 to £35,000. The main disadvantage of this scheme was that it was suitable only for the volume of traffic available at the time and left little scope for further expansion. As an alternative, the Captain set forth a project that was much more significant and far sighted. An area known as 'The Mere' lay in the south-west corner of Portland Harbour, this presenting an open site that could be developed as required to deal with increasing trade. It also had the advantage of being near the existing Portland station. He considered that for £50,000 two piers with cranes and buildings, a slipway and repair shops could be built, adding that 'the abundance of stone at hand and the Chesil Beach affords an unfailing supply of shingle for concrete, which would assist in the construction work'.

The latter plan was given enough serious consideration for provisional approval to be obtained from the Board of Customs for a harbour at 'The Mere', and trial bores for foundations were made. The final estimated cost of the plan was about £108,000, and in all probability it was this large sum which caused it to be dropped.

Early the following year two plans were produced to improve facilities at Weymouth. One was for a dock and dock basin to the north of the existing passenger pier, on a site now occupied by the Pavilion Theatre. The other scheme, which could have affected the Portland branch indirectly, was for the construction of a 10 acre dock on a site in Weymouth Harbour - later reclaimed as Westwey Road and part of the gasworks site - with repair shops and a dry dock, which would have extended over the whole area covered until recent years by the Sidney Hall and Football ground. The rail connection for the scheme was to cross the Backwater alongside the Portland Railway's existing viaduct to join the branch adjacent to the goods shed at Weymouth station.

May 1885 saw the departure from Portland of Mr George Francis Parsons who had been the Island's station master for the past 14 years. He moved to Swanage upon the opening of the branch from Wareham, becoming the first station master there. Whilst at Portland his job had carried the high sounding title of 'Superintendent of the Weymouth & Portland Railway'. His place was taken by Mr George Jeans, who came from the Weymouth Goods Department, this appointment at Portland earning him an annual salary of £130.

Above: Rodwell station master H.G. Day, note the W&PR badge worn on the hat.   *Author's Collection*

Above and below:
Weymouth & Portland Railway buttons, as worn on uniforms by the staff of the branch.   *Author*

Passenger guard Howe wearing the uniform of the Weymouth & Portland Railway Company.   *Author's Collection*

A special train running from Weymouth to Portland late in the evening of August Bank Holiday Monday 1885 smashed through the gates at Littlefield Crossing, the keeper having forgotten the 'special' had been arranged and failing to open the gates. This was not the first time the gates had been demolished! In July 1871, the gate keeper cleared his signals for the 8.30 am from Portland without opening the gates, with the inevitable result that the train smashed through them. The keeper then panicked, locked his house and ran off - although he later returned to the scene of the accident. It transpired that this was not the first time he had caused an accident to happen. Human error such as described could not have happened had the gates and signals been interlocked, a safety feature seldom employed in the early 1870s.

Another demolition job on the gates occurred in 1876 when an LSWR goods train bound for Portland left Weymouth before its booked time. The crossing keeper was walking along the Backwater viaduct towards the crossing to open the gates, but unfortunately the train overtook him and arrived at the gates first with the inevitable destructive results. During 1890 an elevated ground frame with fully interlocked signals and crossing gates was installed at Littlefield Crossing, and as Westham was by that time a fast developing part of the town, the improvements were well timed.

During 1891 a large factory for the manufacture of torpedoes was built on a site adjoining the branch near Ferrybridge, rail access for the supply of raw materials and transportation of the finished product being achieved by a private siding authorised in May 1891. The Whitehead torpedo had been developed by Robert Whitehead, a British engineer who had emigrated and set up a factory at Fiume in Austria during the mid-19th century. The Admiralty became very interested in the invention, carrying out extensive tests, and after evaluating its potential as a weapon of defence, decided to contact the company and inform them that if a contract was signed for a very substantial order for the torpedo, they would be required to set up a factory in Britain. The site chosen at Wyke Regis was ideal, not only because it offered ready-made rail access but also had the adjacent waters of Portland Harbour in which the various designs could be tested.

The rapid development of traffic on the branch had now outstripped the original Portland station facilities. During 1890 94,214 passenger journeys were made and 31,182 tons of goods and minerals handled. The platform was extended by 100 ft to a length of 276 ft in February 1891, making it capable of accommodating eleven 4-wheeled coaches. A month previously the Portland Local Board (the forerunner of Portland Urban District Council) complained to the railway companies that

> . . . owing to the increase of the goods and passenger traffic to Portland, and to the growing importance of the Island, the present arrangements for railway communication between it and London and other places are quite insufficient and greater facilities for the same are required, further, the present station accommodation at Portland is unsatisfactory and deficient in consequence of which the use of the station is often attended with inconvenience and danger to the public.

Replying in the manner of a modern day business which enjoys a monopoly, the railway companies argued that the branch trains made

An early view of the Backwater viaduct looking towards 'Portland Junction'; just to the right of where the viaduct joins the sea wall a raised structure can be seen, this would appear to be the 'raised lever frame' required by the Board of Trade at Portland Junction.   *Author's Collection*

A '2021' class locomotive crosses the old viaduct with a train of four-wheelers bound for Portland, taken not long before the rebuilding of the viaduct, strengthening work to the viaduct can clearly be seen under the locomotive.   *J.H. Lucking Collection*

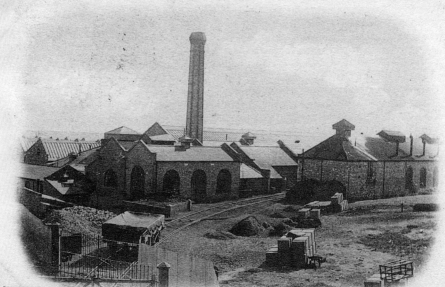

TORPEDO WORKS. WYKE REGIS, NEAR WEYMOUTH.   The 'Progress' Series 133. T. H. S. & CO. B. & C.

A turn of the century view of Whitehead's private siding.   *Author's Collection*

convenient connections at Weymouth with four trains each way to London via the GWR route, and six up and seven down via the LSWR route. Improvements had also been made to Portland station, with extensions, alterations to the goods yard and improved signalling. Although all these statements were correct, the fact remained that the first departure from Portland was not until 7.30 am and, assuming everything went alright, a connection could be made with the 8.30 am train to London, which arrived in the city a little late for businessmen.

What could well have been a serious accident occurred on Sunday 6th November, 1892. The 4 pm train from Portland, hauled by 'O2' class locomotive No. 180, was crossing the Backwater viaduct and only had about 50 yards to go to clear it when the engine and five of the six coaches dropped inside the left-hand rail and ran along the baulks of timber. The cause was faulty rail fastenings, which had allowed the rail to bow out of gauge. Fortunately the train was travelling very slowly at the time and stayed upright, coming to a halt almost immediately with the engine and three of the coaches clear of the bridge. None of the 30 to 40 passengers on board came to any harm, but services were suspended until 7 am the next morning to enable engineers to remove the train and replace the damaged rails.

On Saturday 6th February, 1892 George Jeans, Portland station master for the past seven years, died after being taken ill several days earlier with influenza. His place was taken the following month by Mr James Laver, who for the previous 15 years had been station master of the GWR station at Shepton Mallet.

The platform at Rodwell was extended during January 1894, for by then the Rodwell area was rapidly expanding and more passengers were travelling between Weymouth and Portland. By this date passenger traffic through to Portland was increasing considerably. The facilities at Portland station - still far from ideal - were improved early in 1896 when a wall and cover were constructed on the west side of the station to protect the platform and the waiting passengers from the elements. The platform was resurfaced at the same time.

In that year alone (1896) 291,349 tickets were sold at Portland, of which 158,647 were returns, whilst 13,413 tons of general goods, 43,115 tons of mineral traffic, and 238 wagon loads of livestock were handled at the station. Some of the increase in passenger traffic was accounted for by the large amount of work being carried out on the Island. The construction of the second breakwater had commenced, and this, together with other projects both within and without the breakwater area, created much employment. Consequently more men were travelling between Weymouth to Portland during the early morning and late afternoon, prompting Messrs Hill's (the contractors) to request a special workmen's train. This commenced running on Monday 14th February, 1898, leaving Weymouth at 6 am and returning from Portland at 6 pm at a return fare of 4d. However, this special service was short lived, lasting only until Thursday 7th July. The precise reason for its withdrawal is not known, but a note in the local paper stated that Hill's was considering using a steamer to collect the men.

Complaints concerning the train service continued to appear in the local press, John Merrick Head JP (retired Town Clerk of Reigate and now owner of

The original Backwater viaduct viewed from the west side of the Backwater, in the background many well known buildings, to the extreme left stands Weymouth station Goods shed.

British Railways

A view taken about 1900. An '02' class fitted with its original stove-pipe chimney crossing the viaduct with a Weymouth-bound train. The leading vehicle is a LSWR six-wheel 30 ft passenger brake van.

Adrian Vaughan Collection

Pennsylvania Castle) who was a member of the Dorset County Council writing many letters concerning its inadequacy, and in December 1898 a petition from the Dorset County Council was sent to the Board of Trade protesting about the conditions at Portland. They complained that the sidings at Portland station were so much blocked through the excess of goods traffic that the passenger platform was constantly used for the unloading of cattle, sheep, Naval supplies and other materials, and that the narrow platform was often so crowded that it was difficult to move along it or to pass out of the station, so that the passengers were in imminent danger of falling onto the lines of rails on either side. In the same year Mr Merrick Head complained to Parliament that the New Works Bill for the docks scheme would provide no improvements for the branch.

The *Southern Times* for 7th January, 1899 referred to the previous Monday (the 2nd), when the 7.35 am train from Portland started at 8.17, the unfortunate passengers being left shivering in the booking office or on the platform for three-quarters of an hour! In the evil-smelling waiting room no attempt had been made to light a fire until after 7.30. At Weymouth the usual shunting was anticipated, but a strange thing happened. The railway company had a pilot engine, which they fastened to the other end of the train and brought it into the siding without any shunting. The only explanation that could be given was that it was the New Year and the company had been forming a good resolution. This actually turned out to be the fact, for, like all good resolutions, it was made to be broken. The old shunting went on again when the train returned to Portland.

The mystery of the disappearing driver unfolded itself during the evening of Monday 18th December, 1899. The 6.40 pm from Weymouth had just passed Littlefield Crossing when the fireman, a youth of 18 years of age named Frank Willis, noticed that his driver Percy Nutman was missing from the footplate! He managed to stop the train which was carrying between 50 and 60 passengers, at Rodwell station, and a search of the line immediately commenced. The driver's cap was found on the Backwater viaduct, and it was feared that he had fallen into the Backwater and drowned. For the next three days the Backwater was dragged and a thorough search made, but no sign was found of the missing man. In early January 1900 a reward of £25 was offered by his wife for the recovery of the body; she was by now considering herself a widow, and as such had already made a claim against the railway company under the Employer's Liability Act.

The case was investigated by Chief Inspector Frederick Benton of the Railway Police Detective Department at Paddington. He made extensive enquiries which eventually resulted in the arrest of Nutman on 9th April in the village of Fetcham, near Leatherhead. He had been found living with his wife's sister who was expecting his child, and he had deliberately faked suicide in order to disappear from the Weymouth area. Nutman was brought back to Weymouth to face a charge of unlawfully and wilfully leaving an engine belonging to the Great Western Railway, whereby the lives and limbs of the persons then passing along the Weymouth and Portland Railway might have been endangered. He pleaded guilty, and was sent to the Dorset Quarter Sessions to face the consequences.

Conditions at Portland station were still far from perfect. In 1899 207,000 passengers travelled from the station, and again strong complaints were made to both the railway company and the Board of Trade from the Portland Urban District Council, the Governor of the Prison, and private residents regarding the inadequate accommodation at Portland for dealing with the heavy goods and passenger traffic. Many of the complaints from passengers arose because they had to wait while trucks of cattle were being unloaded onto the passenger platform, and these had to be cleared before the passengers could leave the platform area. This situation persisted because the sidings were still so congested that much of the traffic had to be handled at the passenger station. Until the opening of the Easton & Church Hope line to goods traffic in October 1900, all freight for the Island had to be handled at Portland.

Passenger traffic was also extremely heavy during July 1901, the *Southern Times* being prompted to observe:

> The trains during the week have been excessively crowded with passengers, this especially the case with the late trains. It would be well if the company would provide additional accommodation when The Fleet is in, especially in the shape of 2nd class carriages. The crowd waits on the platform until the porter cries, 'Get in anywhere', and then it is a case of being packed in like sardines in a box.

To cater for the heavy traffic now using the line, the viaduct over the Fleet at Ferrybridge was rebuilt in a more robust form, the original 594 ft, 25 span timber structure being replaced by a 360 ft steel bridge of nine 40 ft 6 in. spans supported on iron cylinders filled with concrete. Constructed by George Palmer & Co. of Neath, stone for the extended embankments was brought from a temporary siding laid near Easton station. The new bridge was erected on the west side of the old viaduct, and was completed in late 1902.

By this time the Easton & Church Hope line had opened to passenger traffic, and the story of the Portland branch moves into the 20th century.

The original viaduct over the Fleet photographed from the Portland Harbour side during 1902, to the right work has just started on the construction of the replacement structure. In the distance Whitehead's factory can be seen.   *British Railways*

Chapter Four

The Easton and Church Hope Railway
1867-1902

The Easton and Church Hope Railway had a very interesting and involved history. It started life as a line completely isolated from any other railway, and was intended to have its own pier for dispatching goods (mainly stone) by sea. This idea never materialised, and when the railway was finally completed it used parts of two other systems to fulfil its limited functions.

The name of the company was itself inaccurate. The word 'Ope' (an archaic term for 'opening') occurs as part of the name of several coves around the Island, and the site of the proposed pier was in Church Ope Cove. The correct rendering would therefore have been 'Easton and Church Ope Railway' - but perhaps 'Hope' is more appropriate in this case, that being about all that kept the enterprise ticking over.

The original plan was to construct a line from a site north of Easton known as Sheepcroft, passing through Easton itself to terminate on the cliff top about ½ a mile beyond a road junction called Perryfields Corner. This last section would actually have formed the headshunt for an incline, in reality two separate lengths of cable-operated incline on a gradient of 1 in 8, giving access to an 'L' -shaped pier in Church Ope Cove.

The very best that such a venture could hope to achieve was to operate as a poor second to the 'Merchants' Railway' already established on the North side of the Island and having the advantage of sheltered moorings. A pier at Church Ope Cove would give little protection from the elements, and none at all in a gale from either South or East!

In November 1866 plans were deposited by Messrs Bircham, Dalrymple, Drake, and Bircham of 66 Parliament Street, Westminster (Solicitors for the Bill), which resulted in the Easton and Church Hope Railway Act receiving the Royal Assent on 25th July, 1867. The Act authorised the construction of three sections of railway, giving a total length of 1 mile 47.86 chains. The capital of the company was £30,000 divided into 1,500 shares of £20 each, with borrowing powers of £10,000.

The first meeting of the Board was held on 14th August, 1867, Robert Amadeus Heath being elected Chairman and John Coode appointed as Engineer. Mr Payne was appointed company surveyor. The registered office of the company was 60 Threadneedle Street, London EC. Two other Directors initially involved with Robert Heath were Lachlan Macintosh Rate and William Amos Michael. Clearly it was not a locally sponsored company, and the most significant choice was that of John Coode as Engineer, this gentlemen having been Resident Engineer to the Portland breakwater project as detailed in Volume One. This small and rather ill-conceived scheme appears to be out of character for a man of such standing, but nevertheless at the first meeting he was instructed to make working surveys for sections of the line.

Two years elapsed before very much else was done. At a meeting held on 8th July, 1869 it was deemed desirable that land sufficient for a double line be

Proposed site of pier for the
Easton and Church Hope Railway Company in 1870

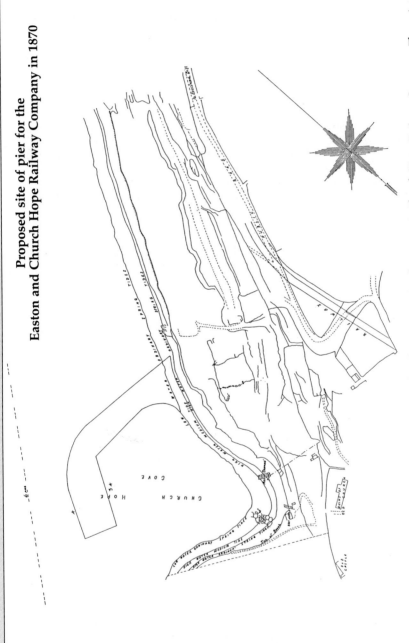

Drawings produced in 1870 for the proposed pier at Church Ope Cove, for the Easton & Church Hope Railway Company. The point where the railway crossed the road near today's Perryfield corner is clearly shown by the word 'Railway' at the bottom centre of the drawing. Note the misspelling of the word 'Ope' for 'Hope' on the engineer's map! This map can be compared with the Ordnance Survey map on page 136 of Volume One.

acquired, and that instruction be given to Mr Coode to prepare the plans accordingly.

The next move resulted in the display of a public notice inviting parties entitled to Common or other rights over certain common or waste land which was required for the building of the Easton and Church Hope Railway to attend a meeting convened at the 'Mermaid Inn' Wakeham, on Wednesday 26th January, 1870. This had been arranged to comply with the Land Clauses Consolidation Act, and was apparently well attended, the *Dorset County Chronicle* reporting that, 'In a small room the commoners stood packed as close as herrings in a barrel, or as thick as Inkleweavers'.

It was not until a Board meeting held on 4th August, 1870 that the solicitor could report that he had held further negotiations with a committee of Portland Commoners to deal with the matter of rights over the land required by the railway, and he could now announce that for a figure of £850 the matter had been settled. Having no doubt struck a good bargain on behalf of the company, he was told to proceed with the agreements and draw up the necessary documents.

By the end of 1872 the powers granted by the Act of Parliament for the construction of the line had expired, and only six furlongs of railway had been completed - and even this was not in operation! Expenses to date had amounted to £20,250, made up as follows.

	£
Legal expenses	2,982
Engineering	1,029
Works	9,626
Land	6,191
General charges	422
Total	20,250

All this expense, and still no operational railway! For the next 10 years little happened to reawaken the company, but in February 1883 Mr W.A. Michael was appointed Chairman following the death of R.A. Heath.

By the end of 1883 things were no better, but the statement of accounts for the half-year ending 31st December make interesting reading. Potentially there were 1,500 shares at £20 each to make up the authorised capital of £30,000, of which shares to the value of £20,250 had been taken up. The total expenditure up to 30th June, 1883 had been £22,671 17s. 4d. The expenses sheet then showed

	£	s.	d.
Legal expenses	3,561	9	1
Engineering	1,029	0	0
Works	9,672	18	1
Purchase of land and compensation	7,582	15	10
General Charges	825	14	4
Total	22,671	17	4

Between 1st August and 31st December additional expenses amounting to £8 16s. were incurred, but much worse was the fact that £2,430 14s. 2d. was owing to sundry creditors.

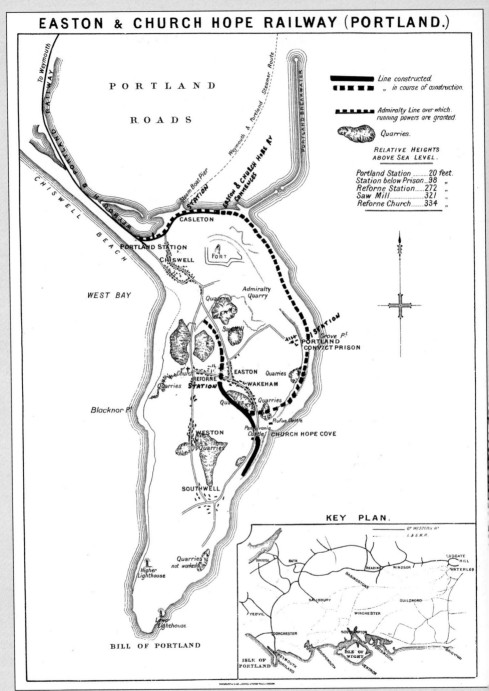

Easton & Church Hope Railway. Plan showing original line and proposed extensions. Note the marked in proposals for stations at Castletown and at Grove Point! Even during the 1930s there was discussion in the local press concerning the provision of halts at Pennsylvania Castle, and the Dockyard. Although both the Grove Point and Pennsylvania Castle schemes were both non-starters, a halt near the dockyard would have proved very useful!

The mileage statement read as follows.

Line authorised	1 mile 5 furlongs, 4 chains 14 yds
Miles constructed	6 furlongs
Miles to be constructed	7 furlongs, 4 chains 14 yds
Miles worked by engines.	Nil

Having constructed just six furlongs of railway in 16 years, the performance of this company cannot have inspired much confidence in anyone connected with it. At an earlier meeting held by the Board on 21st June, both Messrs Michael, the Chairman, and Green, the company Secretary, resigned, their positions being taken by Messrs E. Marchant and H.C. Damant.

By now it was quite clear there was no future for the company in its existing form, and the only chance it had of survival was to join up with the Weymouth & Portland line which had been operational for the past 18 years. Late in 1883 new plans were deposited for three sections of line as follows:

1. An extension from near the 'Mermaid Inn' off the existing line, going westwards for 5 furlongs 15 chains.
2. A short section to Sheepcroft, 4 furlongs 40 chains long.
3. The most important line, 2 miles 5 furlongs 60 chains in length from the 'Mermaid Inn' to join the Admiralty line near the office of the Breakwater Engineer, the line descending 500 feet around the Island's East side to reach sea level.

A Board meeting of Directors was held at the unlikely venue of East Cowes (Isle of Wight) on 4th January, 1884. It was presided over by Mr Marchant, who fully explained the Bill which was about to be lodged in Parliament. He also told the Board that: 'Arrangements for the provisional deposit have been completed, and as one of the arrangements it is necessary that Captain Richard Revett, a Director of the Royal Mail Packet Company, be appointed a Director of this Company'.

The Act of Parliament was passed on 14th August, 1884, giving the company an authorised capital of £50,000 with borrowing powers of £16,000. By obtaining running powers over the Admiralty line at a rent of £900 per year, the Weymouth & Portland line could be reached and direct contact made with the main line railways. Because of the route of the proposed line, clauses were inserted into the Act to prevent the obstruction of Admiralty land and rifle ranges, and also prohibiting the obstruction to or interference with the firing of guns from either the East Weares Battery or the Verne Fort.

After the passing of the Act eight months elapsed with very little construction work being done, and on 19th March, 1885 the Secretary resigned to be replaced by Mr Arthur Lemon. His first task, at the next Board meeting on 25th March at the company offices (which were now at 14 Victoria Street, Westminster), was to inform those gathered that two more Directors, Mr Marchant and Mr J.S. Bush, had also resigned. The meeting agreed that Messrs Baldham and Williams be appointed solicitors to the company, and that a draft contract with William John Alt for the construction of the railway be drawn up.

At the next meeting held (of all days) on 1st April, Thomas Fothergill McNay was appointed Engineer, and at a larger meeting held on the 16th of the month it was resolved that £10,000 be raised by the issue of debenture stock, and a further £50,000 by the issue of £50,000 5 per cent shares as authorised by the 1884 Act. The contract for the construction of the line was duly signed and sealed by Mr W.J. Alt. The terms for payment to the Engineer were settled at £15,000, payable as the work proceeded, and made up of two-thirds in cash and one-third in ordinary shares. Repairs to the old line were also to be paid for as work proceeded - but little work, if any, did proceed.

At this point matters are compounded by lack of detail in the company records, and the employment of sub-contractors. Alt was involved with foreign railways and was Chairman of the Great Southern Railway of Brazil. A sub-contractor brought in at Portland, Messrs Perry, Cutbill & De Lungo, was also involved in a variety of foreign railway schemes.

In November 1885 further plans were drawn up for more alterations to the route of the line, the revised arrangements to be put before Parliament the following year. The modifications concerned firstly the line to Weston Corner, and moved the route to the south of the public highway now known as Weston Street. The 1884 Act had authorised a route which coincided with the middle of the road, but the new one allowed the road to remain where it was and realigned the railway. Secondly, there was a general revision to the route where it approached the Admiralty Railway. Now instead of making a junction right in the middle of the Breakwater Railway complex, it was to cross over the Admiralty incline on a bridge and then run along the base of Verne Hill behind the breakwater works to join the Admiralty line at the west end of the site.

A third line in the revised plans was a completely new one of 4 furlongs 25 chains, to run from Sheepcroft to Priory Corner and join up with the Portland Railway Company, or 'Merchants' Railway'. It was the eventual aim of the company to take over the Portland Railway Company, alter the gauge to the standard 4ft 8½ in. and construct nine chains of railway from Castletown pier to the junction of the Weymouth & Portland Railway and the Admiralty lines, thereby bringing the 'Merchants' Railway' into the main railway network.

Having always paid a good dividend to its shareholders and (as Volume One of this work clearly shows), being a well organised concern, there could be no reason why the Portland Railway should have any interest whatsoever in a company which had not succeeded in running a single train in 20 years - although many shareholders of the Portland Railway were taken in by the dream!

On 23rd August, 1887 the revised Act of Parliament received the Royal Assent, and gave the company £40,000 additional capital and an extension of time, but they were unsuccessful in obtaining a ready-made working system in the shape of the 'Merchants' Railway'.

Three more years passed and still nothing was done, and the legislation passed by Parliament in 1887 ran out of time. Another Act was obtained on 25th July, 1890 giving more time to complete the works and authorising several minor deviations on the East of the Island.

Early in 1892 there was disagreement when Messrs Perry, Cutbill & De Lungo took action against Alt, although this was later resolved. Just how much actual construction work took place is difficult to estimate from the records, for it appears that the sub-contractor's locomotive was sold in February 1894 (*see Volume One*). A year later McNay informed the Easton company he was claiming against them 'for special services and delay in the completion of the works'.

At the same time (February 1895) Alt and Messrs Perry, Cutbill, & De Lungo entered into an agreement by which they surrendered their interest in the contract. There was then, not for the first time, a pause in the progress of the railway! Yet again both in July 1894 and August 1896 further Acts of Parliament were obtained for extensions of time.

A Prospectus issued in April 1895 stated that up to the end of 1894 £80,000 had been spent on obtaining land, engineering costs, and legal and other expenses, although it was considered that once the line was working the dividend would be about 4 per cent. When at last serious work was about to start yet another setback occurred. The ongoing dispute with McNay resulted in him withdrawing the plans and drawings pending a settlement. He was promptly dismissed by the company and replaced by Messrs Packman, Popkiss, and Heasman, of Suffolk House, Laurence Poultney Hill, London EC.

At the end of July Mr Alt promised the Board completion of the works by 23rd July, 1898, accepting £89,980 in debenture and preference stock as payment. Again a sub-contractor was engaged to carry out the work, this time it being H.M. Keone of 13 Victoria Street, Westminster, who was also heavily involved in foreign railways!

Work appeared to progress well until problems arose with Portland Council which was seeking an injunction against the company to stop the construction of a bridge in Reforne Road, and also other bridges if certain demands were not met. Work had already stopped on Wakeham Bridge. To add to the problems, the land required at Castletown was not yet in the possession of the company.

Further problems occurred with contractors and sub-contractors in October 1897. In a letter dated the 22nd from H.M. Keone to Packman, Popkiss & Heasman it was stated 'one engine has been purchased and is being fitted up to be provided as early as possible. Meanwhile we are proceeding with the work by horse traction'.

On 8th November Packman, Popkiss, & Heasman informed the Easton Company, that 'at the time of writing 176 men are at work, 18 wagons out of 30 on ground and 64 wheelbarrows in use - a locomotive and travelling crane expected early this week'. A further letter on the 30th reported, 'no locomotive yet, expected next week. 202 men engaged, 30 wagons, 7 horses, 128 wheelbarows in use, and one steam crane'.

However a letter sent on 6th December reported that the engine, whilst on its way to Portland as part of a normal goods train (a frequent practice at that period), had suffered a broken axle, and was moved to Northam engine shed at Southampton on the LSWR to await a replacement.

The minute books of the Easton company recorded that an engine commenced work in January 1898! A second engine is mentioned in the Minute books in July, when Mr Lano complained that there was a risk of his hayricks catching fire owing to sparks from the 'engines'.

Construction work on the E&CHR taking place over the Admiralty incline, the rails and rollers of which can be seen going down the centre of the photograph. To the right a lightly laid contractor's line, in the background the dockyard.   *Weymouth & Portland Museum Services*

Construction work taking place near Easton on the Easton & Church Hope Railway.
Author's Collection

There were still numerous problems for Mr W.H. Vipan, the Contractor's Agent, who organised work from his office in Straits, Easton. During June workmen kept unearthing various pipes near the Admiralty incline which had to be resited, and further delay was caused by the presence of parties of convicts working in the area, the contractor's men being prohibited from working near prison gangs.

The sands of time once again ran out for the company, and so another petition was put before Parliament for an extension of time. The Act was passed on 2nd August, 1898, allowing until 23rd August, 1900 to complete the works.

On 5th August, 1897 the GWR and LSWR companies completed an agreement with the Easton and Church Hope company. The terms of the agreement - which included the Admiralty line - stated that the works should be completed by 31st December, 1900, the Easton company to provide a station adjoining the Weymouth & Portland station at Portland, whilst the joint companies would staff and operate the line at 2s. 6d. per train mile.

Work was progressing well at Easton, and by June 1898 the station was above the plinth course, the goods shed wall up to the height of 4 ft 6 in. and by October the station roof was ready for slates. The land needed from the Admiralty had been acquired in May 1898, and in January 1899 preparations started for laying the junction with the Admiralty Railway. In the path of this work was the old 'No. 2' signal box which had once controlled the Dockyard system but which, according to a letter received from the Resident Engineer, was now disused. This had to be removed before a retaining wall could be constructed and a bank filled, and eventually the GWR received authorisation to remove the box.

Meanwhile at Easton work was going ahead with the construction of a signal box, this being completed by mid-February, and a short length of track was also laid. Later in the month the work was visited by officials of the GWR and LSWR, and their inspection must have made them wonder what sort of railway they had agreed to operate! The following extract from their report says it all!

The Easton and Church Company have built a station at Easton without first consulting the Joint Companies. It is a matter of regret that plans were not submitted, as suggestions would have been made for materially improving the arrangements and considerable expense would have been saved by the Easton and Church Hope Company. The station and sidings are not laid out to be practical for working, the platform is less than 300 feet long; it should have been 350 to 400 feet. The goods shed, a most unsuitable building, although strongly built of stone, has only a six foot doorway. The yard is not laid out very well and is cramped, and the 1 in 40 gradient at the junction of the main line is a danger. At Sheepcroft the sidings are not good and there is need for backshunt sidings.

In the meantime the case against the Easton company by McNay had been heard in the High Court, it being found 'that the sums paid by or on behalf of the defendant during the continuance of his appointment as engineer were sufficient'. By August 1899 the sub-contractor had become completely disillusioned and refused to proceed with the works, and by the end of the month only about 30 men were left working on the railway. Early in September W.J. Alt removed the sub-contractor, H.M. Keone, and made a final settlement with him, the work being taken over by Frank Chauntler who was Resident Engineer of the Easton company. According to the various correspondence between the persons

Construction work at Red Bridge Wakeham, a typical contractor's wagon in the foreground, the locomotive behind is probably Manning, Wardle No. 1211 *Hornby*.   *Author's Collection*

concerned, it would appear that the contractors plant used by H.M. Keone was used to complete the work (this not being auctioned at Portland until February 1901, by which time H.M. Keone Ltd was in liquidation).

Further problems assailed the Easton company during the year, when the GWR and LSWR sold their share of the Admiralty line to the Admiralty who then became the sole owners, the joint companies each receiving £10,550 for the transaction. This appeared to be a blocking move against the Easton company, or at least it was in very bad taste! The Admiralty then insisted that the Easton company pay the entire cost of upgrading the line for passenger carrying.

No telegraph wires then existed between the Admiralty Junction and Portland station, and this caused yet another disagreement. The Easton company insisted that as it was Admiralty property it was their responsibility, whilst the Admiralty authorities took the view that as they did not run passenger trains it was the problem of the Easton and Church Hope company. However, despite the general air of discord, the pointwork at the junction with the Admiralty line was laid in during early November.

The question of a joint station had arisen several times over the past two years. In January 1900 its estimated cost had been between £17,000 and £18,000 exclusive of land, the Easton company having to provide £2,000 of the required capital. At a meeting held at Waterloo on the 5th July, the company readily accepted this suggestion, doubtless realising that it would be released from the greater expense of providing its own station.

Lt-Col Yorke, Chief Inspecting Officer of the Board of Trade, inspected the line on 3rd July, 1900 and he at once noticed that the railway was not laid out as shown on the plans, but as many of these were over 35 years old it was not surprising in the circumstances! What he did find was a railway laid with 75lb. bullhead rail, except for the Admiralty section which was of the Vignoles type. Col Yorke was not impressed with the bridge over the 'Merchants' incline, this being an original structure of the Admiralty Railway which had carried only freight traffic. As no turntable existed at Easton he insisted that the line be worked with tank engines only, to be fitted with sanding gear and suitable braking, and also suitable for running bunker first, and coal was not to be stacked on the bunker in a manner which would obstruct the driver's vision.

The provision of gates where Quarry Tip Siding crossed the public road and the fitting of catch points needed attention. Although the Easton line was acceptable, the Admiralty section over which all trains would have to pass was not up to standard and the bridge over the Portland Railway needed replacing.

The section from Castletown to Portland station lacked signalling arrangements for allowing passenger trains to enter Portland station, and his report concluded, 'The line is not sufficiently complete to use, and therefore I am unable to recommend its opening'.

Although it was clear from the Board of Trade report that passenger traffic could not be operated, there was nothing to prevent a goods service being worked over the line, and the company decided to do so in order to earn some badly-needed revenue.

This action brought protests from Mr Merrick-Head, of the Portland Local Board, who had previously complained about the state of Portland's railways.

The end of the line at the top end of Sheepcroft yard, a view taken during construction work. After the opening of the line the gantry was used to load stone into wagons standing on the line below.   *Weymouth & Portland Museum Services*

'G6' class No. 263 stands at Easton station shortly after the opening of the line to goods traffic in 1900. Standing on the locomotive from the left are an unidentified porter and Frank Spinney the guard, whilst Fred Stevens the fireman stands on the footplate. Alongside the centre of the engine is the driver Harry Rendall and at the rear assistant guard Mr Davis. *Author's Collection*

On this occasion he ran his own 'Health & Safety' campaign, stating, 'The lives of Railway Officials, Engine Drivers, Guards, and other employees are as much entitled to be protected as ordinary passengers, and that dangers also apply to them. Particularly by the working of the quarry on the cliff'.

As a prelude to this limited opening an inspection train ran over the line on Tuesday 25th September, the public goods service commencing on Monday 1st October, 1900 when the first train departed from Easton consisting of only an engine, two brake vans, and one truck of dressed stone destined for Chatham from the yard of Messrs Webber & Pangbourne.

As the weeks went by traffic failed to increase to any extent, and this prompted a visit from officials of both the GWR and LSWR on Wednesday 21st November, 1900 to investigate the conspicuous lack of stone traffic. The *Southern Times* summed up the situation by saying, 'This is accounted for by two reasons: 1. The loading depots are not near enough to the source of the traffic; 2. The high rates charged'.

It should be remembered that the 'Merchants' Railway' reached directly into many of the quarries, whilst others were served by traction engines which had now become established on the Island. The latter were able to haul stone easily to a loading point on the 'Merchants' Railway' or take it direct to Barnes' yard alongside Portland station. The Easton and Church Hope railway had come too late!

At this time the Admiralty terminated an agreement with the joint companies for the maintenance of their line, thus forcing the Easton company to apply to Parliament for powers to carry out the work itself. The appropriate Act was obtained on 9th August, 1901. During May the inevitable happened. Having existed for many years like Charles Dickens' 'Mr Micawber', its luck and credit had run out. Immediately the Chairman of the company, Colonel Robert Williams MP of Bridehead, Dorchester, and fellow Director David MacIver MP of Liverpool, were appointed Receivers for the Easton and Church Hope Railway. There was only one way out of the predicament that now faced the company - to get the line open to passenger traffic - but this could not be done until the bridge over the 'Merchants' incline was replaced, the Admiralty line relaid, and proper signals and station facilities provided at Portland.

Messrs Packman, Popkiss and Heasman ceased to be the company's Engineers, and the firm of Livesey, Son & Henderson, of Broad Street Avenue, Bloomfield Street, London EC was appointed in their place.

During September 1901 as a result of quarrying at Shepherds Dinner Quarry, on the cliffs above the line near Church Ope Cove, a lump of stone considered to weigh 10 tons fell onto the line causing damage to the permanent way. This event plus other small rock falls that had taken place caused the Local Board to inform the Easton company of their concern that such workings were allowed immediately beside a passenger railway.

The station work at Portland was no problem as this was being undertaken by the joint operating companies, but for the other outstanding work, Livesey, Son & Henderson estimated the cost at £4,113, but made no allowance for the scrap value of the existing rails or the bridge to be replaced. The Secretary wrote to Mr Stanier, the GWR's stores superintendent at Swindon, to enquire about hiring a locomotive and wagons to assist with the work, a little money now being available from a loan of £11,000 at an interest rate of 5 per cent which had been secured to cover the cost

EASTON & CHURCH HOPE LINE

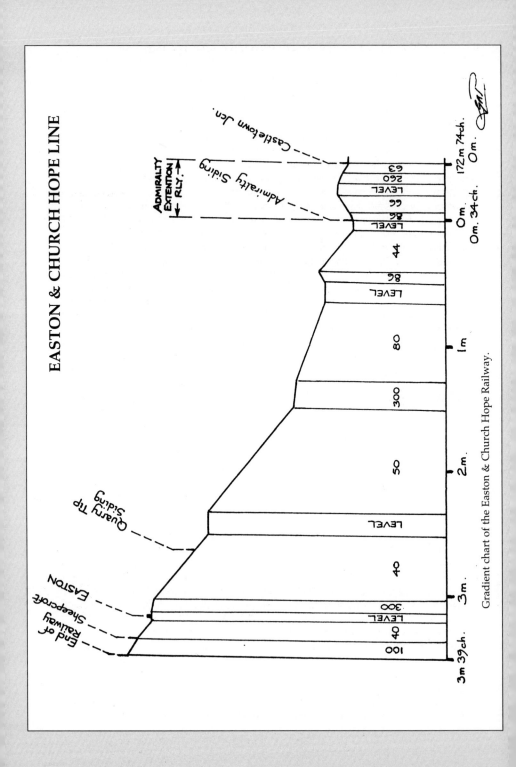

Gradient chart of the Easton & Church Hope Railway.

of the alterations. The request resulted in '850' class saddle tank engine No. 1226 and the necessary wagons being hired to the company, and work then proceeded well. A new bridge with a span of 40 ft 6 in. to cross the 'Merchants' incline had been ordered from the Horsehay Company - perhaps a little prematurely for it was not immediately required and the Horsehay Company was asked to keep it in its yard until needed. When it did eventually arrive on site several complications arose concerning its erection at Castletown. However at the end of September it was finally in place, and by 17th December all the permanent way on the Admiralty line had been relaid except for the crossing at Castletown.

Indeed, things had never gone smoothly for the company, and even at this late stage the Directors were beset with the most unlikely problems. Early in 1902 they were obliged to take action against their own station master at Easton, this official apparently using the station as a dwelling house without authority.

A visit to the Admiralty section by Lt-Col Yorke on the morning of 19th March was yet another complete disaster! When he tested the ground frame controlling the entrance to the stone sidings at Castletown, he found that the Train Staff could be withdrawn from the lock with the points set for the sidings - a situation completely contrary to all the rules of signalling! Even worse, he found that there was no locking whatsoever on the section of line into Portland station. There must have been some very red faces amongst the assembled railway officials! Clearly the Colonel was not amused, for he declined a lunch that had been arranged for him and returned directly to London. An inspection of Easton station made by the officers of the joint companies on 24th April, 1902 also failed to impress, a typical comment being, 'As there is no footpath in the approach road to the station, passengers will have to wade through mud'.

The proximity of the War Department rifle range to the line at East Weares also gave cause for concern. In true Easton company style it was suggested that a flag pole be erected and a man stationed behind a bullet-proof shield, his duty being to hoist a flag as a signal to stop firing when a train approached. The LSWR, who were understandably worried that they might be held responsible for passengers who got shot, wanted an indemnity from the War Department!

At Portland work started on the erection of a temporary wooden platform with a small shelter upon it, situated on the 5-chain curve between Portland station and Castletown Road bridge. This platform was connected to the original Portland station by a footpath, and it was completed by the 19th July and inspected by the Board of Trade on 14th August, 1902. Colonel Yorke was not happy with the curve, but as this was only a temporary arrangement pending building of the new station he was prepared to accept it.

His official report was scathing over the whole affair, particularly over the need for passengers to change trains and walk to and from the original station which was unlikely to encourage them to use the new railway as it was so inconvenient. The Colonel was at pains to point out the folly of this temporary structure, considering that more effort should have been put into the construction of a much needed new station to replace 'The miserable structure belonging to the Weymouth & Portland Railway'.

By this time a signal box to control the run-round loop at the temporary station was in an advanced stage of construction, but there remained the

The temporary passenger platform, shelter and signal box constructed at Portland for the opening of the Easton section to passenger traffic, are shown in the background of this view of Naval ratings undergoing rifle drill. The new Portland station signal box of 1905 was built just to the right of the temporary structure.   *Author's Collection*

A set of LSWR four-wheelers head into the cutting under Red Bridge on an Easton-bound train, shortly after the opening of the line.   *Author's Collection*

problem of the telegraph wires which had never been settled. The Admiralty had not given way on this point, so an independent line was provided by the National Telephone Company between Admiralty Junction and Castletown Junction via the 'outside' network.

Mr Kislingbury, the GWR divisional superintendent, went over the line with the Easton company Engineers on Wednesday 23rd July, and on Thursday 14th August Colonel Yorke again visited the line. This time all was in full working order, including the temporary station and signal box. It must have been a great relief to everyone concerned when he passed it as suitable for passenger traffic.

Little time was lost in organising a train service, the first train to Easton leaving Portland at 7.10 am on Monday 1st September, 1902. The service was of a limited nature as there was no signalling between the Weymouth & Portland line and the Easton line. The physical connection was part of the siding to Castletown, so the Easton service had to be operated by a separate train consisting of four 4-wheeled coaches.

Detonators on the line marked the departure of the first train to Easton and the return journey. History does not record how many people travelled on that first journey, but 200 passengers booked from Portland to Easton that day. The local press reported a rush to obtain the first tickets of all six different types-Single and Return for first, second, and third class passengers. A total of 351 tickets were sold at Easton, and it would appear that a rather small ticket stock was held as by lunchtime the booking office had run out of second class tickets! Excluding through bookings from the Weymouth end, 551 passengers travelled over the line on the first day.

The euphoria quickly subsided; on the second day when only 137 passengers travelled over the line, 63 of whom booked from Easton, a total of one, 35, 24, and 14 passengers respectively travelled to Easton on the four trains from Portland, and these numbers soon decreased further when the novelty wore off of the spectacular journey over this steeply-graded line, which first clung to the cliff edge and then turned inland through a deep cutting in solid rock to reach Easton in the centre of the Island. It had taken over 35 years and nine Acts of Parliament to get the railway to Easton - surely a record for a line of such modest length.

The two mile marker post of the Easton & Church Hope Railway, in true Portland tradition it was carved from stone!   *J.H. Lucking*

Chapter Five

The Joint Railway
1902-1939

A continuous line of railway was now open between Weymouth and Easton, the entire route being worked by the Great Western and London & South Western companies, although the Weymouth & Portland, the Easton and Church Hope, and the Admiralty railways were still owned by their respective companies. The entire railway will be dealt with as one unit hereafter, with reference being made to the companies involved where necessary.

One might have expected the year 1903 to have brought success now that the whole line was fully operational, but things continued much as before with disaster following disaster. In January it was announced that a new railway station for Wyke Regis would be provided as soon as possible, but time went by and no work started. However, work did commence on a new station for Portland, the contractor being Messrs J.H. Vickers of Nottingham. This work soon came to an abrupt halt because Messrs Vickers were in financial trouble and the company was about to be wound up, but fortunately it was soon resumed, Mr J.M. Vicker personally taking over the contract.

At a Weymouth & Portland Board meeting held on 13th August, 1903 Mr Leslie Blunt was appointed Secretary following the death of Mr Fraser, who had been ill for a considerable time. The company offices were moved to 95 Gresham Street, EC the premises of Messrs Blunt and Company, Solicitors.

Meanwhile, on the Easton section matters were far from satisfactory. Both goods and passenger receipts were poor, and the train service left a lot to be desired. During the Summer months there were only four trains on the new line, departures from Portland being at 7.07, 11.17 am, 2.22 and 4.52 pm with return trains from Easton at 9.05 am, 12.40, 3.05 and 5.20 pm. On Saturdays there was a late train, the 9.19 pm from Portland, which returned from Easton at 9.40 pm. As the first train of the day from Easton to Portland did not leave until 9.05 am the service was of no use to workmen from Easton who wanted to reach the Dockyard or Weymouth in time to commence work. Anyone wishing to be in Weymouth early had to make their own way to Portland Victoria Square and then catch either the 7.10 am or the 8.25 am to the mainland. As the last train to Easton from Portland was at 4.25 pm, the return journey for anyone away for the day was equally frustrating.

On the goods side there were two trains each way daily from Portland to Easton, the first at 11.40 am returning at 1.05 pm, and the second at 3.55 pm returning at 4.20 pm. During the shunting of one of these trains in Sheepcroft Yard on Saturday 26th September the first spectacular accident occurred on the Easton and Church Hope section. An LSWR engine was at the far end of the line when the coupling between the engine and the first truck parted. As the line at this point was on a falling gradient of 1 in 100, the 15 wagons (with no guard's van) were quick to make their escape. The gradient soon steepened to 1 in 40 and, gathering speed, the wagons rushed through Easton station. An alert signalman saw them coming, and managed to divert them into the spur siding at the Portland end of the run-round loop, where they smashed into some stationary wagons which resulted in many being shattered beyond repair. Others were described by a railway employee as being 'only slightly warped', but few escaped serious damage. The line into the station was completely blocked by this incident, and until the line was cleared on Monday morning passenger trains terminated on the Portland side of the obstruction, passengers walking the remaining distance to Easton station.

Despite fatal accidents the number of people still using the line as a footpath was unbelievable. One report suggested that on some mornings over 100 people walked the line from the direction of Weymouth to reach Whitehead's factory at Wyke Regis, but sailors bound for Portland Dockyard also developed this dangerous habit. On a wet windy morning in October , four sailors who were walking along the track were killed in the cutting at Wyke Regis by a light engine travelling towards Portland to work the Easton train. Warning whistles were given by the driver, but a full application of the brakes could not prevent the terrible accident that followed. A Naval petty officer who had also been walking the track but who was not involved in the accident stayed to protect the scene, while the engine and crew proceeded to Portland to telephone for assistance. Meanwhile the first passenger train from Weymouth arrived at the scene and stopped. Amongst the passengers on this train was Commander Loring of HMS *Wanderer*, and he instantly took charge of the situation by ordering all naval personnel out of the train to assist in placing the remains in the front guard's van. This done, the train proceeded to Portland.

At an inquest presided over by Sir Richard Howard and held at the Royal Victoria Hotel, Portland, several points were raised. The foreman of the jury, Mr Score, pointed out that the sailors had to be at the Camber Jetty by 7 am, which meant that they could not travel on the first train as its arrival time at Portland left insufficient time for them to walk from the station. He asked if it could be arranged either for the train to run five minutes earlier or for the liberty boats to depart five minutes later, this request being greeted with cries of 'hear, hear' from all around the room. In his summing up Sir Richard said, 'The railway companies ought to take much stricter measures against trespassers upon their lines', to which Detective Inspector Stannard of the London & South Western Railway Police replied, 'When we do prosecute, Sir, only very small and insufficient fines are imposed'.

In the early hours of 28th November, 1903 flames were seen coming from Easton station. The Portland Tophill Fire Brigade was called but arrived too late to save the building, which was reduced to a shell. It was thought that the blaze was started by a spark from a coal fire in the station office. Incidentally, this was the first time that a new system for calling the fire brigade had been used, for just the previous day the National Telephone Company had completed the installation of a telephone link between the house of the fire chief, Captain A.G. Coombe, and certain members of the crew. It would appear from the records of the event that the first fireman to arrive, fireman Fitkins, turned up 20 minutes after the alarm was raised, but despite the time-lag he was presented on the following Thursday with a special badge for being the first on the scene!

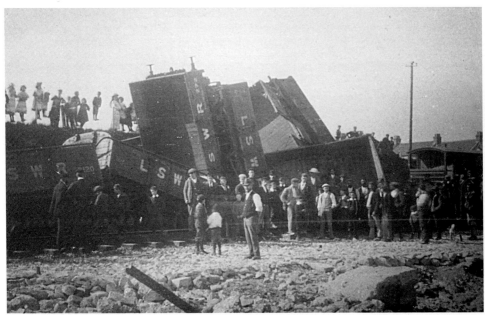

Two views of the scene of the derailment of wagons at Easton on 26th September, 1903, following their runaway from Sheepcroft yard.   *Author's Collection*

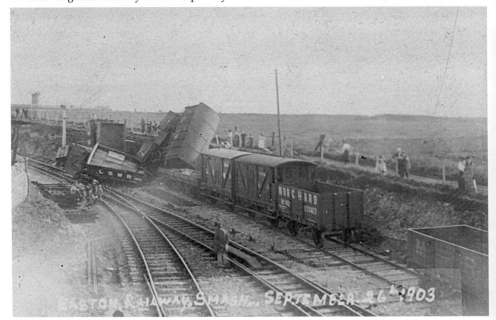

The burnt-out shell of Easton station following the fire of 28th November, 1903.

S. Morris Collection

Rodwell station complete with station staff and passengers; taken pre-1907, the main station buildings and original signal box are shown in detail. *Lens of Sutton*

END ELEVATION

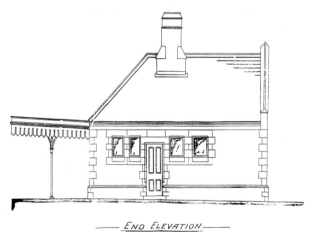

END ELEVATION

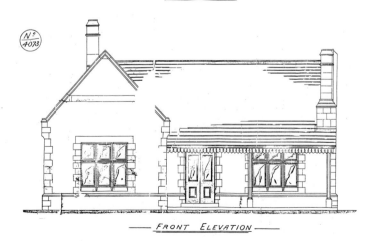

FRONT ELEVATION

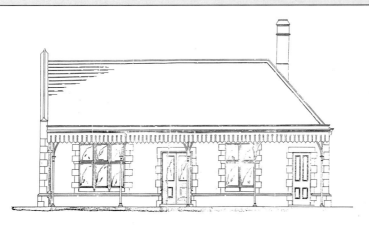

ELEVATION FACING R^Y LINES

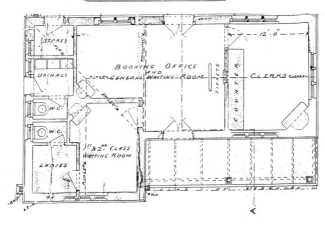

STORES

URINALS

W.C.

W.C.

LADIES

BOOKING OFFICE
AND
GENERAL WAITING ROOM

1ST & 2ND CLASS
WAITING ROOM

12'·0"

TICKETS

COUNTER

CLERKS

LINE OF VERANDAH

PLAN

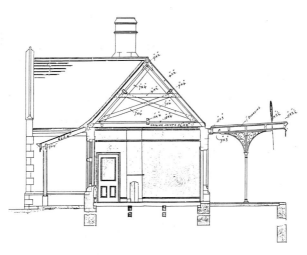

The fire did not affect the train service, and as Easton was not the busiest of stations, the inconvenience caused was not too great. The Easton and Church Hope Railway had insured the station building with the Commercial Union Assurance for £1,000 and they eventually made a claim for £386 for the rebuilding of the structure.

By the end of 1903 plans were again being advanced to involve the Portland branch in a new docks scheme for the Channel Islands trade. Captain Leckey was still trying to get the shipping out of Weymouth. The agreement between Weymouth Corporation and the GWR, signed in 1888 when the Great Western took over the Channel Islands services, had expired, and Captain Leckey still saw Portland Harbour as the answer. In 1897 when work was about to start on the northern arm of the breakwater, he had proposed a dock within the harbour under the cliff at Bincleaves, but the Admiralty had objected to this. The Great Western then proposed to construct a harbour outside the breakwater in Newton's Cove, and as the Admiralty raised no objections to this a Bill went before Parliament which received the Royal Assent on 12th August, 1898. The whole scheme was to have cost £375,000 and included a 4½ mile branch railway, leaving the main Weymouth to Dorchester line south of Upwey Junction and swinging around the west side of Weymouth to pass under the Portland branch near Sandsfoot Castle, thence along the shore to Newton's Cove. Some of the land for the scheme had been purchased and work on the breakwater was already going ahead. The Great Western assumed responsibility for some of the alterations at the shore end, and by 1902 a little of the construction work had been put in hand - mainly to satisfy the Admiralty. A lattice girder footbridge was built to span the approach road, thus preserving the continuity of a public footpath along the cliff top, but little else was done.

The GWR was now heavily involved in many other important and expensive schemes throughout its system, including a major harbour construction at Fishguard which was costing far more than anticipated, and there was a need to cut expenditure. The planned line from Upwey was therefore dropped and replaced by a short line from a point near Rodwell which included a 598 yds-long tunnel. In this connection it was proposed to double the Portland branch from the new junction to Weymouth, the revised scheme reducing the cost to £259,000. The Admiralty approved this amended scheme and work was expected to commence early in 1904, but very little happened. As recorded later in this chapter, the rebuilding of the Backwater viaduct in 1908 made no provision for double track. Up to 1903 almost £70,000 had been spent on the harbour scheme, but in the end the grand plan for the 56 acre dock (which would have been shielded by two breakwaters) came to nought, and Weymouth harbour remained the port for Great Western cross-Channel shipping. There is little doubt that the capital required to execute the scheme was just not available, and in 1913 an Act of Parliament was obtained to abandon the works and hand over to the Admiralty what had already been constructed.

In January 1904 the working of the Portland branch became the responsibility of the LSWR, and shortly afterwards the following comment appeared in the *Southern Times*: 'The carriages on the main line look very nice now, but it probably won't last! T'will soon be a case of "The dirt that won't come off"'. It is assumed that the term 'main line' referred to the section between Portland and Weymouth, and distinguished it from the Easton service.

During the same month an additional coal siding at Sheepcroft was completed and work on the new Portland station restarted, and by the end of the month between 7,000 and 8,000 tons of stone had been tipped as a foundation for the station site, this material being brought by rail from Pearce's quarry at Easton. Early in February it was decided to raise the level of the new station by another two feet, recent floods having proved that the foundations were still too low, and this resulted in another 4,000 tons of filling being required.

In May 1904, Messrs Jesty & Baker made a start on the rebuilding of Easton station, and this was completed by the end of September. By that time the foundations for an engine shed at Easton had also been laid, this work and the construction of a line of railway cottages at the top of Reforne being carried out by Wakeham Bros of Plymouth. The five cottages, costing £1,894, were rented to members of the permanent way staff at 4s. per week each.

The revised timetable for July 1904 caused some comment locally, as the departure time from Portland to Weymouth was brought forward on several trains. In particular the 5.45 pm from Portland was brought forward 15 minutes, and the *Southern Times* remarked,

> There is one great fault in the service as altered, and that is the dockyard employees who leave work at 5.30 pm will have to wait until 6.50 pm to get home, whereas the old 5.45 pm they could manage to catch.

The same paper commented further on 10th September,

> The morning and afternoon times leave little to be complained of, but after 4.25 pm the service is only fit for the wilds of Central Asia. The Manchurian Railway is managed better, for it is said the trains will wait for people who want them, but here they are timed to leave Portland just before passengers get to them. The 5.30 pm is a wretched train, and hundreds of Breakwater people have to hang around Portland from 5.30 pm until 6.50 pm for the sake of 15 minutes.

Work on the new Portland station was progressing well, and a suggestion was made that a footpath should be provided to connect the station with Castletown. Subject to certain conditions the Admiralty were willing to give land for the purpose, and the terms were referred to a Council Committee.

At the Clifton Hotel, Weymouth, on 31st October, 1904, Mr E.T. Targett, the LSWR station master at Weymouth was presented with a marble clock at a retirement party to mark the end of 47 years service. He had entered the company's service at Romsey where his father was station master, and after serving at Leatherhead he moved to Portland to become the first station master of the branch. Five years later he moved to Weymouth as the LSWR station master, as at that time there were separate station masters to look after the interests of the GWR and LSWR at the station.

The year 1905 was only 18 days old when the 6.15 am train from Weymouth to Portland ran past the signals at Littlefield Crossing and demolished the gates, the local press being quick to point out that this had happened on previous occasions!

The exterior of Portland station photographed in April 1904, the condition of the road surface in Victoria Square is clearly visible.   *British Railways*

Portland station looking looking towards the buffer stops on 21st April, 1904. Just visible under the canopy is a Victorian weighing machine. To the left is the goods shed, whilst on the right open wagons stand at the platform behind LSWR coach No. 020.   *British Railways*

Easton engine shed was completed and came into use on 5th February, 1905, a Great Western locomotive having the honour of being the first inhabitant. However, this did little for the train service on the Easton section which had still not improved, and if anything just the opposite! There were trains to Portland at 8.00, 11.55 am and 5.05 pm with return journeys to Easton at 9.30 am, 2.55 and 5.30 p.m. On Wednesdays and Saturdays there was a late service leaving Portland at 9.55 pm and returning from Easton at 10.20 pm. Even the goods service had fallen to one regular train per day, with a second trip run only if required.

The Finance Committee of Portland Council tried to press the Easton & Church Hope Railway for a train from Easton at 3.05 pm to connect at Portland with the 3.25 pm train to Weymouth. They had been complaining about the service from the moment that the line opened, but their complaints had fallen on deaf ears! A reply was now forthcoming from the railway company, but it was not in the least helpful. The Easton and Church Hope Secretary, Arthur Lemon, wrote to point out that the line did not pay at that time (which is not surprising), and continued by threatening the Council by saying that if they pushed too hard or took the matter before the Railway Commissioners, the company would either run still fewer trains or take the service away altogether.

The bright spot of 1905 occurred on Sunday 7th May, when the new Portland station was opened, although part of the new platform had been in use since January for Easton passengers. The new structure had been erected on the 7-chain curve leading around to the Easton line and had cost £10,000, although the buildings were mainly of timber and corrugated iron. It was built six feet above the level of Victoria Square to avoid flooding. The platforms were 500 feet long, which was ample for the type of trains handled, and this ended the problem of lack of space which had plagued the old station. It also dispensed with the use of the temporary platform. Two new signal boxes were brought into use at the same time, one at Portland Goods Junction, and the other at Portland station, the previous arrangements being abolished.

The new station has been constructed at equal cost to both of the operating companies, and in order to discharge the Easton company from its obligation to provide an independent station it had to pay the joint companies an annual rental of £80, or a once for all payment of £2,000.

In March a trial run was made to Easton with a steam railmotor, but little is recorded of the event. On 1st May railmotors had been introduced by the GWR on local services between Weymouth and Dorchester, new Halts being opened at Radipole, Upwey Wishing Well, and Monkton & Came for this service. The steam railmotor was the railway's answer to the electric tram, then becoming very popular in larger towns and having a serious effect on receipts from local passenger traffic in many areas. Public opinion was to a certain extent in favour of a local tram service, it being the 'in thing' at the time for a town of reasonable size to have its own system. An editorial in the *Southern Times* said, 'If Bournemouth could run trams to Christchurch and Poole, why could not Weymouth operate a service from Upwey to Portland?'

The village of Wyke Regis was growing rapidly, but despite Whitehead's factory having been open since 1891 and employing a considerable amount of local labour, there was still no station or halt to serve the factory's requirements.

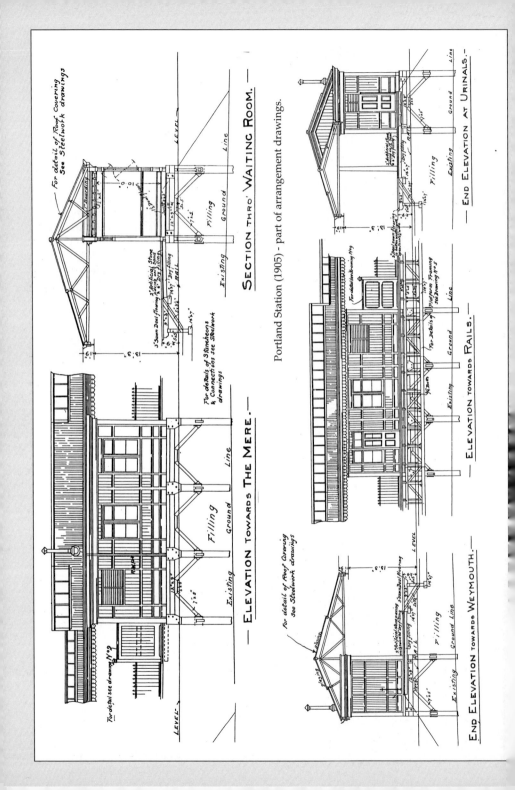

Portland Station (1905) - part of arrangement drawings.

The new Portland station under construction looking in the Easton direction. To the right can be seen the signals, hut and part of the platform of the temporary station used by Easton trains.
British Railways

The new Portland station under construction looking in the Weymouth direction. To the extreme left there is a glimpse of the temporary station used by Easton trains.   *British Railways*

The landslip at Grove Point on 27th November, 1907 looking northwards.

J.H.Lucking Collection

A Great Western 'Dean Goods' 0-6-0 tender locomotive with a ballast train at Grove Point during the rebuilding of the line following the landslip of November 1907. This is the only known photograph of a tender locomotive working on the Easton section, which under normal circumstances was always worked by tank locomotives. *Author's Collection*

This was all the more surprising since the railway ran alongside the factory and a siding entered the works, and no other transport was available to the workers. Without doubt an electric tramway along this route would have carried a great many people. The *Southern Times* had taken note of the success of the Weymouth to Dorchester railmotor service and remarked,

> We would suggest to the Company that a similar car running between Weymouth and Portland, with extra halts say, at Westham, Sandsfoot Castle, and the Torpedo Works, timed for the numbers of working men to go to and from their work, would be received with warm appreciation.

The tramway proposals were not proceeded with, but on 1st July, 1905 the GWR started to operate a motor bus service in the Weymouth area. The service operated hourly from Radipole Spa Hotel to the Wyke Hotel. In September it was announced that a railmotor service would be introduced between Weymouth and Portland in the New Year (1906), the cars running every hour between the ordinary trains which would also run an hourly service. How this intensive service was to be operated over a single line without passing loops and with the additional inconvenience of the shunting required to enter Weymouth station was not explained! In November it was announced that the proposed railmotor service would be extended to Easton.

Mr Palmer who had been station master at Rodwell from the opening of the station retired in October 1905, having been employed in the railway service since 1857. To mark his retirement he was presented with a gold Albert Signet from the joint GWR and LSWR staff, and a purse of gold from the residents of Weymouth, Rodwell and Portland. His place was taken by Mr E.J. Smart, who had previously been employed as ticket collector at Rodwell.

The promised railmotor service failed to materialise, and 1906 was an uneventful year for the branch. One development was at Portland, where the disused terminus was converted into a goods depot, thus providing much improved freight facilities on the Island.

During August tenders were invited for the reconstruction of the viaduct over the Backwater at Weymouth and the building of a station nearby to serve the branch trains. At a Board meeting of the Weymouth & Portland company on 31st May, 1907 a letter from the GWR outlining the proposals for the rebuilding of the viaduct was studied. The Secretary was instructed to reply that the Board would concur in the proposed arrangements providing that the land required was purchased and the works carried out at the expense of the Great Western company, and that the Weymouth & Portland be at no cost for legal expenses. This approach was hardly surprising since on 1st August the Weymouth & Portland company's bank balance stood at only £2,226 10s. 3d. However, work commenced on the new viaduct in September 1907, the contractor being the Cleveland Bridge and Engineering Company of Darlington.

The destination board as used on GWR steam railmotors.   *Author*

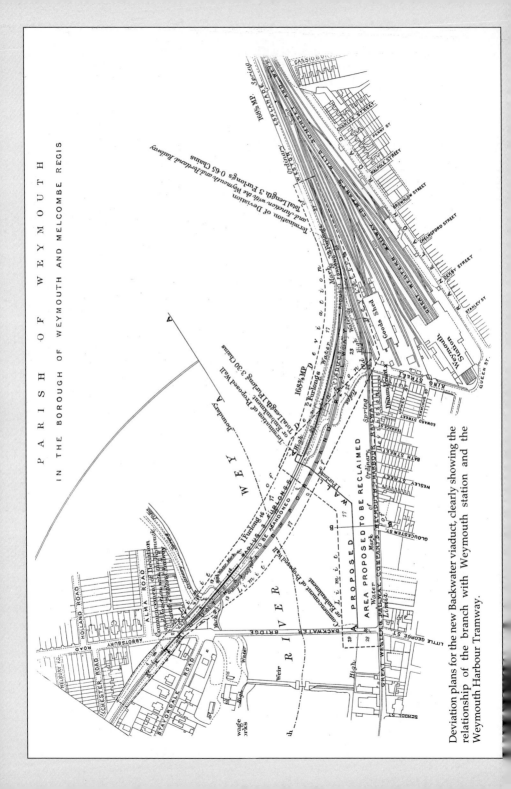

Deviation plans for the new Backwater viaduct, clearly showing the relationship of the branch with Weymouth station and the Weymouth Harbour Tramway.

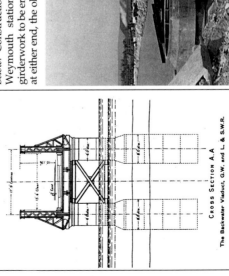

Elevation and Plan of the new Backwater Viaduct, Weymouth, Great Western and London & South-Western Railways.

Above and left: Backwater viaduct, 1909 reconstruction plans.
Right: Early stages in construction of the new Backwater viaduct in 1908. A steam crane working from a temporary staging assists in the construction of one of the piers.
Brian Smith Collection
Below: Construction of the new Backwater viaduct in 1908, looking towards Weymouth station. The piers have been placed in position and await the girderwork to be erected upon them. Already the embankments have been built up at either end, the old viaduct is shown in the background. *Brian Smith Collection*

ELEVATION.

PLAN

CROSS SECTION A.A
The Backwater Viaduct, G.W. and L. & S.W.R.

Work on construction of the brick arch at the Westham end of the viaduct has just commenced.
Brian Smith Collection

Three GWR 2-6-2 tanks and an 0-6-0 saddle tank carry out deflection tests on the completed
Backwater viaduct on 3rd February, 1909.   *Author's Collection*

Weymouth Town Council had reached agreement with the railway companies concerning the reconstruction of the viaduct and other works that were to be carried out at the same time - which included reclamation of part of the Backwater on which to build the new station - but they were still debating the cost as the work went ahead. Included in the plan was the building of a wall and filling in part of the Backwater along the upper part of Commercial Road down as far as Westham Bridge, this reclaimed site later becoming Melcombe Regis Gardens.

On 27th November a landslip occurred on the Easton & Church Hope line just below Grove Point, where the line was constructed on a cliff ledge. Railway engineers stated the cause to be coastal erosion, and calculated that 30,000 cubic yards of earth and rock had moved over a length of 300 yds. It was a mammoth task to replace this material; in one day alone 120 trucks of ballast from South Wales were emptied into the gap, and ash and other material was also used. One wonders why this course of action was adopted at a place where plenty of loose stone was readily available, especially as the ash filling was to cause further trouble for the railway at a later date. Altogether 50,000 cubic yards of material was used to reinstate the line, which remained closed until 23rd December.

The end of 1907 brought retirement for two members of the branch staff. Owing to indifferent health, Mr E.J. Smart retired in November from the position of station master at Rodwell, an appointment he had gained only two years previously. He had commenced work with the Great Western in 1877 and had spent 27 years at Rodwell - most of them as ticket collector. In December Mr G.F. Parsons, a former station master of Portland, retired from his position as station master at Hampton Court, a situation he had occupied for the past 4½ years. Previously he had been station master at Swanage, and was at Portland from 1871 until 1885.

Work on the construction of the new Backwater viaduct was proceeding well, but owing to the temporary closure of the Easton line caused by the landslip the trains of stone required to fill in part of the Backwater in connection with the new works could not start running until 1st January, 1908. By March 14,000 tons had been used to build the embankment approach and the site of the new station at the Weymouth end of the viaduct.

Meanwhile the saga of the phantom steam railmotors continued. The *Southern Times* for 15th February reported:

> Rumour says the railway company contemplate running motor trains between Weymouth and Easton, with intermediate halts at Littlefield Crossing, Rodwell, Ferrybridge, Portland Breakwater and Wakeham.

In May Weymouth Town Council approved a plan submitted by the GWR, for the erection of a footbridge over the level crossing at Littlefield, but they did not vote any money towards its cost! The previous year the GWR divisional superintendent, Mr Kislinbury, sent a letter to the Council pointing out that if the bridge was erected the wicket gates would be removed as the bridge would enable people to cross the line at any time, but the Council were not happy about the removal of the gates.

On 25th July, 1908 the first steelwork of the new viaduct was placed in position. Much was now being done to improve the public appeal and efficiency of the branch. Rodwell station was being enlarged, a new signal box

Working from a barge, workmen remove the piles of the original viaduct.
Brian Smith Collection

The completed new Backwater viaduct viewed from the South side.   *British Railways*

and extra platform being provided as the station was to become a crossing place for trains. This work was carried out by Messrs Bolton & Paul of Norwich. To end the year another statement was made on the steam railmotors, this time in the *South Western Gazette*, the staff magazine of the LSWR:

> It is proposed to substitute the present Weymouth-Portland service with railmotors to be the joint property of the London & South Western and the Great Western Companies.

The year 1909 started rather badly, for in the early hours of Friday 15th January a landslip was discovered near Sandsfoot Castle, and the first train out of Weymouth had to be stopped at Rodwell. Fortunately since the opening of the engine shed at Easton, a locomotive was kept on the Island overnight, and this was brought into use to run a shuttle as far as the slip. Passengers then left the train and walked past the slip to another train on the Weymouth side, and in this manner a service was maintained between Weymouth and Portland but the Portland-Easton service was suspended.

The new viaduct was completed in January, and during the morning of 3rd February Colonel Yorke, RE of the Board of Trade tested and inspected the new work. Three Great Western 2-6-2 tank engines and an 0-6-0 saddle tank coupled together ran up and down the bridge for about an hour while tests were carried out. Having successfully passed the test no time was lost in putting the viaduct into use, the first train to cross being the 9.25 am from Weymouth on Sunday 7th February. The old timber bridge had been in use since 1865 and had shown signs of weakness for some years. The new viaduct consisted of five spans of lattice steel girder work, each 108 feet long, supported by cast iron cylinders of 6 feet diameter filled with concrete and stone. The Weymouth end of the viaduct was approached by a 700 ft bank which also formed the base for the new station, and at the Portland end a bank of tipped material 250 feet in length carried the line to Littlefield Crossing. A 25 ft brick arch set in this embankment provided a scouring current between the bank and the foreshore to prevent the build up of weed and mud. In all, 30,000 tons of stone were used for the approach embankments. No time was lost in removing the old viaduct and filling in the site at the Weymouth end, which was needed for the approach road to the new station then rapidly nearing completion. The station was opened in April 1909, and called Melcombe Regis. As all trains to Portland thereafter started and terminated at the new station the punctuality of the service was greatly improved, the shunting into and out of Weymouth station having long been a source of delay.

Mr W.E. Edwards, an official of the GWR who wrote an article on the Portland branch in the September 1909 *Railway Magazine*, remarked of Melcombe Regis,

> The fact that the new station is of a temporary character appears to point to the carrying out of a contemplated scheme whereby Melcombe Regis will one day become an annexe to a rebuilt Weymouth terminus.

How far this scheme was actually taken is not known, except that plans for one large signal box at Weymouth Junction to control the entire station were drawn up and referred to Weymouth Town Council.

The completed new Backwater viaduct viewed from the North side.   *British Railways*

The scene of the landslip near Sandsfoot Castle in January 1909. A GWR saddle tank passes with a Weymouth-bound train.   *W. Macey Collection*

Melcombe Regis station under construction.   *Brian Smith Collection*

Melcombe Regis station almost ready for opening, a contractor's crane stands in the
background, note the original station canopy, entirely unsuitable for such an exposed location.
It was later replaced by a larger structure, and a windscreen was erected along the site of the
railings.   *Lens of Sutton*

A pre-1914 view of Melcombe Regis station, before the reclamation of much of Radipole lake to form Radipole Park Drive and gardens.   *Author's Collection*

A GWR '850' class 0-6-0ST awaits to depart Melcombe Regis with a Portland train shortly after the opening of the station in April 1909, showing the original canopy, this was later replaced by a standard GWR structure. The remaining supports of the original viaduct can be seen on the extreme right. Behind the station stands Weymouth goods shed, curving away to the left the Backwater wall and the line towards Weymouth Junction. Standing on the platform, railway staff and passengers including sailors and young girls; within a few years world events were to change their ways of life for ever.   *Author's Collection*

In June 1909 Halts were built at Westham and Wyke Regis, and these were later inspected by Col von Donop of the Board of Trade and passed as suitable for public use. At last, on Thursday 1st July, the long-awaited improved rail service became a reality with 13 trains each way daily operating between Weymouth and Portland, plus nine railmotors. There were trains from Easton at 9.08 am, 1.08, 3.10 and 6.33 pm which made connections at Portland for Weymouth. The Sunday service consisted of seven trains each way.

The new timetable was not without its problems because only the railmotors served the new Halts at Westham and Wyke Regis, and as they did not run on Sundays these places were not served on the first day of the week. The situation was not eased by the withdrawal of the Radipole - Wyke Regis bus service by the GWR in early September, thus cutting off all forms of public transport between these fast-growing communities on Sundays.

Having had their railway facilities vastly improved during the past few years, Portlanders were quick to find fault with the new arrangements. The *Southern Times* for 24th July, 1909 stated,

The wretched apology for a railway station at Melcombe Regis has been the cause of even more anathema than the huge pneumonia trap at Portland, and the inconvenience of a broken journey has been felt by all who have had occasion to travel.

In a letter to the Board of Trade from Portland UDC complaints were made that trains from Weymouth Quay were blocking the road and causing passengers to miss connections by not being able to get through, and there were difficulties in the transfer of luggage. Although a hand cart was provided the service depended on the size of the tip given! The prison authorities were also unhappy about having to march convicts along the public road between the stations, which resulted in their being brought from Portland by horse-drawn carriage direct to Weymouth station.

Two other matters soon became talking points; in October 2nd class travel was abolished on the branch - a move considered scandalous by the class conscious local society! The situation came about as the railmotors only had 1st and 3rd class accommodation, but holders of 2nd class through tickets were allowed to travel 1st class. There was also the matter of cheap day return tickets, it being thought grossly unfair that these were available from Weymouth to Portland but not Portland to Weymouth.

A further slip occurred at Sandsfoot Castle on Friday 29th October, 1909. This was not as severe as the previous movement and by the afternoon the railmotors were able to proceed with caution, heavier traffic having to wait until later.

The question of a footbridge at Littlefield Crossing had never been resolved, but the introduction of the increased train service over the branch again brought it to the fore. The cost of a bridge had been put at £400, and the Town Council were expected to make a contribution towards it. During 1910 agreement was finally reached between the Weymouth & Portland company and Weymouth Town Council resulting in the GWR Directors authorising the work to be carried out.

The railway strike of August 1911 had little effect on the passenger traffic of the branch, the LSWR men not joining the strike, although parcels and goods traffic was delayed from other parts of the country. On Monday 22nd July, 1912 the GWR motor bus services were reinstated in the Weymouth area.

Workmen just putting the finishing touches to the newly constructed Wyke Halt in 1909, and watching the arrival or departure of a GWR steam railmotor and trailer.   *K. Bakes Collection*

A Drummond railmotor locomotive approaching Wyke Halt shortly after its opening.
K. Bakes Collection

The Easton section was inspected on 20th September by Mr Venton, district superintendent of the LSWR, accompanied by other senior officers and including Mr Arthur Lemon, the Easton and Church Hope Secretary. After visiting Sheepcroft and other parts of the line, the party arrived at Quarry tip siding. This siding was part of the original Easton & Church Hope Railway, and headed in the direction of the proposed pier in Church Ope Cove (which was never built) and had been used only as a contractor's depot during the construction of the line. Since the opening of the line it had come into use as a siding for tipping rubble over the edge of the cliff. The United Stone Firms Ltd had just opened a new quarry nearby and were making good use of Quarry Tip Siding to dispose of their waste, using a small locomotive to haul the trucks of rubbish.

Mr Lemon was utterly astonished to see the locomotive working on the siding, and he was even more surprised to hear from Mr Venton that it had been working there for several days as provided for in an agreement between the two operating companies and the United Stone Firms. Mr Lemon retorted that as the Easton company actually owned the line they had the right to be consulted, particularly as the operating companies had always insisted that the Easton company was responsible for the maintenance of Quarry Tip Siding beyond the trap points which protected the Pennsylvania Road. The condition of the line beyond the road did not help matters, and Mr Lemon was far from pleased with what he saw. Much of the waste, instead of being tipped over the cliff, had been dumped on railway property. The rails in places had been taken up and roughly relaid, and in one place he found that the rails had been relaid 4 feet above their original level.

The stone company had a man in charge of the catch points and gate at the level crossing, and he was keeping a tally of the number of waggons passing through the gate each day. Mr Lemon discovered that the tip waggons were of 2 ton capacity, but they were being overloaded to hold nearer 3 tons. Although the operating companies did not maintain this section of the line they were still taking their 1d. per ton as a tipping charge. Indeed it was quite clear to Mr Lemon that the Easton company was being taken for a ride.

In a subsequent report on this inspection prepared by Mr Venton many points were mentioned. Most of them were of a minor character, but they had to receive attention to ensure the legal rights of all parties concerned. The report more or less admitted that the Easton section was always the 'poor relation' of the branch, very little repair work being done until it became absolutely essential. However, the gantry crane at Sheepcroft was now in need of urgent repair, Venton noting that 'The ironwork shows signs of rusting and the timbers are rotting for the want of re-tarring and painting'.

The discovery of the body of a newly-born female child in a Portland train at Weymouth station during the early hours of Monday 13th January, 1913 aroused much local excitement. The body, found by a cleaner, was wrapped in brown paper and left under the seat in a 3rd class carriage. Police enquiries established that it was the illegitimate child of a girl in service at Rodwell. She had apparently delivered the child herself but it had died. She then wrapped it up and deposited it in the train at Rodwell station during the evening of 11th January. The accused appeared before Weymouth Magistrates on Monday 27th January, and was committed to the Assizes on a charge of manslaughter.

Rodwell station about 1908, a Weymouth-bound train consisting of a selection of elderly Great Western coaches stands in the up platform.   *Lens of Sutton*

A very detailed view of Rodwell station, a GWR saddle tank pulls away with a Weymouth-bound train consisting of clerestory stock. Taken from this angle it is also revealed that the station master had a second greenhouse tucked away behind the rear wall of the one usually shown.   *Author's Collection*

Portland station pre-1910. Two '02' class locomotives shunt trains, the one nearest the camera hauling a bogie coach and an LSWR close-coupled set. To the extreme left is Portland Goods Junction signal box, and standing at the end of the siding a LSWR gas tank wagon.
Gordon Weddell Collection

A view towards Portland Goods Junction signal box shortly after its opening, a LSWR 0-6-0 locomotive shunts a goods train whilst to the right the construction of oil tanks for the Royal Navy has commenced.   *Bill Macey Collection*

In January 1913 Littlefield Crossing once again come under attack, this time from the Dorset County Council. They claimed that the Weymouth & Portland Railway Company had encroached upon the road with the crossing gates, the latter replying,

> There has been no alteration to the position of the gates or the fencing at the crossing, and it is our opinion that any claim by the Dorset County Council is barred by lapse of time and acquiescence, and we are not prepared to pay for any alterations.

The train service at the time gave little cause for complaint. The 22 trains daily of 1909 had been increased slightly to 23, and Westham and Wyke Regis Halts were now being served by the Sunday trains of which there were seven each way, both Halts having been lengthened during February 1913. The year 1914 was to be one of great change. It started well, with the Weymouth & Portland company paying a dividend of £4 9s. per cent per annum for the last six months on consolidated Ordinary Stock, but it was to be the last Summer of peace and tranquillity for some considerable time, and the last Summer in which Britain could boast of an Empire on which the sun never set. War was declared with Germany on 3rd August and at midnight on 5th August both the Weymouth & Portland and the Easton & Church Hope companies came under the direct control of the Government - as did all other railways throughout the Country.

Traffic patterns on the branch quickly altered. The Home Fleet was now at sea, but there were still many ships using Portland Harbour - most of them coal burners requiring the contents of many wagons to fill their bunkers. During 1915 casualties from part of the Indian fighting force in France were landed at Portland and taken by special ambulance trains to other parts of the Country.

In May Thomas Loosemore, station master at Rodwell since 1907, resigned and returned to his home in Devon. Before taking up his post at Rodwell he had been employed by the LSWR starting his career at Tipton St Johns in 1892. Mr Loosemore was a founder member and Hon. Secretary of the Weymouth and District Society of Devonians, and on 9th June this Society held a presentation in his honour at the Crown Hotel, Weymouth at which he received a silver cigarette case. His place at Rodwell was taken by Mr H.G. Day, who had previously been station master at Upwey on the Abbotsbury branch.

The fighting never reached our shores, but it was never far away in the minds of the people. Ammunition was being loaded daily into ships anchored in Portland Harbour and destined for France, and in 1916 a special workmen's train ran from Easton to Portland at 6.20 am at a fare of 4d. return to transport the men engaged in this loading work. Extra men were employed in the Dockyard to receive the many ships damaged by torpedo attacks and carry out the necessary repairs, and in most of these cases the ship's cargo had to be off-loaded and sent to its destination by rail.

Whereas many branch lines were having their services withdrawn or drastically reduced, the Portland branch with its important war functions maintained a good service. In May 1917 there were 20 trains between Melcombe Regis and Portland and 19 return journeys, four return journeys extending to Easton. On Sundays there was a service of seven trains each way, but no service over the Easton section. In October two trains in each direction were removed from the timetable, these being the 5.20 am Melcombe Regis-Portland, the 10.00 am Melcombe Regis-Portland, and the 10.17 am and 3.35 pm from Portland.

Outward goods traffic increased when the Military Authorities required 40,000 tons of stone debris at Southampton for the wartime train ferry terminal under construction. The first load departed from Easton on 11th May, 1917, two extra sidings being laid in a quarry alongside Sheepcroft yard for loading - which was done with a steam crane - up to 20 wagon loads a day being forwarded.

Despite the grave problems of war, the Littlefield Crossing question was still being discussed by all parties involved. A firm of consulting engineers was called in, and they suggested that the signal box be moved back and that the entrance to the Halt be moved further along the Abbotsbury road to improve the position of the crossing. At a Board meeting of the Weymouth & Portland company in February 1917 consideration was given to the sinking of a subway on the north side of the crossing, the Dorset County Council being required to contribute £500 towards the cost. It was soon decided that this work would be carried out as soon as possible after hostilities had ceased. The crossing problem had been aggravated by the number of extra trains that had to be fitted into the branch timetable. The Whitehead's torpedo factory at Wyke Regis was in full production, upwards of 1,000 men a day using Wyke Regis Halt, whilst special trains brought casualties from the Grand Fleet based at Scapa Flow to the Royal Naval Hospital at Portland. For example, during 1918, 312,213 passengers travelled from Portland - a figure that did not include free warrants and return ticket holders - and as the war drew to a close Australian troops returned home via Portland, adding still more traffic to the branch.

Once the war was over the railway was again able to settle down to its normal daily routine, which was shattered by the tragic death of a ganger on the Easton section on the morning of 16th April, 1919. Working on a curve near the Dockyard Samuel Drake and Henry Goddard were struck by the 9.10 am from Easton; Drake died immediately of his injuries, whilst Goddard although severely injured, survived the incident. At the subsequent inquest the crew of the train said they saw nothing, but a strong wind was blowing at the time and in such an exposed place with a train almost silently running down hill, the dangers of walking on the railway were highlighted.

Disruption was caused by the national railway strike of 1919, which had been sparked off by the threatened loss of war bonus that had been paid to railway workers, and would have resulted in a drop in pay and living standards for all concerned. Trains stopped in the Weymouth area on Saturday 27th September, but Portland services were restarted on Thursday 2nd October, a large number of LSWR men having returned to work.

The Weymouth & Portland and the Easton & Church Hope companies were both omitted from the Railways Act of 1921, but the leasing companies were constituted into new groups formed in 1923. The Great Western remained much the same both in name and nature, but the London & South Western joined the London, Brighton & South Coast and the South Eastern & Chatham Railway to form the new Southern Railway. However this amalgamation had little impact on the branch.

No. 221 has just run around its train after arrival at Easton, the coaching stock on this occasion being the Bristol Division No. 7 'B' set. *Author's Collection*

A 1930s view of Littlefield Crossing looking towards Weymouth, a typical Summer scene of the period as holidaymakers return to their Bed & Breakfast! To the right the wicket gates, to the left the much debated subway. *Author's Collection*

It will be recalled that during November 1907 a serious landslip had occurred at Grove Point on the Easton & Church Hope section, and that some 50,000 cubic yards of ash and dust was brought from South Wales to reinstate the line. In September 1921 this material became a serious source of trouble for the Easton & Church Hope company when the filling under the track suddenly started to burn for no apparent reason. Immediately the fire was discovered, water was poured into the ballast daily in an effort to extinguish it, but this failed, and the line was eventually moved 12 feet nearer the cliff for a distance of 100 yards. A lot of effort was put into trying to reach the cause of the trouble, and holes were dug into the bank to allow water to penetrate the filling. A year later the filling was still burning, and it became a local joke. But it was no joke to the railway company to whom it had become a source of embarrassment and expense. The problems at Littlefield Crossing were resolved in August 1922 with the opening of a subway under the line on the Weymouth Junction side of the level crossing.

The train service on the branch in 1922 consisted of 18 trains daily each way as far as Portland, only five of which were extended to Easton, the first train out of Easton being 9.25 am. The service to Easton had reverted to the level which had caused numerous complaints from the public when the line opened, and it was not until the Summer of 1924 that an early train was reinstated. This left Easton at 8.10 am and gave the Easton section a service of six trains a day.

The force of the sea again caused havoc in the Victoria Square and Portland station area on the morning of 9th January, 1924. During a severe gale the sea surged over Chesil Beach, resulting in the goods yard and line being flooded to a depth of 5 ft in places, and displacing sleepers. The train service was suspended until the water receded and an inspection of the line was carried out. On 17th January the Chairman of the Weymouth & Portland company, Joseph Trumen Mills, passed away aged 88 years. His estate was valued at £4,100,000, a vast difference to the railway where considerable expenses were now being incurred. In 1924 a new roof had to be provided for Portland goods shed at a cost of £100, and £250 was spent on repairing a landslip at Rodwell. In October 1925 another slip at Rodwell cost £340 to put right.

Mr H.G.Day, the station master at Rodwell, was transferred to Pilning in 1925, thus saving his salary of £250 per annum. Thereafter the station staff consisted of two 'grade one porters' at 49s. a week, and two signalmen at 55s. a week. Mr Day retired from Pilning 10 years later after 40 years railway service. During his time at Rodwell he had been a member of the Weymouth Town Council, and an active member of the GWR Ambulance Corps. In 1921 he was awarded a silver medal for attending a man injured in a motor accident on the Wyke Road. The following year Day was one of the principal instigators in the formation of the St John's Ambulance Brigade in Weymouth, and was their first divisional superintendent. However, this was short-lived, for in July 1923 Day - a well respected councillor in the town - suddenly stopped attending Council meetings, and only attended 23 out of 53 first aid drills. For reasons never explained the pages covering this period have been torn out of the Brigade minute book, and later, Day was asked to resign!

The Portland branch did not escape the General Strike of 3rd May, 1926, the train service coming to a standstill. The strike ended on Wednesday 12th May, and the following day a service of five trains, using one locomotive and crew ran over the branch as far as Portland, the first departing Melcombe Regis at 10.30 am, and the last returning from Portland at 5 pm. By the 17th of the month a full service had resumed. The Great Western bus service ran during the strike with a reduced service until Tuesday 11th, when a normal service operated. However, the bus service operated by the National Omnibus & Transport Company was not effected, and no doubt the small independent operators also took advantage of the situation, enabling most people to travel between the Island and Weymouth. It is a certainty that a few people remained bus passengers after the strike was over!

The dangers of 'occupation' crossings were clearly demonstrated on 6th August, 1925, when a car being driven across the line at a crossing near Sandsfoot Castle was struck by the 3.35 pm train from Weymouth and carried for a distance of 500 ft. The driver was thrown from the vehicle and down the embankment into an allotment, but unfortunately despite prompt first aid, and removal to hospital in Weymouth's new motor ambulance, later died from his severe injuries.

On 4th August, 1926 Mr Sidney Dunn, station master at Easton for the past 13 years, left to take up a new post at St Mary Cray, Kent. He was presented with a silver cigarette case by the railway staff before his departure. Easton was a post for a 'grade 4' station master at an annual salary of £210, and the vacancy was taken by Mr A.J. Pike, station master at Toller (on the Bridport branch) for the previous 5½ years.

In the years following the Great War the railways no longer enjoyed their earlier monopoly, and loss of trade, increased running costs, and wages were occupying the minds of management a great deal. In 1925 the staffing cost of the branch stood at about £6,800 a year, not including engine crew, permanent way and other support staff.

By June 1927 the members of the Great Western and Southern Companies Joint Officers' Conference were taking a very serious look at the branch, and had to admit the physical features of the lines made them costly to work and maintain. In a report they concluded,

> The freight train traffic on the Easton & Church Hope Line, consisting mainly of stone outwards and coal inwards, is of a weighty character, and the limitations of the loads imposed by the gradients involves the employment of locomotive power beyond the average. The freight traffic has, however, a heavy contributive value to the main line owing to the long haulage of the stone and coal.
>
> The passenger traffic of this line consists principally of workmen employed in the various Naval establishments and quarries who travel in considerable numbers at certain times of the day, necessitating the provision of an unusual number of coaches for such a short mileage. Ticket issue is mainly local at short fares, and the passenger traffic has therefore little contributive value so far as main lines are concerned. There is heavy road competition along the whole line of route, the motor omnibuses having the advantage of passing through the principal business and residential areas of Weymouth and Portland, whereas the stations at Easton and Melcombe Regis are not favourably situated for the attraction of local traffic.

The Easton section caused the greatest concern. A census carried out during March 1927 revealed that just over 800 passengers per week travelled over this line. The first train of the day, the 8.10 am Easton to Weymouth, carried just over 60 passengers each day, Monday to Friday, whilst the 4.30 pm from Melcombe Regis returned with roughly the same number. Many of these passengers were pupils attending Weymouth Grammar School. The number of people travelling for the remainder of the day just reached double figures for each train except on Saturdays, when a considerable number of people travelled to Weymouth for the day.

It was considered that closing the Easton section to passenger traffic and replacing the train service with railway owned motor buses might be the answer, and that this would bring about a great saving in maintenance and staff costs by converting the line from Portland station to Easton into a 'freight only' branch. Portland to Easton would then be controlled by wooden train staff and the signal boxes at Portland station and Easton abolished, a ground frame controlled from Portland Junction box being installed at the Easton end of Portland station to control run-round movements in connection with Weymouth and Portland trains. The estimated saving on traffic staff expenditure was £763 18s. per year, accounted for by the wages of two signalmen at Portland station box, one at Easton, a porter-signalman, and the Easton station master. On Easter, Whitsun, and August Bank Holidays, when there was the chance of heavy traffic to Easton, it was proposed to run passenger trains under special regulations.

The train service between Weymouth and Portland was also examined, but owing to the nature of the traffic little could be done. The possibility of withdrawing the Sunday morning service and reducing the afternoon service to a level which required only one shift of staff to be booked on duty was also examined, but as the 10.00 am train from Melcombe Regis carried an average of 70 passengers and many more when the Fleet was in, this idea was not pursued. Various suggestions for improving the train working were put forward, including the closure of the Southern Railway engine shed at Weymouth. This housed three tank engines for the service, and employed seven drivers, six firemen, three cleaners and two coalmen. Two alternatives for stabling the engines were discussed, the Southern locomotives either being accommodated at the Great Western shed, or the latter supplying the motive power for the branch.

Despite all these ideas for saving money none were carried out directly, not even the closure of the Southern shed, a move that would not have affected the travelling public. The buses continued to make progress, their fares being 4d. from Easton to Victoria Square against the train fare of 5½d. whilst a fare of 1s. 6d. from Easton to Weymouth was common to both forms of transport. The last paragraph of the Joint Officers' report clearly sums up the situation.

The geographical situation in respect to the railway and road routes is greatly in favour of the latter. The most populous parts of the Island lie on the omnibus route, including the village of Southwell. The modern vehicles, regular service, and cheaper fares will undoubtedly cause a continuous reduction in our receipts.

Visits by the Royal Family and foreign Heads of State to the Navy at Portland required the working of special trains over the branch and such was the case on Tuesday 3rd April, 1928 when His Majesty the King of Afghanistan, whilst on a state visit, inspected the Atlantic Fleet at Portland. The special, consisting of Pullman cars and hauled by engine No. 850 *Lord Nelson*, left Waterloo at 8.40 am. On arrival at Weymouth Junction the main line locomotive was replaced by two immaculately polished '02' class engines for the journey over the branch to Portland. Whilst the train was stationary King Amanullah looked out of the saloon car window and waved to a crowd of onlookers assembled along the footpath between Ranelagh Road (Weymouth) and Alexandra Bridge. The crowd, all eager to see the King, pushed against the railings, which gave way and resulted in many of the spectators tumbling down the bank, fortunately without serious injury.

At 11.10 am the train arrived at the Dockyard, where a special platform had been constructed near the Camber Jetty. Following the usual introductions, presentations, and the inspection of a Guard of Honour, the King continued by Admiral's barge to the flagship, HMS *Nelson*. A day of Naval manoeuvres in the English Channel had been planned, but due to inclement weather the full programme of events had to be curtailed. At 6.00 pm HMS *Nelson* arrived at Spithead, where His Majesty disembarked.

November 1928 saw the replacement of the footbridge which crossed the railway just south of Easton station. The original bridge was of lattice construction, but the replacement was of the plate girder type and cost £290.

There is little doubt that the heavy vehicular traffic using the road bridges on the Easton section of the branch did little to prolong the life-span of these structures. Heavy traction engines hauling trailers loaded with blocks of stone weakened the road bridge in Reforne, and in March 1929 it had to be replaced at a cost of £850. Cranes as well as bridges were showing signs of their age. In 1927 the Portland 10 ton hand crane was condemned and was replaced by a 12 ton model, whilst the following year the 2½ ton crane at Sheepcroft had to be replaced, this time by one capable of lifting 6 tons. During 1930 improved waiting accommodation at Westham Halt cost £90, and £110 was spent at Wyke Regis.

From the outset the Portland branch had been operated jointly by the London & South Western (now the Southern Railway) and the Great Western Railway, but in 1931 the branch was brought into line with other pooling arrangements where these companies had been operating a joint service. The Southern Railway took over the entire operation of passenger services on the line, and it remained that way until nationalisation in 1948.

To meet increased competition from the motor bus it was decided to construct an additional Halt at Sandsfoot Castle, and work started in July 1932. The Halt, which had a 300 ft platform, cost £340 to construct and it was estimated to bring in an annual revenue of £70. It opened to passengers on 1st August, bringing the remains of Henry VIII's castle within easy reach of rail travellers. A footpath from the Halt led down to Sudan Road from where access to Clearmount Road was obtained via an underbridge, the right of way having been granted in April 1930 after a footpath and underbridge further north had been closed and sealed up.

The Easton and Church Hope company was still not making much profit from its line, although the joint companies were paying them £2,000 per annum for its use irrespective of the amount of traffic carried. However, the local company did have a small income from surplus land which had originally been purchased for the construction of the railway but not used. For example, £1 per quarter was received from the lease of land and stables at Easton.

What could have been a more serious mishap occurred at Easton on 30th August, 1933, as 'O2' class tank No. 201 was approaching the station with the afternoon goods, the left side connecting rod snapped. The rod flew around smashing a sleeper before punching a hole in the footplate of the engine, and causing the other connecting rod to bend.

King Edward Vlll, the uncrowned King, visited Portland to inspect the Fleet on 12th November, 1936, this being his last Naval engagement before his abdication. He had attended the Armistice Day Remembrance service at the Cenotaph in London previous day and had travelled by Royal train to Portland overnight, arriving at 4.30 am. It was a rough night and the sea had broken over the Chesil Beach and caused flooding to a depth of two feet in the station yard an hour after the King's arrival. Two officers of the Dorset Constabulary were guarding the Royal Train overnight, but as the water rose they had to move to higher ground. The first train from Weymouth at 6.15 am conveying almost 1,000 sailors returning from Weymouth was held at Rodwell, and the three following trains were cancelled. As the water subsided the 6.15 am managed to arrive at Portland by 8.30 am, and there followed a mad scramble to the Dockyard and aboard liberty boats to the various ships!

Meanwhile the King had slept aboard the Royal Train in the middle of Portland goods yard, completely surrounded by water, and at 9.35 am the Royal Train was shunted through the subsiding flood into the station where the King alighted to be welcomed by Mr J.A. Attwooll, Chairman of Portland Urban District Council, Mr H.J. Sansom, President of the Portland branch of the British Legion, and Mr E.J.N. Carter, the station master. The King asked, 'Do you often get weather like this on Portland?' After paying his respects to 200 ex-servicemen lined up in the station approach, the King travelled to the dockyard by car - despite the fact that Victoria Square was still partly flooded!

During 1937 the enamel sign 'Season Tickets must be shown here' disappeared from Melcombe Regis station, probably becoming a prize trophy on the mess deck of one of His Majesty's warships in Portland Harbour! With so many servicemen travelling over the line, many after a good night out in Weymouth, acts of drunken bravado were bound to occur, but they were never of too serious a nature. It was not always naval personnel who caused complaint, for during November the conduct of pupils from a Weymouth school travelling home on the 4.38 pm to Portland caused public disapproval, but this matter was summarily dealt with by their headmaster the next day.

A new housing estate at Southlands had been built on the opposite side of the line to Sandsfoot Castle Halt, and although it was only a stone's throw from this estate to the Halt, it took a good walk to reach it as the only access was by way of the underbridge at Sudan Road. In an effort to attract traffic from this new development a footbridge was erected to give direct access from the houses to the Halt.

The Summer of 1937 had some glorious days when the temperature soared, and one such was 7th August when the heat twisted the rails at Ferrybridge,

With a background of posters extolling the virtues of 'Glorious' Devon, Warwick Castle, and other exotic places to visit, station master Pike stands on the platform of Easton station.

Author's Collection

resulting in the cancellation of four trains. The business affairs of the Easton &
Church Hope company improved during the year to furnish gross receipts of
£3,644, as against £3,568 for the previous year, whilst expenditure had been
reduced from £4,297 to £4,158. This resulted in an overall loss of £514 on railway
working for the 12 months, but miscellaneous receipts of £70 reduced the deficit
to £444. There was no doubt that the improved bus service offered by Southern
National from Tophill was having an effect on passenger receipts, and from the
commencement of the 1937/8 Winter timetable two daily trains were
withdrawn from the Easton section to reduce operating costs, leaving a five-
train daily service.

The plain fact was that the Easton section was just not a viable proposition,
having been in Receivership since 1901. The line was also worked under the
original 1897 agreement, under which the joint companies paid a fixed rate of
2s. 6d. per train mile, this being the estimated costing for one goods and six
passenger trains daily. However the Easton company had expected a far larger
return, particularly from stone and general goods traffic, which never
materialised. There was constant wrangling in later years between the Easton
and joint companies every time the annual accounts were presented.

The problem was the usual one of continuously rising operating costs and
falling receipts, passenger figures declining rapidly from the early 1930s (enter
the motor bus!). Stone also declined, but although parcel traffic remained steady
the revenue from it also fell. It was against this background that the Easton
company struggled on with mounting interest charges and debts. At the end of
1938 it owed the Admiralty £14,480 for use of their line, but the outbreak of war
and Government control saved the Easton & Church Hope company from
further embarrassment

By contrast, in February 1915 the Weymouth & Portland company declared a
half-yearly dividend at the rate of £4 9s. per cent, per annum, less income tax on
the consolidated ordinary stock of the company, and this was to continue until
1925 when a dividend of £2 15s. less income tax at 4s. 3d. in the pound was
declared. However by the end of that year it was back to £4 9s., remaining so
well into the 1930s.

The 1939 half-yearly meeting of the Weymouth & Portland took place on 8th
February with Mr Leonard Mortimer in the chair, aided by Arthur C. Blunt, the
Secretary. The General Account stood at £1,663 6s. 7d. and the Dividend
Account at £1 11s. 2d., Directors fees amounted to £7, and it was declared that
£1,209 16s. 11d. would be divided among the holders of consolidated stock.

By this time the GWR had decided to build a new station at Weymouth, with
platforms 1,000 feet in length, at an estimated cost of £80,000, and in anticipation
of this work the Southern Railway engine shed was closed in the January of
1939 and demolished shortly after. Thereafter SR engines used the GWR shed
as first suggested back in 1927.

Record crowds arrived at the station for the August Bank Holiday, and on
Saturday 23,342 came in via the Great Western and 10,823 by Southern Railway.
Improved facilities were urgently needed, and work was about to start on
reconstruction, but due to the situation then developing in Europe the project
was shelved.

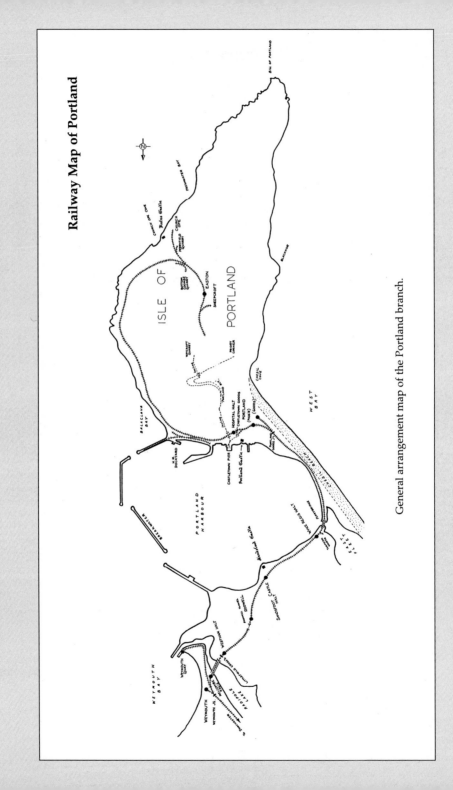

Railway Map of Portland

General arrangement map of the Portland branch.

Chapter Six

The Route Described

The Portland branch is difficult to describe at any particular period of time. Much of the line - particularly in the Weymouth area - is of a suburban nature, and throughout the working life of the branch there has been considerable residential development along the route, unlike the usual country branch line where very little change occurred. However, it has been decided to take an imaginary trip along the line from Weymouth to Portland during the Summer of 1939, just before the war changed so many things and post-war development altered the landscape.

Although passengers join the train at Melcombe Regis station, the starting point for the train is Weymouth Junction signal box, where the engine runs around its stock after the previous journey and takes on water. With tanks suitably replenished the empty train travels the 27 chains to Melcombe Regis station. The first few yards are on double track until a scissors crossover is reached, at which point the Harbour Tramway and the Portland branch divide. The line now becomes a single track curving right and crossing the road at the entrance to a section of the Weymouth goods yard. Here a flagman protects the train from any coal merchant's or carter's vehicles that might be entering or leaving the yard. Only a few yards further on the line crosses a public footpath, which is ungated but provided with a tremulous bell operated from the signal box to warn pedestrians of the approach of trains. Just beyond this foot crossing stands Melcombe Regis station. The 400 ft platform is on the left-hand side of the track, and is the starting point for all Portland services.

The station is built on land reclaimed from the Backwater, and the buildings are constructed of corrugated iron. The platform was originally of timber construction but was rebuilt with stone blocks during the late 1930s. It is protected to some extent from the elements by an iron screen erected along the right-hand side of the line, the site being otherwise exposed to the vast expanse of Radipole Lake. At this point the line is on a rising gradient of 1 in 96. At the far end of the platform there is the massive 180 yds-long five-span steel viaduct across the Backwater - a stretch of water and reed beds known as 'Radipole Lake' since the building of the embankment and Westham Bridge in 1921.

Pulling away from the station the train threads the girder work of the viaduct on a gradient of 1 in 98, easing to 1 in 143. At the end of the viaduct a short stone embankment is crossed, followed by a brick arch. On the right is the Littlefield Crossing keeper's cottage, and the train now crosses the Abbotsbury Road on the level. To the left, after the gates and opposite the 169 mile post, stands Littlefield Crossing ground frame.

The train now stops at Westham Halt (169 m. 3 ch.), with the platform on the right-hand side of the line, just beyond the Littlefield Crossing gates. The platform is faced with stone, and upon it stands an iron shelter with a flat roof. At the entrance gate in Abbotsbury Road there is a small wooden hut for the ticket collector who is in attendance at certain times of the day. The gradient at

WEYMOUTH

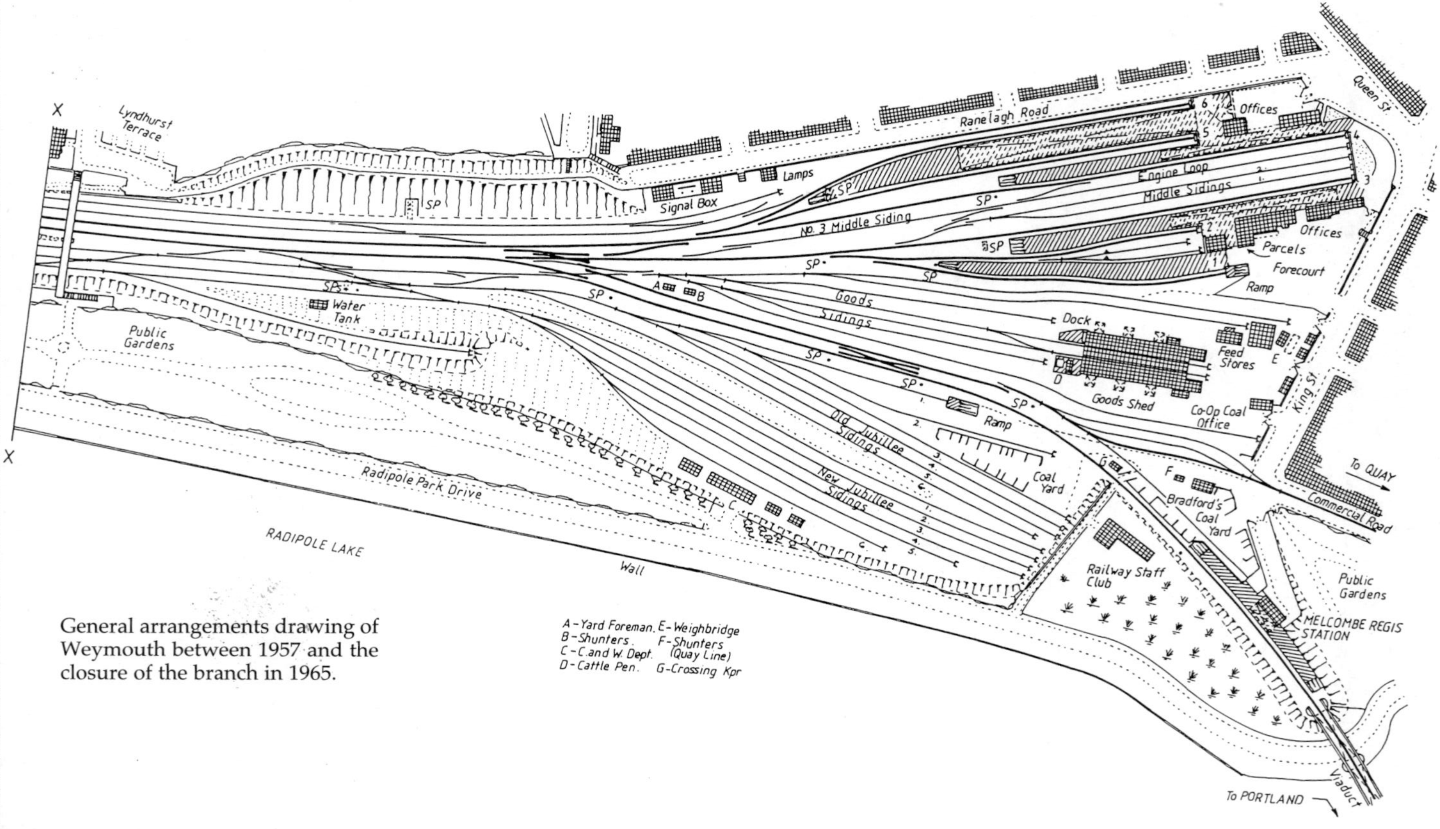

General arrangements drawing of
Weymouth between 1957 and the
closure of the branch in 1965.

A – Yard Foreman. E – Weighbridge
B – Shunters.   F – Shunters
C – C and W. Dept. (Quay Line)
D – Cattle Pen.   G – Crossing Kpr

To QUAY

To PORTLAND

Commercial Road
King St
Public Gardens
MELCOMBE REGIS STATION
Viaduct
Queen St
Offices
Offices
Offices
Parcels
Forecourt
Ramp
Feed Stores
E
Engine Loop
Middle Sidings
Co-op Coal Office
Bradford's Coal Yard
F
Railway Staff Club
Ranelagh Road
Dock
Goods Shed
SP
BSP
Ramp
Coal Yard
No 3 Middle Siding
Goods Sidings
Old Jubilee Sidings
New Jubilee Sidings
Lamps
Signal Box
A
B
SP
SP
SP
SP
SP
SP
SP
SP
SP
Water Tank
Wall
Radipole Park Drive
RADIPOLE LAKE
Public Gardens
Lyndhurst Terrace
X
X

Weymouth station viewed from the top of the water tank during the winter of 1938, with 'T9' class 4-4-0 No. 728 standing outside the Southern shed. The station with its overall roof stands behind. To the right 'Weymouth Station signal box' a structure dating back to the 1870s, and behind the goods shed. *S.C. Townroe*

Although this photograph was taken during the 1930s, little had changed at Weymouth station since the turn of the century when Portland branch trains commenced and terminated there. In this view ex-LSWR 'T9' class 4-4-0 No. E730 prepares to depart with a Southern Railway train, whilst GWR 'Bulldog' class No. 3324 acts as station pilot; to the left stands GWR auto-trailer No. 103 awaiting its next turn of duty. *British Railways*

An exterior view of Melcombe Regis station, the alignment of the original viaduct was along the shoreline of the station approach. In later years the land in the foreground was reclaimed and a putting green laid out on the site.   *J.H. Lucking*

Melcombe Regis looking towards Weymouth Junction, to the left the screen erected to protect waiting passengers from the exposed area of Radipole Lake. In the background between the screen and the station building can be seen the tank traps constructed during World War II as an invasion precaution.   *C.L. Caddy*

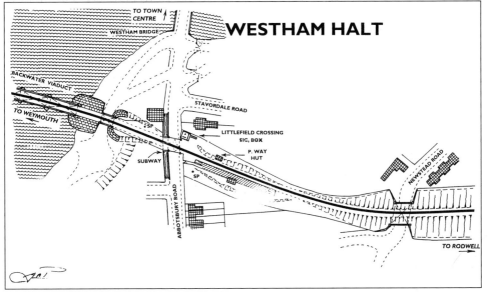

Westham Halt. General arrangement drawing.

Westham Halt during 1951, 'O2' class No. 30229 heads towards Weymouth with the afternoon goods from Portland. Grammar School children wait for the next Portland train near the small ticket hut staffed at busy periods. A drop front pram and gas meter reader on his cycle all add to this delightful period scene. *W. Newman*

'02' class No. 30177 emerges from Rodwell tunnel on 12th July, 1949 heading towards Weymouth with a branch train consisting of former Great Western stock. The bracket signal is pulled off in the down direction because Rodwell signal box is switched out, the up loop being used by both up and down trains.   *D.E.H. Box*

Rodwell station looking towards Portland, the signal box added during 1892 is clearly shown in this view taken about the turn of the 20th century.   *Lens of Sutton*

the Halt is 1 in 98, but immediately on leaving the train has to battle with a climb of 1 in 58 past the end of Illchester Road, which was named after the former owner of the land on which the Halt and railway were built.

The line now curves left and crosses Newstead Road on an embankment, the road passing underneath in a stone arch. From the carriage window the inner harbour, the gas works, Weymouth football ground, and much of the town can be seen to the left, whilst on the right is an area known as 'The Marsh' - land which was formerly waterlogged but was stabilised by the building of the railway. Further over to the north can be seen the rapidly expanding estates at Westham around the western edge of the town.

The line now crosses Chickerell Road, which also passes under the embankment in a stone arch. On the Weymouth side of the arch the Fleur-de-Lys of the Prince of Wales is carved in the keystone. The gradient now eases slightly to 1 in 60 as the train enters the 58 yds-long Rodwell tunnel under Wyke Road, which was built for double track. There are actually two tracks throughout the length of the tunnel, the right-hand one (which ends in stop blocks) acting as a trap siding for the up loop.

On emerging from the tunnel the train reaches Rodwell station (1 m. 16 ch.). Nestling in the deep cutting driven through the Lansdowne Estate, this station was thought by many to be one of the prettiest in England. The sides of the cutting are covered with fine trees, and during the Spring and Summer the flower beds are a riot of colour. No wonder that Rodwell was frequent winner of the 'Best Kept Station' Competition. Rodwell is rather unusual in being a fully-fledged station with no goods facilities, the only access being on foot either down a sloping path from Wyke Road, or by a much longer path along the top of the cutting from Buxton Road. The main building, of stone construction, is on the left-hand (or down) platform, whilst the up platform has a waiting hut in the GWR 'Pagoda' style and a brick signal box of standard GWR design. A lattice footbridge connects the two platforms.

As the train leaves Rodwell station the summit of the Weymouth section of the line is reached, having climbed 80 feet in just over 1½ miles. Descending now at 1 in 66 the line passes under a three-arch brick bridge carrying Buxton Road and curves to the right, at which point several glimpses of the sea can be obtained through the trees before the train stops at Sandsfoot Castle Halt (1 m. 53 ch.). The platform, on the left-hand side of the line, is a simple structure 300 ft in length faced with sleepers to hold back the solid ash filling. A small hut is provided as shelter for passengers. To the right is the Southlands Estate containing roads of semi-detached houses, all recently built. A lattice footbridge and short footpath give access from the estate to the Halt, which derives its name from the Castle built by Henry VIII in 1541, the ruins of which are situated in the nearby public gardens.

On leaving Sandsfoot Halt the whole of Portland Harbour comes into view, backed by the large hump of the North side of the Island. This view, seen from the left-hand windows of the train, can indeed be a beautiful one on a fine day.

The train is now travelling very near the edge of the cliff, descending for a mile on a gradient of 1 in 88 towards Wyke Regis Halt. Across the fields to the right Wyke Regis can be seen - a village along the main Portland Road which is growing daily with new housing developments.

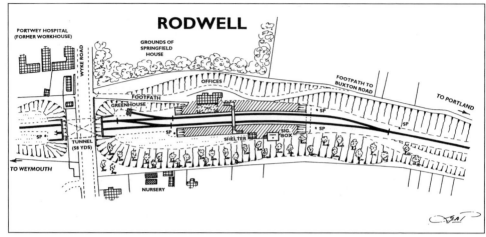

Rodwell. General arrangement drawing.

Rodwell station looking towards Weymouth during 1909, the poster board against the railings on the left proclaims the opening of Melcombe Regis station in the April of that year. Partly obscured by the footbridge is the Rodwell up starting signal with the Littlefield Crossing distant below, (painted red pre-1928). Through Rodwell tunnel can be seen the Rodwell up home signal. Although well within the Borough of Weymouth the station has the feel of a typical GWR country station!   *British Railways*

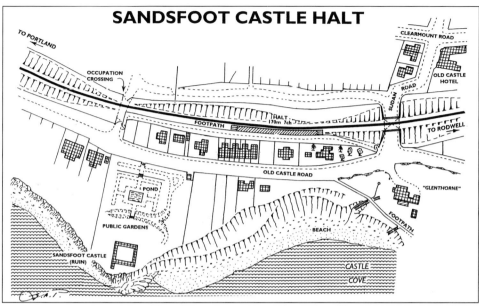

Sandsfoot Castle Halt. General arrangement drawing.

Saturday 1st March, 1952. Parents and their children stand on Sandsfoot Castle Halt watching history take place. Fifty years later the clothing worn by the bystanders clearly demonstrates the fashions of the period. *Author's Collection*

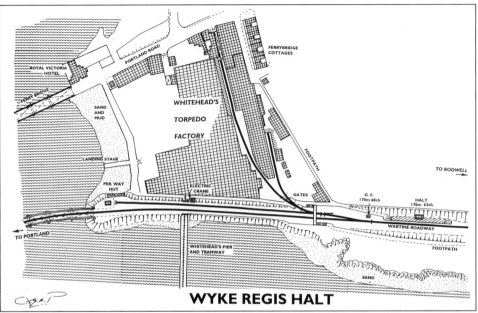

Wyke Regis Halt. General arrangement drawing.

Wyke Regis Halt looking towards Weymouth, showing the extended platform and second hut added.   *H. Kailes*

The train now enters a fairly deep cutting 500 yards in length to emerge at Wyke Regis Halt (2 m. 29 ch.). The simple stone platform, upon which are two huts, is on the right of the line. One of the huts (the original) is of the 'Pagoda' type, but the other with a flat roof is a later addition. A footpath leads from the Halt up the side of the cutting to the main road and to Whitehead's Torpedo Factory, which is situated a few yards away. Whitehead's is a large employer of local labour, and its workers account for most of the traffic at the Halt. A private siding to serve the factory goes off to the right immediately at the Portland end of the platform, and at the same point a plate girder footbridge crosses the line giving access to a cliff top footpath. Projecting out into Portland Harbour is a pier 1,060 yards in length, along which a 2 ft gauge railway worked by battery-powered trolleys operates to take men and equipment between the factory and the boats. The pier tramway passes under the railway to gain access to the factory, and an electric crane stands adjacent to the bridge for transferring loads between the narrow gauge line and main line wagons standing in a siding parallel to the running line.

Leaving Wyke Regis behind and passing Whitehead's factory the Fleet is crossed at (2 m. 79 ch.) on a 360 ft nine-span plate girder viaduct. Then, after a slight descent of 1 in 205, the line runs beside the sea-shore towards Portland. On the left the great ships of the British Navy lie at mooring buoys in Portland Harbour. When the Navy is 'in' many types of vessels can be seen with such names as *Nelson*, *Royal Oak* and *Barham*, together with four-funnel cruisers, destroyers, and a host of other ships that make up the Royal Navy. Behind them stand the breakwaters surrounding the harbour, and in the distance the cliffs of East Dorset stretching away past Lulworth Cove to St Aldhem's Head. To the South the steep North face of Portland can now be clearly seen standing 500 feet above the Dockyard - an awe-inspiring sight which gave Thomas Hardy, the Dorset novelist, the inspiration to call Portland 'The Gibraltar of Wessex'.

Close to the line, and away to the right, Ferrybridge can be seen carrying the only road to the Island, with the famous Chesil Beach towering behind it. The line curves gently to the left and an occupation crossing, known as 'Mere Crossing' (3 m. 67 ch.), is passed. From this crossing right into Portland station the left-hand side of the line is flanked by large oil tanks, each containing a million gallons of fuel oil for Navy ships, and the road and railway run side by side separated only by a stone wall six feet high, built specially to prevent trains frightening horses.

Portland signal box is passed on the left and it is here that the single line staff is given up. Opposite the box the spacious goods yard fans out, most of it occupying the site of the original passenger terminus, the buildings of which still do duty as a goods depot. The buildings are of local stone and are set out across the platform ends in true terminal style. The train curves sharply to the left and enters the new Portland station (4 m. 25 ch.) which has been built on a sharp left-hand curve of 7½ chains radius. The buildings are a mixture of brick, corrugated iron, and wood, a light form of construction made necessary because the station was built on land reclaimed from the harbour. The two platforms are joined by a covered footbridge, and passengers leaving the train have a short walk down an approach road which leads past the original station into Victoria Square. Portland gas works is situated on the left and near the approach road gates.

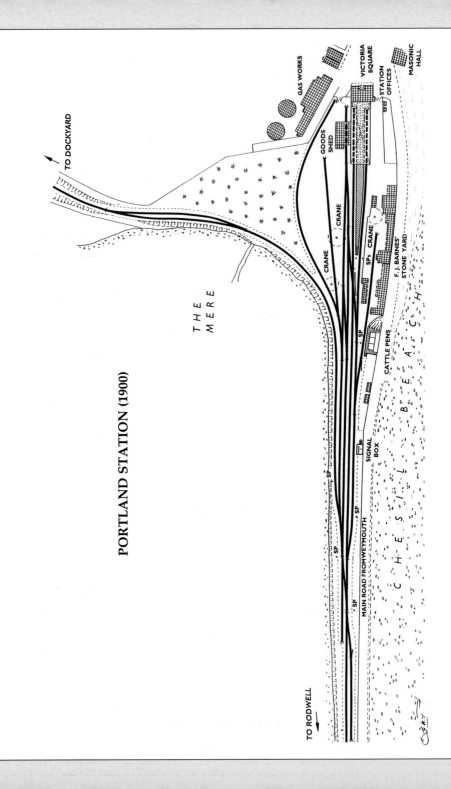

PORTLAND STATION (1900)

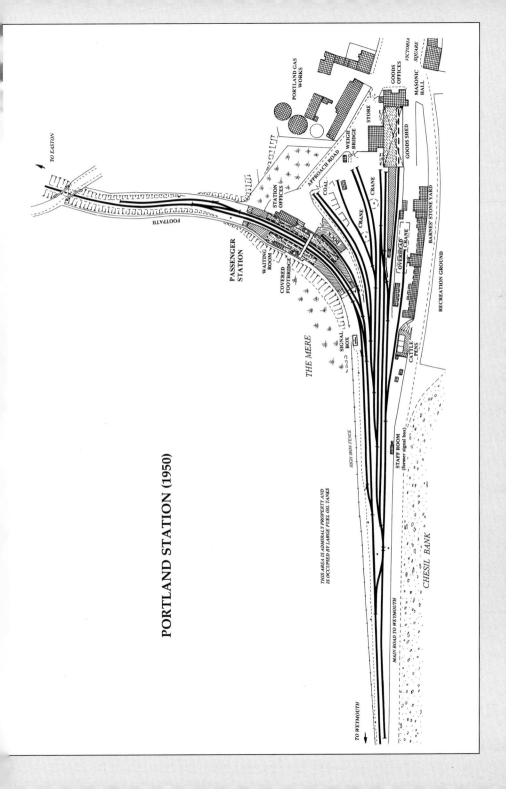

PORTLAND STATION (1950)

Exterior view of the original Portland station taken during the late 1950s.   *Lens of Sutton*

'O2' class No. 207 awaits to depart from Portland with a Weymouth-bound train, on the adjacent platform kit bags as always are awaiting collection.   *Lens of Sutton*

Portland looking towards Weymouth. To the right is the new Portland signal box opened in October 1935 and bombed on 11th August, 1940, to the left the original signal box of 1877 used as staff hut, and between the box and the platform a GWR concrete signal post. *A.B. Macleod*

A view from the new signal box of 1935 looking towards Portland station and yard, the new passenger station to the left, the old station serving as a goods shed centre right, and F.J. Barnes' stone works extreme right. Behind the two coaches are the buildings of Portland Gas Works.
Maureen Attwooll Collection

CASTLETOWN YARD

Castletown Yard. General arrangement drawing. The Admiralty Railway commenced just to the Easton side of Castletown Junction ground frame. Detailed maps and drawings of this area are contained in Volume One.

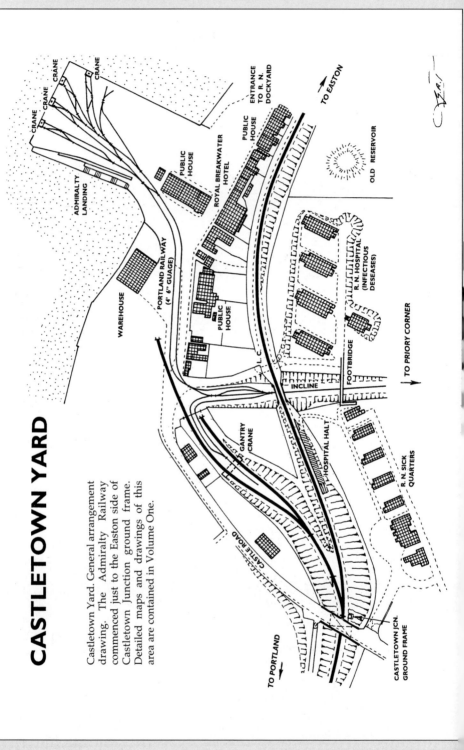

CRANE
CRANE
CRANE
CRANE
CRANE

ADMIRALTY LANDING

WAREHOUSE

PORTLAND RAILWAY (4' 6" GUAGE)

PUBLIC HOUSE

PUBLIC HOUSE

ROYAL BREAKWATER HOTEL

PUBLIC HOUSE

ENTRANCE TO R. N. DOCKYARD

TO EASTON

OLD RESERVOIR

R. N. HOSPITAL (INFECTIOUS DESEASES)

TO PRIORY CORNER

INCLINE

FOOTBRIDGE

GANTRY CRANE

HOSPITAL HALT

R. N. SICK QUARTERS

CASTILE ROAD

TO PORTLAND

CASTLETOWN JCN. GROUND FRAME

The next section of the line between Portland and Easton is one of the most spectacular on any railway line in the Country. The train leaves Portland station on a rising gradient of 1 in 216, which changes to a much steeper 1 in 48 as the line passes under a bridge carrying the road to Castletown and the Royal Naval Dockyard. On the left are Castletown sidings (4 m. 40 ch.) which are spanned by gantry cranes for the transfer of stone from the wagons of the 'Merchants' Railway' into standard gauge wagons waiting in the sidings.

From the junction with Castletown sidings the train travels over the line which forms part of the Admiralty Railway, and to the right can be seen a platform 60 feet long serving the Royal Naval Hospital (4 m. 48 ch.). At the end of the platform a girder bridge carries the line over the incline of the 'Merchants' Railway', and looking up to the right the cable-operated incline can be seen climbing up in a straight line high onto Verne Hill. After the bridge there is an occupation crossing leading into part of the Naval Hospital.

The line now curves to the right and runs on the level behind the houses and shops of Castletown Road. On the right-hand side Verne Hill drops steeply to the railway, the last few feet being held in place by a retaining wall. The gradient now changes to 1 in 66 (falling) to reach 'Admiralty Junction' - the point where the Dockyard sidings leave the Easton line, and the actual starting point of the Easton and Church Hope Railway. The Dockyard lines pass through a gate, and are separated from the public railway by high iron railings.

Leaving Admiralty Junction behind, there is immediately a short climb of 1 in 44 onto the lower edge of Verne Hill. A girder bridge takes the line over Incline Road, formerly the site of the Admiralty incline, and to the left there is a close view of the breakwater. In the south entrance to the harbour the rusting hull of HMS *Hood* can be seen rising from the water at low tide, this vessel having been sunk at this spot in 1914 to protect Portland harbour from U-boat attacks.

A pre-1900 view of Castletown sidings complete with overhead gantry cranes, running down the centre can be seen the narrow gauge line and wagons of the 'Merchants' Railway'.   *J.H. Lucking*

The 60 ft-long platform adjoining the Naval Hospital situated just beyond Castletown sidings. At the far end of the platform the girder bridge carrying the Easton line over the 'Merchants' incline can be clearly seen.   *Author*

The train climbs at 1 in 80 around the north-eastern corner of the Island and then takes a right-hand curve to pass HMS *Osprey* the Naval anti-submarine school. Above on the sheer face of Verne Hill, the East Weares Battery looks out over Weymouth Bay.

Near HMS *Osprey*, Incline Road goes to the top of the Island in three stages marking clearly the course of the former Admiralty incline. To the right is the rifle range and at the top of the hill stands Nicodemus Knob - a pillar of rock and relic of former quarrying operations, now used as a navigational landmark.

Gradually the train climbs the side of the Island, the gradient changing for one mile to 1 in 50 as the line clings to the cliff edge. To the left are the scars of old worked-out surface quarries leading down to the sea, and from here (on a clear day) the Shambles Lightship can be seen at anchor 4¾ miles off shore. To the right and high above the railway are the gaunt buildings of the Borstal Institution, the former convict prison, perched on top of the Island.

Numerous rock falls have occurred along this section of the line, and on the right near Grove Point the railway is protected by a 'screen' consisting of wires strung between poles which operate signals in the event of fresh falls of debris. The line now curves slightly to the right and passes St Paul's Quarries on the left. It was from here that Sir Christopher Wren obtained the stone for his famous cathedral in London.

The line at Grove Point in later years looking towards Portland station, the wire screen can be seen to the left running alongside the track, to the right the notice board giving warning of the Admiralty rifle range. *Author*

The train now turns inland through a deep rock cutting and climbs at 1 in 50 under Yeolands Bridge (known locally as Red Bridge) towards the centre of the Island. This was the section that caused many problems for the builders of the line, for it is no ordinary cutting through which we are now passing. It was cut and blasted out of solid rock, and the sides are vertical rock cliffs towering high above the tiny train.

Still in this deep cutting and climbing, the line passes under Wakeham Road bridge, after which there is a right-hand curve. Quarry Tip Siding now comes in on the left, this being part of the original Easton and Church Hope Railway, but destined only to serve a stone works and quarry waste tip. Now climbing steeply at 1 in 40 and still curving, the line comes up towards Easton. A siding to the right goes off into Bottom Coombe Quarry, shortly followed by another into Webber & Pangbournes yard. Journey's end is now in sight, for under a footbridge the line opens out into Easton station (7 m. 47 ch.). The line has curved through 180 degrees in just under one mile to reach its destination.

Easton station is built of stone, and stands at the end of an approach road leading from Easton Square. The goods yard, small and cramped, has a 3 ton crane and a small goods shed of the side loading type standing on a loading dock. Opposite the platform and beside the run-round loop stands the small signal box

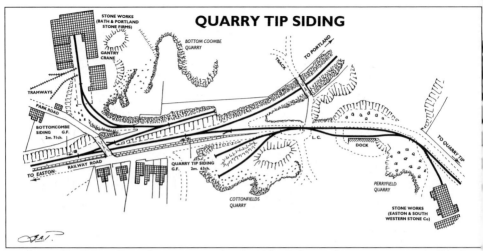

QUARRY TIP SIDING

STONE WORKS
(BATH & PORTLAND
STONE FIRMS)

BOTTOM COOMBE
QUARRY

TO PORTLAND

TRACK

GANTRY
CRANE

TRAMWAYS

PARK ROAD

BOTTOMCOMBE
SIDING   G.F.
         2m. 71ch.

L.C.

DOCK

TO QUARRY TIP

QUARRY TIP SIDING
G.F.   2m. 63ch.

RAILWAY ROAD

TO EASTON

COTTONFIELDS
QUARRY

PERRYFIELD
QUARRY

STONE WORKS
(EASTON & SOUTH
WESTERN STONE Co)

Quarry Tip Siding. General arrangement drawing. The Ordnance Survey map on page 136 of Volume One shows the full extent of Quarry Tip Siding.

An 'O2' class locomotive propels a train of loaded stone wagons out of the South Western Stone firm's yard at Quarry Tip Siding back onto the branch towards Easton station. The regulations for working the branch obliged the engine to be at the Portland end of the train to avoid a runaway in the event of a coupling breaking. When this picture was taken shortly before World War II, the land behind the train was being quarried (Park Quarry). Today most of it has been built on.   *R.E. Diment Collection*

Easton station looking towards Portland. An '02' class tank can be faintly seen inside the engine shed to the right.   *Author's Collection*

Easton goods shed. Note the very small side door and narrow platform!   *C.L. Caddy*

EASTON

Easton. General arrangement drawing. The 1902 Ordnance Survey map of Easton station can be found on page 142 of Volume One.

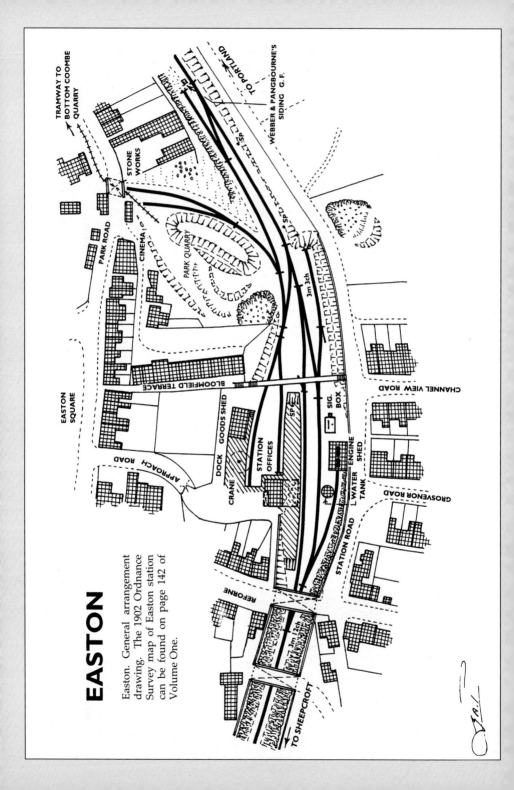

A general view of Easton station on 10th April, 1939, with No. 221 awaiting departure for Weymouth.   K.O.B. Nichols

built of stone and timber. Next to it is the engine shed, which is also constructed of local stone, and a conical water tower to serve the needs of the locomotives.

Before leaving the station the fossils displayed on the platform are worth inspection, they were collected by station master Pike from the railway cutting and the quarries of the district. Inside the station entrance glass-fronted cases filled with fossil shells, fish and other items collected over the years form a fascinating display.

Easton is the end of the line for passenger trains, but the rails continue under Reforne Road and climb for a short distance at 1 in 40, easing to 1 in 100 into Sheepcroft Yard (7 m. 74 ch.), where a trailing connection leads into Sheepcroft Sidings. These consist of two short loop sidings in front of a loading dock and a third much longer siding serving a coal yard which once extended westward into a group of quarries. One of the sidings is served by a 10 ton hand crane.

The main line continues for about ¼ mile beyond the points, coming to an abrupt end in a stone cutting at 8 m. 5 ch. In earlier days a gantry crane spanned the top of the cutting to load wagons from a nearby stone yard. There is no stop block, the rails ending against a solid wall of stone - the material that made the building of the railway such an attractive proposition.

As No. 233 approaches Easton the fireman holds out the single line staff ready for the signalman. To the right is the siding which was the scene of the 1903 runaway. K.O.B. Nichols

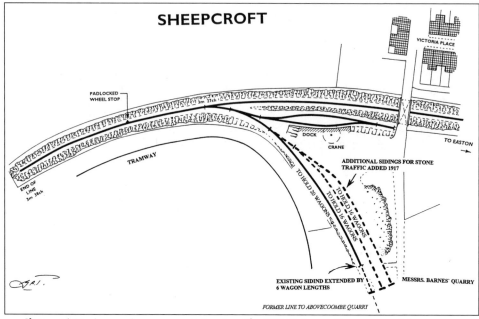

Sheepcroft Yard general arrangement drawing. The 1902 Ordnance Survey map of the area can be found on page 140 of Volume One.

Class '2' 2-6-2 tank No. 41294 marshals up the last freight train to leave Sheepcroft Yard on Tuesday 9th March, 1965. The branch can be clearly seen dropping away towards Easton under the bridges in the background.   *J.H. Lucking*

Chapter Seven

Motive Power and Rolling Stock

The best remembered locomotives used on the Portland branch were the Southern Railway 'O2' class. However, being a joint line without too many restrictions, a wide variety of engines were to be seen over the years, and it would be an impossible task to list all those that have worked the line. A brief outline of the more common types and notes on various locomotives of interest will give a good impression of the motive power provided.

Being constructed to mixed gauge, the line as opened in 1865 could be worked by the engines of both the operating companies. Apart from the Board of Trade tests carried out with a Great Western broad gauge 0-6-0 tender engine of the 'Caesar' class named *Clyde*, (which weighed 32 tons 19½ cwt and had 5 ft diameter driving wheels) little is known of other broad gauge locomotives employed in the early years. The Great Western did not participate in the working of the passenger traffic initially, which resulted in their broad gauge engines appearing only on goods trains. The London & South Western started operating the passenger services with their Beattie well tanks, the history of which was quite long and complicated. To many, the 'well tanks' are synonymous with the Wenford Bridge branch in North Cornwall, but although derived from the same class, the 'famous three' were considerably rebuilt over the years. The remainder of the class had been withdrawn by the late 1890s.

In 1858 three 2-4-0 well tanks of the 'Nelson' class were built, Nos. 143 *Nelson*, 144 *Howe* and 145 *Hood*. These had 5 ft diameter driving wheels, and cylinders of 15½ inch bore and 20 inch stroke. *Hood* was used for the testing of the line on 19th May, 1864. Still wishing to improve the well tank design, Joseph Beattie put three more into service in 1859, No. 154 *Nile*, No. 155 *Cressy* and No. 156 *Hogue*, these having 5 ft 9 in. diameter driving wheels and 14½ inch diameter cylinders. They carried 485 gallons of water and 15 cwt of coal. *Nile* is reputed to have hauled the first train on 16th October, 1865.

In 1863 the first of the standard well tanks was introduced. It was an improvement on the two previous types , and 85 of these engines were eventually built. There were various detail differences, full details of which are well described by D.L. Bradley in *Locomotives of the LSWR - Part 1* (published by the RCTS). The driving wheels were of 5 ft 9 in. diameter, and the cylinders (according to the batch of locomotives) being 15, 15½, or 16 inches diameter, a diameter of 16½ inches later becoming standard as the engines were overhauled. Various other small alterations took place over the years. Weather boards were fitted to the bunkers to give the crew a little more protection, and No. 208 actually received a cab roof! This was regarded as sheer luxury in the days when enginemen were still exposed to the elements except for the minimal protection of the front spectacle plate.

These little engines were of elegant appearance with all the brass work polished. In their early days they were painted in a chocolate livery with lining executed in black edged with white, but in 1872 the livery was changed to a

Well tank No. 156 *Hogue* withdrawn in September 1882 after working her last few years on the Portland branch.   *Author's Collection*

Well tank No. 214 worked on the Portland branch during the mid-1870s.   *Author's Collection*

Line drawing of GWR 0-6-0 'Caesar' class broad gauge tender engine. *Clyde* of this class hauled the broad gauge Board of Trade inspection train before the opening of the branch. *Clyde* and other members of the class undoubtedly hauled broad gauge goods trains pre-1874.

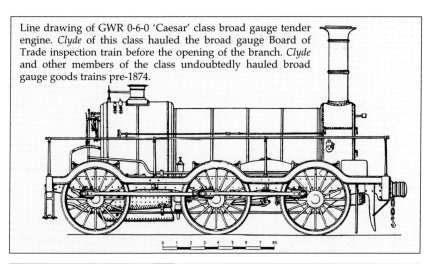

Line drawing of 2-4-0 Beattie well tank *Hogue* used at the opening of the branch.

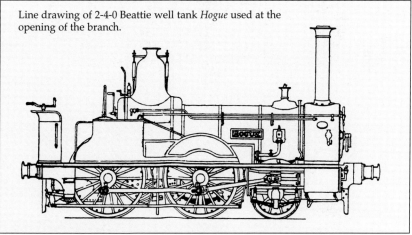

Line drawing of '329' class Beattie well tank.

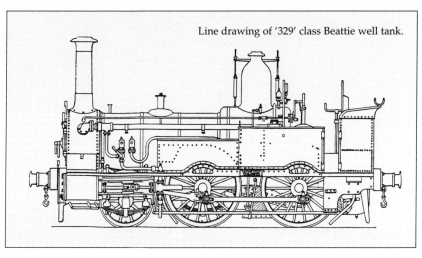

paler shade of chocolate known as 'purple brown'. The use of feed water heaters on earlier engines was discontinued, as was the fitting of running plate-mounted boiler feed pumps, although those already fitted lasted until 1880 when a start was made on their removal. In June 1865 the LSWR Locomotive Committee placed an order with Beyer, Peacock & Co. Ltd for six standard well tanks, Nos. 209-214, ostensibly to work the Winchester-Alton and Portland branches, the order being completed by May the following year. Which of these locomotives (if any) were sent to work the Portland branch is unclear, as frequent changes of allocation took place.

Dorchester Shed was responsible for supplying the branch engines, and No. 115 *Cressy* was working the branch during 1867; Dorchester had No. 143 *Nelson* as a spare engine during the early 1870s, and she was often used on the branch. Following the removal of the broad gauge and the working of the passenger service in alternate years by each company the demand on the class was less. By the mid-1870s standard well tanks Nos. 203, 208 and 214 were the regular branch engines, and at the same time No. 145 *Hood* made a brief re-appearance on the line. By March 1878 the allocated engines were Nos. 246 and 248, No. 155 *Cressy* returning during 1880/2. In March 1890 Nos. 327 and 246 were working the branch, although by then the introduction of the '02' class was shortly to bring about their demise.

With the construction of new locomotives the well tanks were progressively displaced from the London suburban area, but as their use in country areas required a greater water capacity for longer runs, a number of the class were converted to tender engines. In June 1888 Nos. 177, 178, 180 and 181 were stationed at Dorchester for local work. Whether they actually worked on the Portland branch is a matter for conjecture, but it seems likely they put in an appearance at some time. These locomotives, as with all the remaining well tanks were re-numbered in the duplicate list to allow their original numbers to be used by the '02' class then under construction.

In 1878 William Adams succeeded W.G. Beattie as mechanical engineer of the London & South Western Railway, and on 12th December, 1889 the first of his highly successful '02' class 0-4-4 tank engines entered service. By 1895 sixty of these very useful machines had been built at Nine Elms works, each costing £1,500, which also happened by coincidence to be the yearly salary of their designer! The driving wheels were 4 ft 10 in. in diameter, and the bogie wheels 3 ft. The cylinders had a 17 in. bore and a 24 in. stroke, except Nos. 117-196 which were built with 17 in. cylinders. Their water tanks carried 800 gallons, and the bunker held 1½ tons of coal.

As with all Adams designs they were aesthetically pleasing, and when new they were painted in a delightful pea green. Various shades of green remained their livery until World War II, when black was substituted as the engines were repainted. After nationalisation, black with red, cream and grey lining became the livery for many the class, and it suited them well when kept clean. Some minor alterations were made to the class over the years, the original stove pipe chimneys being replaced by the Drummond type after 1900, and coal rails were fitted to the top of the bunkers which allowed an extra ½ ton of coal to be carried. In June 1907 No. 223 was fitted with a new boiler with Drummond mountings, the main difference from the Adams' type being the fitting of the safety valves on the steam dome instead of over the firebox. Fourteen more of these boilers were constructed at Eastleigh after 1923, and at different times fitted to various locomotives as required. Compared with their Adams' counterparts they were poor steamers and not so popular with the crews. However, the engines themselves were very popular, and could manage the severe gradients of the Easton section without difficulty. Another good feature was the steam brake, which was much in demand on the return journey - particularly with a loaded stone train!

The system of replacing a locomotive with one of the same class at a depot when a visit to works was due caused a great many changes in allocation. Once overhauled, an engine could well be sent to another shed to replace the next of that class in line for attention. No. 180, built in April 1890, was soon put to work on the branch. During November 1892 she was involved in a minor derailment on the Backwater viaduct. Between May and August 1902 this engine was converted to burn oil on the Howden system as an experiment, during which time she worked in the London area. Although the trials were successful, coal cost only 17s. 5d. per ton whereas oil was £1 2s. 5d. per ton, so the engine soon reverted to normal use. She was transferred to the Isle of Wight in May 1927 where, as No. 31 *Chale*, she operated until the last steam train ran on 31st December, 1966, then being one of two retained to haul engineer's trains during electrification work.

Three engines built during April 1892, Nos. 214, 215 and 216, were fitted with steam sanding gear and sent to work the branch. During 1896 Nos. 215, 216 and 221 were recorded as working on the branch. No. 214 was an early casualty being withdrawn in July 1940. No. 215 was transferred to the Isle of Wight in June 1924 and renumbered No. 22 *Brading* surviving there until December 1966. By June 1914, No. 216 was working the Yeovil Town-Yeovil Junction shuttle service, and by the early 1930s she had moved further into the West Country. She was finally withdrawn in November 1957. After various transfers No. 221 was again at Dorchester in 1939, being withdrawn from service in August 1953.

Coal returns for August 1911 give details of locomotives in use on the branch,

Engine No.	Miles passenger	Miles goods	Coal burnt per mile (lbs.)
202	2,444	509	40.3
214	916	978	39.4
234	995	986	42.0
233	1,950	333	42.0

Of these engines, No. 233 was used by the War Office for a period during the World War I, as were two other branch engines Nos. 178 and 197. No. 185 was the only Adams' engine to carry a name. On 12th July, 1890, named *Alexandra* for the occasion, she hauled a special train conveying HRH Princess of Wales over the Bisley branch.

No. 213, employed on the Portland branch during the 1920s, was loaned to the War Department between 1941 and 1943. The first of the class to be built, No. 177, spent a considerable part of her life on the Portland branch. During 1900 she was working on the LSWR section of the Chard branch, and between

Line drawings of Adams 'G6' class 0-6-0 and '02' class 0-4-4 tank as in original condition with stovepipe chimney.

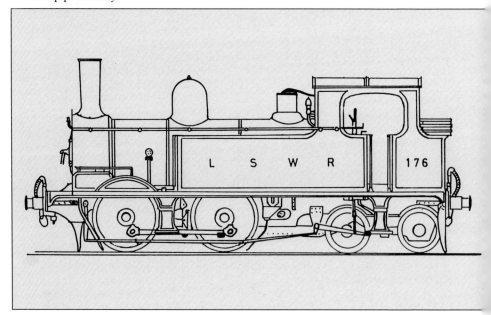

1907 and 1914 worked the Lyme Regis branch. By the mid-1920s No. 177 had appeared at Portland and she was to maintain an association with the branch for many years. In August 1951 she was painted in British Railways' lined black livery, and in spotless condition had the distinction of hauling the last regular passenger train.

During 1932 Nos. 202, 213 and 224 were to be seen on the branch, whilst by late 1934 Nos. 193, 201, 203 and 213 were the usual branch engines, but various changes took place. In August 1937 the following Dorchester-allocated engines were available for branch service: Nos. 177, 181, 213, 221, 223 and 229. By August of 1939 Nos. 181 and 213 had been replaced by 185 and 233. It is recorded that in August 1943 Nos. 177, 221 and 223 were working the line whilst No. 229 appeared by late 1945, when the branch engines were listed as Nos. 177, 221, 223, 229 and 233. Following nationalisation the class were renumbered into the 30,000 series, each engine receiving the prefix '30', the December 1948 allocation being 30177, 30179, 30223, 30229, 30233, and during the final years of passenger operation Nos. 30177, 30179, 30197 30223 and 30239 were the usual branch locomotives.

By the late 1890s the 'G6' class had arrived at Dorchester for use on local shunting duties and the Portland goods trains. These 0-6-0 tank locomotives entered service in 1894, also designed by William Adams and costing £1,480 each, they were robust shunting engine with 4 ft 10 in. driving wheels and cylinders of 17½ in. bore with 24 in. stroke. Their tanks held 1,000 gallons of water and the bunkers carried two tons of coal. Weight in working order was 44 tons 3 cwt. Similar to the 'O2' class in appearance (apart from the wheel arrangement), they were fitted with a stove-pipe chimney when new. No. 258 was one of the first of the class to be allocated to Dorchester, and often worked Portland goods traffic.

During 1901 No. 273 appeared at Dorchester followed later that year by No. 263. As first built these engines were provided only with a handbrake and it was not until the late 1920s that vacuum brakes were fitted. It took 20 years to fit this refinement to the whole class! In May 1922 No. 263 was fitted with the vacuum brake as an experiment and ran trials over the Portland branch. However she was considered less successful than the 'O2' class, and after removal of the vacuum fittings she returned to yard shunting duties.

The railmotor era can be best described as a short experiment in cost-cutting, made necessary mainly to meet competition from trams and motor buses. Compared with those on the Great Western, the LSWR cars had a short life. Fifteen were constructed but the last one was withdrawn from service in October 1919, whereas the Great Western had a total of 99 cars, the last of which survived until 1932. The LSWR cars were successful only if used on a line with limited traffic and without severe gradients, but if extra traffic appeared they were in trouble! Hauling a trailer was just too much for them.

In 1905 Halts were opened between Weymouth and Dorchester at Radipole, Upwey Wishing Well, and Came Bridge, the GWR starting up a service of steam railmotors to serve them, and soon afterwards railmotors appeared on the Abbotsbury branch.

Not to be outdone, the London & South Western conducted trials on Wednesday 29th March, 1905 between Dorchester and Easton using railmotor

No. 198 in LSWR livery stands at Easton. This locomotive was one of the last 'O2' class to be shipped over to the Isle of Wight in April 1949, where she was renamed W36 *Carisbrooke*. She survived until June 1964 and when withdrawn from service, had travelled 1,599,478 recorded miles.   *S. Morris Collection*

LSWR steam railmotor No. 5. For a short time she was used between Weymouth and Portland.
Lens of Sutton

No. 2, which was jointly owned by the London & South Western Railway and the London, Brighton & South Coast Railway for use on the Fratton to Southsea branch. Although only two years old, No. 2, and her sister No. 1, had already received new boilers in an attempt to improve their efficiency, but they were still incapable of hauling a trailer. It was also sometimes rather difficult to stop them, as they were fitted only with a handbrake! One wonders how Drummond could report in April 1905 that trials on the Portland branch had been a success!

Between October 1905 and February 1906, seven railcars of the 'H13' class were constructed and worked various branch lines, and another six were soon added. The entire class was equipped with horizontal boilers (which were in fact miniature locomotive boilers working at a pressure of 165 psi). The two 10 in. diameter cylinders had a stroke of 14 in., and the coal capacity of 1 ton was carried in a bunker alongside the boiler. On the other side was a 485 gallon water tank.

The engine and boiler unit was contained within the main bodywork of the coach, the length of which was 52 ft 7 in. The total weight was 32 tons 6 cwt. Built to the general outline of London & South Western passenger stock of the period, the livery was dark brown lower panels with salmon pink above the waistline, the engine bogie frame and cylinders, etc. being locomotive green. Seating inside was for 40 passengers - eight in the first class saloon and 32 in the third. The floors were covered with linoleum and the first class seats were upholstered, whilst in the third class seating consisted of curved plywood panels with perforated patterns cut into them - an idea very popular at the time. The entrance was between the two compartments by way of an open vestibule protected only by lattice gates, from which doors led into each compartment.

Although they appeared throughout the South Western system, the cars never came up to expectations. Hauling themselves along was an effort enough and as already mentioned towing a trailer was not far short of impossible. In service the lot of the crew was not to be envied, for in order to keep a good head of steam expert firing was required. However, if this was attempted whilst the engine was pulling hard, the mere act of opening the firehole door soon reduced the steam pressure, and the only way out was to have a good stoke up at a station stop and hope that it would last until the next. There is little doubt that their generally poor performance was the downfall of the class, the entire fleet being withdrawn during the Great War and converted into push-pull trailers.

By 1908 the Portland branch had been losing money for several years, and it was agreed between the operating companies to improve the service by making use of railcars, the agreement being signed (perhaps not inappropriately) on 'April Fools Day' 1st April! The Great Western for its part was to build two large capacity cars costing £2,350 each, but for reasons not fully explained that company soon withdrew.

There is little doubt that the Great Western realised the limitations of these machines. There is photographic evidence of a GWR railmotor and trailer on the branch at Wyke Halt in late June 1909, and from the allocation records it is reasonable to assume that this was either car No. 44 or 46, as No. 36 did not arrive at Weymouth until that July, with No. 46 departing in September. Allowing for railmotor operation of the Dorchester local service and the

Abbotsbury branch, with an average allocation of three railmotors there was little or no reserve to operate a regular service to Portland.

The LSWR was therefore left to operate the service from 1st September, 1909, car No. 12 being the first to be regularly used on the line, she was joined by No. 4 at the end of the year, and No. 13 also appeared at various times. Of the railcars known to have worked on the branch, No. 4 managed to clock up 96,329 miles by the time she was withdrawn in July 1919, her boiler then being sold to Bournemouth Corporation to heat the Council greenhouses.

The railcars were certainly unsuitable for the branch, and Drummond was considering the idea of fitting one car with a high pressure boiler designed by Vickers and using a four cylinder engine unit. To reduce the weight of the vehicle by 12 cwt 3 qr the fitting of light weight seating and a new trailing bogie was also considered, a total cost of £410 being involved. Intended for service on the Portland branch, the boiler was purchased, but the modified unit never materialised. As the details of this conversion came from a report by Drummond himself, he had virtually condemned the class by his own hand! He had obviously realised the limitations of the railcars very quickly for no sooner had they entered service than he ordered 10 small 2-2-0 tank locomotives to haul auto-trailers, thus allowing the engine to be changed without affecting the coach.

Although the Great Western railmotors had been more successful than those on the LSWR, that company also quickly came to favour the idea of a separate engine. But as the locomotives used were of tried and tested design the GWR suffered none of the frustrations endured by the LSWR.

The Drummond 2-2-0 tanks cost £875 each, and were built at Nine Elms works. Classed as 'C14', their cylinders, motion and wheels were the same as used on the railmotors. The boiler worked at a pressure of 150 psi. The side tanks (which almost extended the full length of the boiler) held 500 gallons of water, and the small bunker carried 1 ton of coal. Intended to operate push-pull trains, the necessary wires and pulleys were fitted to the cab roof.

As with the railmotors, which engines of the class actually worked the branch is not fully recorded. In May 1907 No. 744 was in operation, and in 1911 No. 738 was to be frequently seen at Portland. In November 1907 the following notice appeared:

The small railmotor engines and trailer cars on the Portland line to be restricted to 15 mph and to run with the engine leading in the down direction. Additional cars are not to be attached. These engines and trailers not to be used in high winds.

It is clear that these units were not at all versatile, in fact 'handicapped' is an apt word for them! Before the building of Melcombe Regis station the distance from Weymouth to Portland was 4½ miles. At 15 mph the journey took 18 minutes, (not allowing for reversal at Weymouth Junction and a stop at Rodwell). When allowance is made for acceleration and braking distances the average timing of 20 minutes for the journey must have pressed these engines to the limit. In fact, to arrive on time must have involved breaking the speed limit!

Like the railmotors they replaced, these units were under-powered when it came to hauling extra stock, and the class was withdrawn from regular passenger service to end up either in store or doing very light work. Members of the class were eventually sold to private owners, except for three which were converted into 0-4-0 tanks for use in the Southampton area. The 'C14' in this rebuilt form was clearly the nearest thing to Frank Hornby's famous 'M3' tank, but without the hole for the key! No. 3744 (as British Railways No. 30589) had a final swan song on passenger work on 14th June, 1952, when she hauled an RCTS special on the Bishops Waltham branch, on which she reached a speed of 34¾ mph! Both the railmotors and the 'C14' class were a conspicuous failure on the Portland branch, and the '02' class regained their control of the branch for the working of LSWR trains, and as already mentioned Nos. 202, 214, 233 and 234 put in 6,305 miles hauling passenger trains during August 1911.

Far from being a typically quiet branch line, Portland could become very busy, and it only needed a ship to arrive with Naval personnel going on leave or going out for a night on the town in Weymouth for the branch train to become very well loaded. Extra stock could be hauled by an '02', but that had been out of the question for the railmotor units. As a result the 'O2' class remained firmly in charge of LSWR (and later Southern) trains until the end.

Following the re-construction of both the Fleet and Backwater viaducts many restrictions were lifted, and a variety of engines have worked over the branch, particularly as far as Portland station. The Drummond 4-4-0 'T9' class were frequent visitors on specials such as Naval trains between Portland and Portsmouth, as were the Drummond 4-4-0 'K10' class. During the Great War munition trains, consisting of about 30 covered vans with a heavy brake van each end, were double-headed by these locomotives, Nos. 334, 347 and 394 being used on these duties for which they carried large fire extinguishers as a precaution against fire in the van roofs caused by sparks. Again during World War II the 'K10' class worked over the line, often piloted by an '02'. Amongst the various movements recorded during November 1941, 'K10' No. 387 and 'T9' No. 284 were noted hauling a Naval special to Portland.

Any engine allocated to Dorchester and suitable for use on the branch could by used, and before World War I Drummond 'Black Motor' '700' class 0-6-0 tender engines were to be seen. In 1927, '0395' class 0-6-0 goods engine No. 083, (built in 1885) was recorded as being in charge of the branch goods. This engine was not withdrawn until February 1953, having travelled a recorded 1,723,902 miles. Dorchester allocated 'A12' 0-4-2 ('Jubilees') also worked over the branch. During 1917 '330' class 0-6-0 saddle tanks Nos. 0217 and 0334 were sent to Dorchester to assist with the extra shunting at Weymouth caused by the heavy Naval traffic to Portland, and it is almost certain that these and many other locomotives found their way onto the branch. Definite information is lacking, but it must be remembered that the Portland branch was not the best place to be seen with a note book and camera in times of war!

In later years 'Q', 'Q1' and 'U' class locomotives were often used on the branch, especially working empty stock trains. Before moving on to the motive power of the Great Western Railway, it is interesting to note that during the summer of 1960 'M7' class No. 30377, was allocated to Weymouth, the motive

A Drummond railmotor locomotive with a Weymouth-bound train hauls two trailers along the shoreline towards Sandsfoot Castle, during the short period these locomotives operated on the branch. *Author's Collection*

Two 'T9' class locomotives head past Westham Halt towards Weymouth with a special train, complete with Union Jack and other decorations on the front locomotive. It is either a Coronation Special, or 'Pompey for the Cup'. *W. Newman*

power depot by that time being under the control of the Southern Region. On at least one occasion she was noted hauling the Portland goods, the final visit of a former LSWR engine to the branch.

Owing to the fact that the GWR was less heavily involved in the operation of branch train services than the LSWR (and later the Southern Railway), there is not so much documented material available on the subject, particularly during the Broad Gauge period. The Gooch 0-6-0 'Standard Goods' no doubt worked much of the freight traffic, assisted by any other suitable broad gauge engine available.

Saddle tanks were in use on the line from the time of the gauge conversion, At first the '850' class appeared, to be followed after the turn of the century by the '2021' class built at Wolverhampton Works between 1897 and 1905. Their cylinders had a bore of 16½ in., and a stroke of 24 in., the six-coupled driving wheels having an overall wheelbase of 14 ft 8 in. and the complete engine weighed 40 ton 13¾ cwt making them a very useful locomotive. Various members of the class, including Nos. 2031, 2038, 2044, 2046, 2059, 2086, 2093, 2124, 2125, 2126, 2132, and 2147, are known to have worked over the line.

No. 2044, the Easton engine in January 1906 and again in 1909, was fitted with a drumhead extension to the smokebox about 1911, and operated on the branch in that condition. Like most of her sister engines she lasted many years, being converted to a pannier tank in March 1926, and not withdrawn until July 1951.

In the years following the Great War several of the '1076' (or 'Buffalo') class could be seen at times on the line, Nos. 1239 and 1281 being allocated to Weymouth. These had been built at Swindon in 1877 and subsequently had an interesting history. Like most tank engines of the period they were fitted with saddle tanks and were later converted to pannier tanks. No. 1239 was rebuilt as a broad gauge engine in June 1887 for work in the West Country, and following the abolition of Brunel's famous 7 ft way in 1892 she was restored to standard gauge. Both of these locomotives survived until 1935.

Following the Great War operation of the regular passenger service was completely in the hands of the Southern Railway, the Great Western working only their own goods trains and other special traffic as required. Weymouth had acquired five of the '655' class tank engines by 1938. These engines dated from between 1892 and 1897, and like those mentioned previously were built at Wolverhampton and started life as saddle tanks. By the time they appeared at Weymouth they had become pannier tanks, and some were fitted with enclosed cabs. With the approach of World War II Nos. 1775, 1782, 1789, 1831 and 2710 were based at Weymouth, although this allocation varied. In May 1943 No. 2720 was seen shunting at Portland, whilst 1789, withdrawn in September 1939, was reinstated that December and survived at Weymouth until withdrawn in October 1950. In her 56 years of service she travelled a recorded 1,069,716 miles, a record for the class.

Just after the end of the war the newer '57XX' pannier tanks started to appear, including Nos. 4660, 7782 and 9628, and thereafter any members of that class allocated to Weymouth would work the traffic. Over the years many of these locomotives were constructed and full details of the various small alterations are to be found in *Locomotives of the Great Western Railway, Part 5*, published by

GWR '2021' class saddle tank No. 2044 photographed at Portland between 1908 and 1912, during which time she was fitted with an extended smokebox. To the left is fireman George Gould, standing alongside driver Fred Hooper. *Author's Collection*

GWR '45XX' class locomotive, No. 4536 climbs away from the Backwater viaduct towards Littlefield Crossing with a Portland-bound goods on 22nd July, 1939. *W. Newman*

the RCTS. Of the more interesting was No. 3765, built in March 1938, which fell victim to a derailment in October 1949 when the line was flooded, and No. 9642, for many years allocated to Weymouth and now preserved by a group based at Swansea, South Wales.

Very little is known about the use of Great Western steam railmotors over the branch, it would appear that they were little used, although one was tested over the line to Easton. The GWR preferred to retain the use of conventional trains. Likewise the Great Western 'auto-trains' were never put to regular use on the line, although at one stage during the 1930s and 1940s one morning trip, the 7.38 from Melcombe Regis, was operated by an auto-engine before it went to work on the Abbotsbury branch. Amongst the other Great Western types used on the line, the '45XX' class 2-6-2 tanks often worked as far as Portland with goods traffic. During 1937 experimental loadings were carried out with '55XX' class tanks on the Weymouth-Portland section, allowing a maximum of 26 loaded wagons to Portland and 38 Portland to Weymouth, or 34 and 50 empties. '43XX' class 2-6-0 Moguls also appeared on the branch, these being permitted to work as far as Portland. This restriction also applied to the 0-6-0 '2251' class. In earlier years the '2301' class 'Dean Goods' frequently appeared on the line, and like the other larger locomotives, they were not permitted beyond Portland. However, one was recorded along the Easton section with a ballast train during a landslip. A story (unsubstantiated) was told by the older staff for many years concerning a 'Hall' class 4-6-0 working a special over the branch during the war years and striking the platform edge at Portland with her cylinder block. However as a '47XX' 2-8-0, a class banned south of Castle Cary managed to arrive at Weymouth during 1943, anything was possible!

Early in 1964 the last GWR pannier tank left Weymouth, the duties being taken over by Ivatt '2MT' 2-6-2 tanks, and Nos. 41261, 41284, 41298, 41305 and 41374 worked the branch in its final year. Even these engines were not without interest. No. 41284 had previously worked on the non-electrified section of the London Transport system, between Rickmansworth and Amersham, whilst No. 41298 arrived at Weymouth in 1963, and remained there until October 1966 when she moved to London working empty stock trains between Waterloo and Clapham Yard. When steam working finished on the Southern Region in July 1967 she was purchased by The Ivatt Trust, and stored on the Longmoor Military Railway in Hampshire until December 1970, when she was moved to the Quainton Railway Centre in Buckinghamshire for restoration.

The GWR introduced its diesel railcars onto the Weymouth-Bristol service in January 1936, and later onto both the Weymouth-Dorchester-Yeovil local service and the Abbotsbury branch. A comment in the local press on 21st March, 1936 stated:

The *Southern Times* understands that consideration has been given by Weymouth Railway officials to the future possibility of operating a diesel car service between Weymouth (Melcombe Regis) and Portland.

As far as is known the idea was never followed up and the only time diesel traction ventured over the Portland branch was when trains from the Abbotsbury branch ran into Melcombe Regis station, which was used as an extra arrival platform for Weymouth station during busy periods.

A pair of GWR '43XX' class Moguls pass Westham Halt with a special for Portland.
W. Newman

Owing to congestion at Weymouth station certain Abbotsbury branch trains terminated at Melcombe Regis at busy times, and as far as is known a GWR diesel railcar never ventured further along the Portland branch. *Author's Collection*

The general locomotive restrictions of the branch did not apply to the section between Weymouth Junction and Melcombe Regis station, and often 'King Arthurs', 'West Countries', and 'Halls' were to be seen, and on at least one occasion a Great Western 'Castle' had pulled well forward onto the Backwater viaduct. But with all the various engines that have worked the line, anyone looking back nostalgically to the days of the passenger service will always cherish the memory of the '02' tanks, faithful to the end, and at 60 years of age a credit to their designer for reliability and Victorian elegance.

Rolling Stock

With very few exceptions most types of rolling stock appeared on the branch, ranging from primitive four-wheelers to modern post-war main line vehicles. Details of early coaching stock are generally sketchy, and full details of branch line stock almost non-existent.

According to W.E. Edwards, writing in the 1909 *Railway Magazine*, amongst the early stock used on the line was a set of six LSWR four-wheelers, one of which is reputed to have been a former Royal saloon constructed in 1851 for the use of Queen Victoria's children. Having been stripped of its Royal fittings and re-upholstered, it appeared in normal service as a first class saloon. Later sold to the Plymouth, Devonport & South Western Junction Railway, it had moved on to the Kent & East Sussex Light Railway by 1914, on which (as first class No. 10) it remained until 1936 when it was exchanged with the SR for a more modern coach. The body was sold to a Sussex farmer, and survived until the early 1960s.

Both companies used four-wheelers of various vintage, and generally they had seen good service before their arrival on the branch. The earlier vehicles were not fitted with any form of continuous brake, and when it did appear it was not very reliable, as was proved by the accident of September 1876. The *Southern Times* for 29th September, 1877 gave the reassuring news that 'several new coaches with continuous brake have been put on the Portland line'. These were the GWR vehicles involved in the December 1877 accident, the train on that occasion consisting of a 1st/2nd composite, 1st class, brake 3rd, two 3rds, 2nd, and brake 3rd.

In August 1880, at a meeting of the officers of the Joint Committee, it was revealed that when the LSWR Company operated the passenger service trains of more than six coaches required two guards as the brake was not continuous throughout the train. The Great Western objected to this - not on the grounds that unfitted stock was used, but to sharing the expense of the additional guard! The following year the LSWR decided to adopt the automatic continuous vacuum brake as standard, and within a few years it was in general use. The illumination of coaches at that time was also poor, oil lamps being the usual form of light. These were later replaced by Pintschs Patent Gas Lighting. There were many complaints concerning the condition of the trains, but to be fair they were no worse than those used on many branch lines.

In general both companies used four-wheel coaches until the introduction of the steam railmotors. During 1904 the LSWR trains consisted of 28 ft and 30ft

'O2' class No. 229 stands at Melcombe Regis station, waiting to depart for Portland with a train of four-wheel coaches. Taken just after the opening of the station in 1909. The area in the foreground was later infilled to form Melcombe Regis Gardens.
R.S. Carpenter Collection

LSWR four-wheel stock standing outside Portland station c. 1910. They appear to be (from the left) a 32 ft brake third of c. 1891, a 34 ft third of 1882, 32 ft composite of 1881, two 32 ft composites of 1880, a 32 ft brake third, and a 34 ft brake third of either 1882 or rebuilt from a third. In the background (below the oil tanks) stands an LSWR 2-coach set. In the right background is Portland station signal box.
Author's Collection

coaches dating from the early 1880s, one such vehicle being No. 020, a 28 ft brake third of 1881, its three compartments each seating 10 passengers. It should perhaps be added that compartments in LSWR stock were of generous proportions compared with those found on some railways.

Even as late as 1910 LSWR four-wheel coaches were to be seen on the branch, a typical rake of the period consisting of a 32 ft brake third, a 34 ft third, a 32 ft composite, two 32 ft composites, a 34 ft third and a 34 ft brake third - all dating from 1880-82. The opening of the Easton extension to passenger traffic and the use of a separate train on that service initially provided the LSWR with a good excuse to give some antique stock an outing, the train of four-wheeled vehicles consisted of two brake thirds, a four-compartment composite, and a five-compartment composite.

Likewise the Great Western used four-wheel stock almost until the Great War, and trains of up to 12 of these vehicles were not uncommon, it being the practice at that time to add the Abbotsbury branch set to the train. One reason for doing this was to increase the seating capacity of the service, but the other was the lack of siding accommodation at Weymouth to hold the stock. Gradually the Great Western introduced better vehicles, and older main line bogie coaches, usually of the clerestory type, appeared on the branch.

Three special LSWR coaches that should be mentioned as they almost certainly appeared on the branch during their lives, were a special coach constructed in 1869 to convey convicts, and a later vehicle of the same type built in 1882 and also an Admiralty ambulance coach of 1899. The introduction of the steam railmotors and the trailer sets provided the public with a standard of comfort never before experienced on the island. The trailer cars, with their centre entrance protected by an iron gate, were synonymous with the branch until the early years of World War II. As with previous steam railmotors, these vehicles had more than a passing resemblance to a tramcar. The gated entrance, the interior layout with well upholstered seating, a section of which was placed longitudinally, the handrails and straps, all combined to give that impression. The 'gate sets' totalled 31 coaches, all built between 1903 and 1914, of these 15 were reconstructed from steam railmotors after the Great War. Nine gate-type vehicles are known to have worked regularly over the Portland branch

During 1909 three trailer cars specially for working the Portland branch were constructed at Eastleigh works. Each car was 56ft long and two were of the composite type carrying 10 1st class passengers and 40 third class. Luggage space and a driving compartment were also provided. The third class car seated 38 smoking and 30 non-smoking passengers; steam heating and gas lighting were provided. All cars were gangwayed, and could run as a three- or two-car set which was probably just as well when a 'C14' class tank provided the motive power! The set was originally fitted with the LSWR wire and pulley push-pull gear, which was only used during the brief stay of the 'C14' tanks, the '02s' never working on the branch push-pull fitted. The push-pull equipment was eventually removed from the set in October 1933.

When built, the two brake composites carried the numbers 7 and 9 and the third saloon number 8, these being later renumbered 4301, 4302 and 4254 respectively. They were again renumbered by the Southern Railway as Nos.

Three-coach gate set consisting of open brake composites Nos. 6543 and 6544 and open 3rd No. 736 standing outside Portland station. It was painted in the salmon and brown livery of the LSWR. This set was constructed in 1909 especially for the Portland branch, and later became set No. 370.   *Author's Collection*

End detail of trailer set No. 371, as engine No. 229 takes water before the return journey to Weymouth.   *A.B. Macleod*

6543, 6544 and 736 and run as set No. 370. During October 1937 brake composite No. 6543 was withdrawn and brake composite No. 6553 was placed in the set, this vehicle having previously run on the branch as steam railmotor No. 12 before conversion.

Two other former steam railmotors came to the branch as trailers, No. 740 was formerly LSWR 'H12' class steam railmotor No. 1, built in 1904 and converted into a trailer with a seating capacity of 64 third class in October 1922. No. 743, formerly one of the two joint LSWR/LBSCR steam railmotors used on the Southsea branch, was rebuilt as a trailer in February 1922. It had seating capacity of 56, the centre section seating 32 in conventional fashion whilst at each end longitudinal bench seats catered for another 24. One of the original brake composites, No. 6543, was withdrawn in October 1937, being replaced by brake composite No. 6553 which was a rebuild of former LSWR 'H13' class steam railmotor No. 12. Two other brake composites, Nos. 6554 and 6555, and former 'H13' class steam railmotors Nos. 13 and 14, were also working on the branch, No. 6554 having previously appeared on the line as a railmotor. In their rebuilt form they had a capacity of 54 passengers, six first class on longitudinal seats in a compartment between the entrance and the guard's van, and 48 in conventional seating in the main compartment. Sixteen of these seats were provided by the conversion of the original cab/boiler room into a compartment. There was also some variation in the type of gate used on the stock. All the rebuilt vehicles used the original Bostwick-type lattice sliding gate, whereas the three 1909 vehicles used had conventionally-opening iron gates of the 'garden' type. Needless to say, once inside the entrance vestibule, there were sliding doors into each compartment.

Two sets of coaches were required to cover the basic service, although the set system was far from permanent, and over the years many changes were made. The following are just some of the combinations recorded at various times.

Set 370
6543 736 6544 in 1910.
6543 736 743 6544 in 1930s
6543 740 742 6544 in 1930s
6543 736 743 6553 in 1937
6543 736 740 743 6553 on one occasion
6544 736 743 6553 in 1937
6543 736 in 1928, 1930 and 1933
6544 6553 in July 1939

Set 371
6544 743 in 1928
6554 740 late 1920s
6554 743 in 1930 and 1933
6554 6555 in July 1939
6554 740 742 6555 in 1930s
6554 743 6555 on one occasion.
6544 6555 in 1939/41

Set 372
6544 743

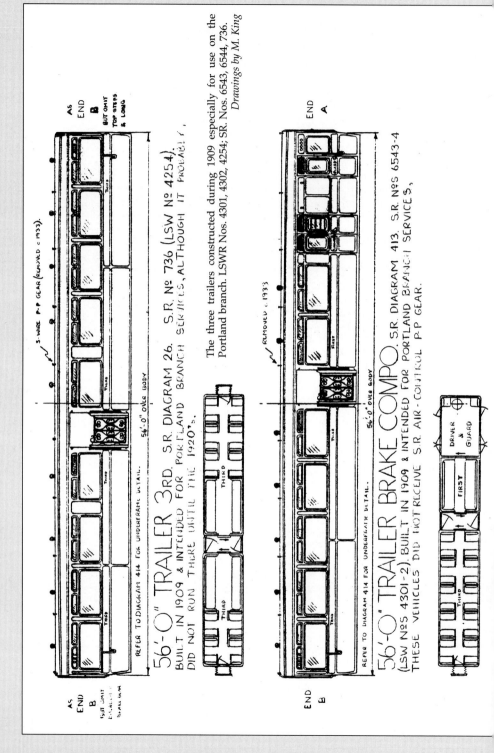

56'-0" TRAILER 3RD. S.R. DIAGRAM 26. S.R. N° 736 (LSW N° 4254).
BUILT IN 1909 & INTENDED FOR PORTLAND BRANCH SERVICES, ALTHOUGH IT PROBABLY
DID NOT RUN THERE UNTIL THE 1920's.

REFER TO DIAGRAM 414 FOR UNDERFRAME DETAIL.

56'-0" OVER BODY

AS END B BUT OMIT TOP STEPS & LONG

AS END B BUT OMIT BRAKE GEAR

3. WIDE P.P GEAR (REMOVED c 1933).

The three trailers constructed during 1909 especially for use on the
Portland branch. LSWR Nos. 4301, 4302, 4254; SR. Nos. 6543, 6544, 736.

Drawings by M. King

56'-0" TRAILER BRAKE COMPO. S.R. DIAGRAM 413. S.R. N°s 6543-4
(LSW N°s 4301-2). BUILT IN 1909 & INTENDED FOR PORTLAND BRANCH SERVICES,
THESE VEHICLES DID NOT RECEIVE S.R. AIR-CONTROL P.P GEAR.

REFER TO DIAGRAM 414 FOR UNDERFRAME DETAIL.

56'-0" OVER BODY

END A

END B

REMOVED c 1933

DRIVER & GUARD

FIRST

During the late 1920s the Joint Station Committee suggested that the four-coach sets be reduced to two vehicles for off-peak services, but although several sets were listed as two coach units, there is no photographic evidence of two-coach gate sets in operation. In fact, it would have caused many problems to split and reform sets for odd trains at different times of day.

Apart from time away for overhauls and repaints, the gate sets served faithfully until 11.20 pm on the night of Sunday 4th May, 1941 when, during an air raid, two bombs were dropped near Weymouth Junction causing much damage and a fire which destroyed vehicles 736, 740, 742, 743, 6544, 6553, 6554 and 6555. This brought to an end the gate-set era on the branch. Ironically, had the branch not been closed that day following earlier air raid damage, at least one set would not have been at Weymouth Junction at that time of night!

Gate Set trailers known to have operated on the Portland Branch

LSWR No.	SR No.	Built	Wdn	Notes
4254	736	12/09	7/41E	50 ft 3rd trailer.
4258	740	8/04*	7/41E	48 ft 3rd trailer. Ex-SRM No. 1 R/B 10/22.
4260	742	2/06*	7/41E	50 ft 3rd trailer. Ex-SRM No. 10 R/B 10/19.
4261	743	4/03*	7/41E	53 ft 3rd trailer. Ex-SRM No. 2 (note A).
4301	6543	12/09	10/37	56 ft brake open.
4302	6544	12/09	7/41E	56 ft brake open.
4311	6553	11/06*	6/41E	50 ft brake open. Ex-SRM No. 12+ R/B 10/19.
4312	6554	11/06*	6/41E	50 ft brake open. Ex-SRM No. 13+ R/B 10/19.
4313	6555	11/06*	7/41E	50 ft brake open. Ex-SRM No. 14 R/B 10/19.

A former LSWR/LBSCR joint railcar No. 2.
* Built as Steam Railmotor (SRM).
E destroyed by enemy action at Weymouth 4th May, 1941.
+ previously worked on Portland branch as SRM.

The gate sets were assisted by other mixed stock over the years. By 1910 a two-coach set, consisting of a 48ft brake third and a brake composite, was working over the branch with other odd stock kept in reserve. During 1926 the stock required to operate the branch consisted of two four-coach gangwayed sets, one two-coach non-gangwayed set, and six thirds for strengthening purposes. From 20th December, 1926, in an effort to reduce expenses, a GWR two-coach 'B set' which stood idle at Weymouth between main line duties replaced the Southern Railway two-coach set during the Winter months. However as the GWR set was required for other work during the Summer the Southern set returned. It would appear that this process continued for some years. In the January of 1929 the *Dorset Daily Echo* commented,

> The two old coaches on the Melcombe Regis and Portland branch have been withdrawn and replaced by two from the Tavistock branch, coaches with padded seats, and windows and doors which will readily open and shut whenever required. There is quite a run on the accommodation provided by them and the regular passengers are hoping that they will remain on the branch as long as the Southern Railway are working it.

Following the loss of the gate sets any available assorted stock appeared on the branch for a while. At one stage several GWR auto-trailers hauled by an '02'

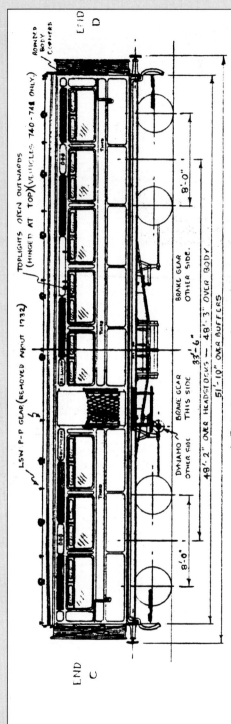

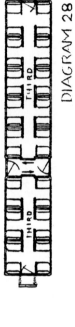

48'-3" TRAILER 3RD. S.R. DIAGRAM 28.

S.R. NUMBERS 740-741 (LSW 4258-4259). REBUILT FROM ORIGINAL LSW ARC-ROOF RAILMOTORS 1 & 2 ABOUT 1919.

DIAGRAM 28

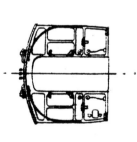

END C

END D

48 ft gate trailer No. 4258. Ex-steamrailmotor No. 1, as rebuilt October 1922.

Drawings by M. King

tank made up the branch train, and during October 1943 two GWR brake composites Nos. 6530 and 6588 were amongst the various coaches in use.

By the end of 1944 the regular trains consisted of two LSWR four-coach corridor sets, Nos. 341 and 475. Until 1947 set 341 was made up of brake composites Nos. 6522 and 6530 with thirds Nos. 702 and 706. In 1948 the set was reduced to three coaches with the removal of No. 702. Set 475 originally contained brake composites Nos. 605 and 608 with thirds Nos. 664 and 686 until May 1947, when brake composite No. 6508 was replaced by No. 6520 and the two thirds by Nos. 693 and 703. The following year the set was reduced to three coaches by the removal of third No. 703. Within a short while both sets were replaced by GWR stock, the branch train usually consisting of three coaches of assorted types of brake composite and third coaches, and on occasions a luggage van. This was later reduced to a two-coach train.

It was not until almost the end of the branch's life that other stock appeared, and for the final 14 months of passenger operation probably the most interesting coaches ever used on the line were to be seen - although it must be said that they did not represent an improvement! Following the closure of the Isle of Sheppey Light Railway in December 1950, the two sets of coaches used on that line were transferred from Kent to the Portland branch. These sets had quite a chequered history. Set 513 was formed by coaches Nos. 3660 (saloon brake third), and 975 (saloon third) painted in Southern green, and set 514 consisted of coaches No. 3561 (saloon brake third) and No. 976 (saloon third) painted in the then standard British Railways 'all red' livery for branch line stock. This set had formed the last passenger train on the Sheppey Light Railway. Both sets were articulated, with a common bogie between the coaches, and it was the only stock of this kind on the Southern Railway. The reason for this was that originally these coaches had formed the carriage section of South Eastern & Chatham Railway steam railcars, No. 3561 being formerly No. 1, 976 No. 2, 3660 No. 3, and 975 No. 8. The 0-4-0 engine units were built by Kitson & Company in 1905/6, and the carriage section was sub-contracted to the Metropolitan Railway Carriage & Wagon Company of Oldbury. The engine units supported the leading end of the coach, and like the steam railmotors of the other companies that later formed the Southern Railway, they were not a success. Following various work in Kent, East Sussex, and the south-east London suburbs, the entire fleet of eight railmotors was laid up by 1920. In April 1924 the engine units were condemmed and the coach sections altered for other work.

Four units were converted into two-coach push-pull sets, the other four becoming articulated units Nos. 513 and 514 but these were not auto-fitted. The brake thirds retained their original seating capacity of 56, whilst the other brake third in each set was converted to a third with the seating increased to 65. Sets 513/514 were not well suited to the Portland branch, their limited brake van capacity requiring each set to be marshalled with a luggage van. Their small low-backed seats, although padded, were not of the greatest comfort, and their only entrances were inward - opening doors at the ends were not ideal for a line with frequent halts. They were not vestibuled, but had doors in the ends (as on underground stock) and chains connecting the two vehicles so that the guard

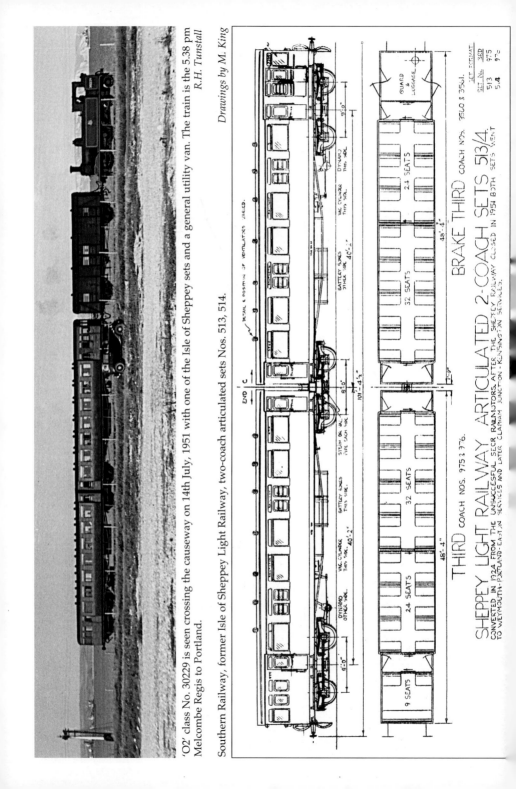

'O2' class No. 30229 is seen crossing the causeway on 14th July, 1951 with one of the Isle of Sheppey sets and a general utility van. The train is the 5.38 pm Melcombe Regis to Portland.

R.H. Tunstall

Southern Railway, former Isle of Sheppey Light Railway, two-coach articulated sets Nos. 513, 514.

Drawings by M. King

DETAIL & POSITION OF VENTILATORS VARIED.

END C

DYNAMO OTHER SIDE.

VAC CYLINDER THIS SIDE. 40'-2½"

BATTERY BOXES THIS SIDE.

STEAM ON INC. PIPE EACH SIDE.

9'-0"

9'-0"

101'-4⅜"

BATTERY BOXES OTHER SIDE. 40'-2½"

VAC CYLINDER THIS SIDE.

DYNAMO THIS SIDE.

9'-0"

THIRD COACH NOS. 975 & 976.

9 SEATS

24 SEATS

32 SEATS

48'-4"

32 SEATS

24 SEATS

48'-4"

GUARD & LUGGAGE

3'-0"

BRAKE THIRD COACH NOS. 3560 & 3561.

SET FORMAT

SET No.	3RD	3RD
513	975	3560
514	976	3561

SHEPPEY LIGHT RAILWAY ARTICULATED 2-COACH SETS 513/4.
CONVERTED IN 1924 FROM THE UNSUCCESSFUL SECR RAILMOTORS. AFTER THE SHEPPEY RAILWAY CLOSED IN 1951 BOTH SETS WENT TO WEYMOUTH-PORTLAND-EASTON SERVICES AND LATER CLAPHAM JUNCTION-KENSINGTON SERVICES.

'O2' class No. 30177 heads across the Fleet viaduct with a Portland-bound train consisting of former GWR stock during 1949. Under the legs of the bridge can be seen a section of Whitehead's pier stretching out into Portland Harbour. *D.E.H. Box*

'02' class 0-4-4 tank No. 30223 heads across the causeway towards Weymouth hauling three GWR coaches on a Weymouth-bound train on 26th March, 1951. Behind the train by the oil tanks can be seen 'Mere Crossing'. Across the harbour the Dockyard is visible, and on top of the Verne the massive mast of the early radar defence system. *Pursey Short*

A builder's photograph of Bath Stone Firms' wagon. Although clearly giving Portland as the main place, the 'small print' reads 'Return to Corsham station'.   *Author's Collection*

Bath & Portland Stone Firms' wagon No. 99, of 10 tons capacity. The gentleman sitting on the left-hand side is George Jenvey, later to become Portland station master.   *Author's Collection*

could pass from one end of the train to the other to issue tickets. Although the vehicles were fitted with electric light, it was certainly a case of turning the clock back as far as passengers were concerned. Following closure of the branch they found work at various places on the Southern Region to end their days, set 513 being withdrawn in October 1957, and set 514 in October 1959.

Although not passenger stock, other important items were the two gas holder tank wagons, LSWR Nos. 7S and 9S. Both vehicles were 4-wheeled and measured 22 ft overall. No. 7S had a cylinder 20 ft long by 4 ft 2 in. diameter with a capacity of 270 cu. ft, whilst No. 9S had five small tanks, 7 ft 1 in. long by 3 ft 1 in. diameter mounted across the chassis, holding 275 cu. ft. Their duty was to travel between the gas production plant at Eastleigh, Weymouth, and Portland to charge up the tanks on the gas-lit stock, there being photographic evidence of this process taking place at Portland. Likewise the GWR had arrangements for its stock to be charged from wagons travelling from its plant at Swindon.

The stone traffic was always important, and many wagons were required to convey this material. Besides the many ordinary wagons used, the LSWR (and later the Southern Railway) built a number of special wagons for this traffic, the original designs of which date back to the 1880s. Basically there were two types: a fixed-side design where the sides were just 10½ in. high, and a four-plank drop side wagon with sides 2 ft 1½ in. high. Of the original wagons that were still running in 1923, the 10 ton single-plank type Nos. 428-434 had timber underframes except for No. 429 which had frames of steel construction, as did the 12 ton wagons Nos. 7570-7586, and the three 15 ton wagons, Nos. 9129, 9131 and 9138. The four-plank wagons, Nos. 9130, 9132-37 and 9139, had been constructed from 1889 onwards as 20 ton fixed-side wagons, being rebuilt as four-plank drop-side wagons during 1907 and reduced to 15 tons capacity. All these were constructed with timber underframes and, as with many other wagons, various modifications took place over the years mainly with the fitting of later types of brake gear. Following the formation of the Southern Railway two 15 ton four-plank wagons were built during 1926, Nos. 61429 and 61030. The final batch of 15 wagons, Nos. 61121-61135 constructed during 1933, were the last Southern Railway wagons built with wooden underframes, although they were of special design with extra longitudinal timbers, it having been found that timber resisted loading shocks better than steel.

Substantially constructed with a timber floor three inches thick, all the wagons lasted well in service, No. 9139 built in 1896 remaining in service until April 1947, whilst the majority of the Southern Railway-built wagons lasted almost until the final closure of the branch. During Southern days they ran in the livery of 'wagon brown' with black undergear and white lettering. Although not being a high priority for repainting many carried their pre-Grouping number and livery well into the 1930s, several examples lasting until 1939. In many cases a layer of stone dust covered the paintwork! Just prior to World War II cast-iron 'Return to Portland' plates were fixed on the side planks, and being used for specific traffic they were not classed as 'common user' wagons.

Although many of the wagons required to handle the stone traffic were supplied by the railway companies, there were also the private owner wagons

Wagon No. 7583, originally LSWR No. 5280, built in 1898 and having a later form of Fox pressed steel underframe. It was a typical two-plank low-sided wagon used for Portland stone traffic, and was photographed at Eastleigh in 1949. Ten years earlier the original brakegear had been replaced by the 'freighter' type shown in the photograph.   *A.E. West*

Wagon No. 61126, a 15 ton four-plank low-sided wagon for stone traffic built by the Southern Railway in 1933. Note the 'Return to Portland' board on the left-hand side. Photographed at Eastleigh in 1949.   *A.E. West*

belonging to the various stone firms. F.J. Barnes owned wagons, although little is recorded of them, and the Bath Stone Company had low-sided wagons painted a straw colour with black undergear and lettering. After 1911 these wagons appeared carrying the lettering 'Bath & Portland Stone Firms'. As this company also had quarries at Corsham its fleet was divided, and for operational reasons some were lettered 'Return to Portland', others 'Return to Corsham'. During November 1909 the Board of the Bath Stone Company agreed to let 50 rail wagons to the United Stone Firms. Wagons owned by United Stone were of a similar type to the Bath company wagons, except their livery was a biscuit brown with black underframes and lettering. Again they were not purely Portland wagons, being also used at the company's other quarry sites.

The Ham Hill & Doulting Stone Company operated a small quarry at Portland although the company was Somerset based, and no doubt its wagons visited the Island at times to collect stone. Other goods stock used on the branch included the usual range required for the normal traffic of the line, ranging from the common 10 ton truck to 'Warflats' for the carriage of tanks.

Having good brake vans was an important item, particularly on the Easton section. The Great Western always used its standard van, known by the telegraphic code name 'Toad', whilst the Southern, in view of the weight of the stone traffic, used its 'Gondola' bogie brake vans. The original batch of those was built in 1934 on the underframes of former London, Brighton & South Coast Railway electric train power cars. These were numbered 56261-56281, and had a tare weight of 28 tons. They were so successful that in 1936 a batch of 25 ton bogie vans was constructed and numbered 56282-56306. There were always several brake vans of both types based at Dorchester to handle both the branch and the Dorchester-Nine Elms goods traffic.

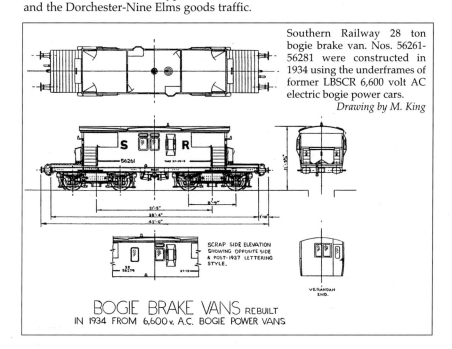

Southern Railway 28 ton bogie brake van. Nos. 56261-56281 were constructed in 1934 using the underframes of former LBSCR 6,600 volt AC electric bogie power cars.

Drawing by M. King

SCRAP SIDE ELEVATION SHOWING OPPOSITE SIDE & POST-1937 LETTERING STYLE.

VERANDAH END.

BOGIE BRAKE VANS REBUILT
IN 1934 FROM 6,600 v. A.C. BOGIE POWER VANS

WEYMOUTH - PORTLAND TRAIN TIMES NOVEMBER 1865

Weekdays

			A	B					
	am	am	am	am	am	pm	pm	pm	pm	pm
Weymouth	7.30	9.30	10.30	11.00	11.25	1.20	3.00	4.25	6.00	8.20
Portland	7.50	9.50	10.55	11.25	11.45	1.30	3.20	4.45	6.20	8.40

			A	B					
	am	am	am	noon	pm	pm	pm	pm	pm	pm
Portland	8.00	10.00	11.50	12.00	12.15	2.00	3.50	4.50	6.30	8.45
Weymouth	8.20	10.20	12.10	12.25	12.40	2.20	4.10	5.10	6 50	9.05

Sundays

	am	am	pm	pm	pm
Weymouth	8.30	10.30	2.40	5.00	7.10
Portland	8.50	10.50	3.00	5.20	7.30

	am	am	pm	pm	pm
Portland	9.00	1.00	4.30	6.30	7.40
Weymouth	9.20	1.20	4.50	6.50	8.00

Notes
A = LSWR goods. B = GWR goods.

Working timetable 1870.

The public timetable as featured in the *Southern Times* in January 1881.

An advertisement for an excursion train from the *Southern Times* of 6th November, 1885.

Chapter Eight

Operation and Traffic

It was quite common in the early days of branch lines for mixed trains conveying both goods and passenger traffic to be operated. However, on the Portland branch this practice ceased after 1st December, 1865, an early demise owing to operating difficulties.

Initially operation of the branch was relatively simple, the Train Staff system, and later Train Staff & Ticket, being able to cope with a service of eight passenger and two goods trains daily in each direction. This type of control allowed a second train, (or more if necessary) to follow in the same direction, the first train (or trains) carrying a written ticket and the last taking the staff. In those days before the Regulation of Railways Act 1889 which stipulated minimum standards of signalling, certain risky practices took place, and several trains simply followed each other on the 'Time Interval' system. The original timetable shows the 12.15 pm GWR goods departing Portland 10 minutes before the 12 noon LSWR goods had arrived at Weymouth. In January 1870 the 11.25 am Weymouth to Portland passenger service departed 5 minutes before the preceding GWR goods had arrived at Portland, and even more startling was the departure of the 12 noon LSWR goods from Portland hot on the heels of the 11.55 am passenger train! The opening of the signal box at Rodwell in 1892 speeded things up a little, and there was the spectacle of three trains following each other between Weymouth and Portland, the 10.20 am GWR goods, the 10.30 LSWR goods, with the 10.45 am passenger bringing up the rear. The return working was not so exciting, only the 12.55 pm passenger train having a 10 minute start on the GWR goods.

By this time the service had increased to nine passenger trains each way daily and five on Sundays, the weekday goods service being two each way with an extra LSWR each way if required. The passenger service was increased to 10 trains daily by 1898.

In 1898 the 9.33 am passenger service from Portland was followed by the 9.48 am LSWR goods, whilst a little later three trains followed each other out of Portland - the 11.00 am passenger, 11.25 am LSWR goods, and the 11.50 am LSWR goods. Earlier in the day there was the same procedure from Weymouth, when the 10.20 am Great Western goods, 10.35 am LSWR goods and the 10.40 am passenger train all followed each other.

The LSWR was responsible for all regular passenger services until the abolition of the broad gauge, after which date the LSWR and GWR companies worked the passenger service for alternating periods of 12 months. When the Easton line opened in 1902 the LSWR provided engine and stock and worked the Easton section until the end of 1903 when, to avoid moving engines from Weymouth, the LSWR took over the working of the Portland branch and the GWR the Easton section.

This arrangement was reversed in January 1905. With the opening of the new station at Portland in July 1905 and through working of the entire line, the Great Western took over all the working until the end of 1909. The LSWR then took

PORTLAND BRANCH.

Single line, worked by Train staff. Assisted by Disc Block Telegraph.

TRAIN STAFF AND TICKET.—Section.—Weymouth Junction Signal Cabin and Portland Signal Cabin.   STAFF and TICKETS:— Red and Square.

DOWN TRAINS.

WEEK DAYS.

Distances	STATIONS	1	2	3	4	5	6	7	8	R 9 R	10	11	12	13	14	15	16
		Pass, S.W. G'ds	S.W. G'ds	Pass,	S.W. G'ds	Pass,	Pass,	G.W. G'ds ST	Pass,	S.W. G'ds	Pass,	Pass,	Pass,	Pass,			
		A.M.	A.M.	A.M.	A.M.	A.M.	P.M.	P.M.	P.M.	P.M.	P.M.	P.M.	P.M.	P.M.			
	Weymouth ---- dep	6 55	8 10	9 15	10 35	10 55	12 25	12 35	2 10	3 15	3 40	4 55	6 25	8 40	--	--	--
	Rodwell ---- "	7 0	—	9 25	—	11 5	12 35	12 45	2 20	3 25	3 50	5 5	6 35	8 50	--	--	--
4¾	Portland ---- arr	7 15	8 30	9 35	10 55	11 15	12 45	12 55	2 30	3 35	4 0	5 15	6 45	9 0	--	--	--

SUNDAYS.

STATIONS	1	2	3	4	5	6	7
	Pass,	Pass,	Pass,	Pass,	Pass,		
	A.M.	P.M.	P.M.	P.M.	P.M.		
Weymouth ---- dep	9 30	12 30	3 0	5 30	8 40	--	--
Rodwell ---- "	9 40	12 40	3 10	5 40	8 50	--	--
Portland ---- arr	9 50	12 50	3 20	5 50	9 0	--	--

UP TRAINS.

ST No128.

WEEK DAYS.

Distances	STATIONS	1	2	3	4	5	6	7	8	R 9 R	10	11	12	13	14	15	16
		Pass,	Pass,	S.W. G'ds	S.W. G'ds	S.W. G'ds	Pass,	G.W. G'ds	Pass,	S.W. G'ds	Pass,	Pass,	Pass,	Pass,			
		A.M.	A.M.	A.M.	A.M.	A.M.	P.M.	P.M.	P.M.	P.M.	P.M.	P.M.	P.M.	P.M.			
	Portland ---- dep	7 35	9 45	10 0	11 30	11 55	12 55	1 45	2 40	4 0	4 15	5 30	7 0	9 10	--	--	--
	Rodwell ---- "	7 45	9 55	10 0	11 40	11 55	1 5	1 55	2 50	4 10	4 25	5 40	7 10	9 20	--	--	--
4¾	Weymouth ---- arr	7 55	10 5	10 20	11 50	12 20	1 15	2 5	3 0	4 20	4 35	5 50	7 20	9 30	--	--	--

SUNDAYS.

STATIONS	1	2	3	4	5	6	7
	Pass,	Pass,	Pass,	Pass,	Pass,		
	A.M.	P.M.	P.M.	P.M.	P.M.		
Portland ---- dep	10 0	1 0	4 0	6 0	9 10	--	--
Rodwell ---- "	10 10	1 10	4 10	6 10	9 20	--	--
Weymouth ---- arr	10 20	1 20	4 20	6 20	9 30	--	--

M.J.T.

Working timetable 1885.

over for five years which would have ended in 1914. However with the Great War and Government control of railways it was decided that in view of the situation no change could be made to the arrangement, but that future policy would be agreed at the end of Government control. By then the general situation was changing, and the matter was left in abeyance until 1931 when, to bring the branch in line with other pooling arrangements where these two companies were operating a joint service, the Southern Railway took over the entire operation of the passenger services. This arrangement remained in force until closure.

In the early days of the line freight traffic was very heavy. In 1898 the LSWR ran three goods trains in each direction and the GWR two, but after the Great War this had tailed off to one train a day by each company. Goods to Easton was usually worked by the LSWR.

Prior to 1911 each company worked its own freight traffic over the Weymouth & Portland section. In that year, as an exercise in economy for both companies, it was arranged to use the available engine power to the best advantage by conveying any traffic on the freight trains irrespective of which company worked them. By the late 1920s the daily freight service consisted of three trains each way between Weymouth and Portland; two worked by the SR, and one by the GWR. Shunting at Portland was performed by either company's engine, assisted by the Southern passenger engine if required, and goods trains between Portland and Easton were worked by the Southern company, who also provided the heavy brake vans required on this section.

In later years the goods train timetable was revised so that the GWR goods departed from Weymouth Junction at 8.53 a.m. arriving at Portland at 9.17 am, and after shunting Portland Yard returned to Weymouth (arriving 12.06 pm), having shunted Whitehead's siding *en route*. The Southern goods left Dorchester South at 9.19 am and arrived at Portland at 10.30 am. It then performed general shunting before taking traffic to Easton, arriving there at 12.10 pm. After serving Sheepcroft and the various quarry sidings, it returned to Portland at 2.25 pm where more shunting took place before departure at 3.47 pm to arrive at Weymouth Junction at 4.12 pm. The wagons were then marshalled into the 5 pm Nine Elms goods, the branch engine being used to bank this train up to Bincombe tunnel.

The inquest on Thomas Smith, a pedestrian who was killed during shunting operations in 1877, gave a very clear picture of goods train operations at the Portland Junction (Weymouth) end of the branch. The Quay Tramway, although part of the Weymouth & Portland company by virtue of its Act of Parliament, had little in common with the Portland branch proper except for this legal point and the fact that the tramway made a physical connection with the branch. Until 1880 all traffic on the tramway was horse drawn, the wagons being placed at the top end of the tramway by the Portland goods engine. On leaving Portland Junction the formation of goods trains bound for Portland was engine-tramway wagons-Portland traffic-brake van. On arrival in the tramway loop the engine would run-round its train to the rear end and propel it onto the top end of the tramway, where the tramway traffic would be uncoupled and left ready for the horses. The remainder of the train would then pull back onto the loop, where the engine would again run around to the front of the train and then proceed to Portland. It was revealed at the inquest that it was quite common practice to 'fly shunt' the tramway wagons to save some work for the horses, and there were reports of uncontrolled wagons running down Commercial Road!

The point where the Portland branch separated from the Harbour Tramway was crossed by a public footpath which gave access between King's Street and the Backwater side of the railway. In later years this crossing was protected by a warning bell which sounded automatically upon the approach of a train, but unfortunately this refinement did not exist on 10th April, 1899 when Mr E.E. Skidmore, aged 83 years, was killed by the 11.10 am train from Portland. The driver sounded his whistle, but could not stop in time. There had been a fatal accident at this point shortly after the opening of the branch, the operating companies then considering the erection of a footbridge. However, owing to a disagreement with Weymouth Town Council over additional costs if ramps were provided for invalid carriages, no further action was taken.

As with all branch lines there were restrictions on the loading of trains, in particular on the steeply-graded Easton section upon which the Board of Trade had stipulated from the outset that all goods trains were to have two brake vans and a brakesman in each. A train of 20 loaded or unloaded wagons was allowed between Easton and Portland, and 14 loaded wagons between Portland and Easton, this number being reduced to 9 when they were loaded coal wagons.

Originally the Board of Trade stipulated only 10 wagons in either direction, this being altered following talks with the operating companies, as was the original recommendation that four 4-wheel coaches be the passenger train limit, bogie stock was subsequently allowed, but six-wheel passenger stock still remained barred. Following the Easton shunting accident of 1903 the rule that the locomotive had to be at the Portland end of the train whilst shunting was strictly enforced to prevent any further runaways. Owing to the nature of the Easton section, between Portland station and Easton a speed limit was enforced of 25 mph for passenger trains and 15 mph for goods trains in both directions. There were also special working instructions to allow the propelling of stock between Portland station and the Royal Naval Hospital Halt, and the working of hospital trains to and from the Dockyard.

In later years the GWR 0-6-0 pannier tanks were allowed 176 tons between Weymouth and Portland; 193 tons from Portland to Weymouth; 118 tons from Portland to Easton; and 176 tons from Easton to Portland. By 1909 the passenger service had increased to 22 trains each way on weekdays between Weymouth and Portland, nine of these being railmotors. The peak was reached in 1914, with a weekday service of 23 trains each way.

Passenger loading fluctuated according to external circumstances. If the Fleet was in many sailors would be travelling, either into Weymouth or further distances on leave , but when it was at sea there was a marked decrease. There was of course a regular traffic in Dockyard workers, coal hulk gangs, quarrymen, and others travelling to and from work in Portland or Weymouth. Whitehead's torpedo factory also contributed greatly to the revenue of the branch, although during the depression years with reduced staff levels, there was a marked decline in passenger numbers.

In pre-war days workers from Whitehead's factory would travel home to dinner and return within the hour, the 12.27 from Portland being strengthened by spare stock kept at Portland. This train was double-headed, using the engine off the Southern goods as pilot. Arriving at Melcombe Regis at 12.40 pm, and returning at 1.15 pm made it a quick lunch and a mad rush back into the factory from Wyke Halt!

Other train workings reflected the changing times. During the late 1930s there was an interesting working over the branch consisting of a 'B Set' which arrived from Bristol at 11.16 am. This stock formed the 2.10 pm service to Portland, and was on occasions hauled by Southern Railway 'A12' 'Jubilee' 0-4-2 No. 612, although the booked locomotive was a Dorchester 'T9' class 4-4-0, either No. 284 or 286 running tender first to Portland. Upon its return the engine worked the 4.40 pm Weymouth-Bournemouth Central service.

The presence of the Royal Navy at Portland was always an important factor in the operation of the branch, with the arrival of the Fleet and men going on leave creating much work for the staff. Booking clerks would go out to the ships at anchor in the harbour to sell tickets in advance to men going on leave thus avoiding long queues at the booking office, and there were numerous 'Naval specials' - not to mention the many personnel travelling by the ordinary branch services to Melcombe Regis, thence on the regular trains from Weymouth. Even a 'good night ashore' filled the branch train to capacity. Indeed, even in later years there were always sailors coming and going and an endless stream of kit bags in transit.

The guard of the last train to Portland also needed to be of strong character as many of the passengers had sampled the local ale and problems could arise! Overcrowding was also a problem, particularly during the war years, and one guard remembered as many as 900 aboard a four-coach train, many hanging on wherever they could! Expediency and discretion were to the forefront as 'officialdom looked the other way'.

Naval specials were quite common, one such on 19th December, 1921 conveying 60 men with their kit bags and hammocks to Chatham. It consisted of a third class coach and bogie brake van, and left Portland at 8 30 am. Upon arrival at Weymouth the stock was attached to the 9.15 am Waterloo service, which was already conveying 256 extra seamen between Weymouth and Waterloo.

Government traffic did not end with the Navy. The Verne Citadel was an Army garrison until 1948 and generated a great deal of traffic, whilst the prison also used the railway to 'import and export' their inmates. Following its conversion to a Borstal Institution, the first 180 inmates arrived at Portland station by special train on 23rd August, 1921.

Troop specials were a regular event up to the end of World War II. One such arrived on 31st March, 1922, conveying 10 officers, 350 men and 40 tons of baggage of the '2nd Royal Inniskillings' from Dover to Portland. Upon arrival at Dorchester the train, consisting of a brake composite, eight lavatory thirds, brake composite, seven 4-wheel baggage vans and bogie brake van, was divided, the 10 passenger coaches proceeding as one train to Portland to be followed by the baggage vans and bogie brake as a second train. On 5th

WEYMOUTH, PORTLAND AND EASTON.

Single Line, Weymouth Junction to Portland Goods Yard Junction (crossing place, Rodwell), and from Portland Station to Easton, worked by Electric Train Staff

DOWN TRAINS. — WEEK DAYS.

Distance from Pad'ton (M|C)	STATIONS.	Station No.	1 B Pass. RR	2 M Motor	3 B Pass.	6 B Motor	7 G S.W. Eng'n	9 G Gds or Light Eng.	11 B Pass.	13 B Motor	16 B Motor	17 B Pass.	18 K G'ods	19 K Gds.	21 B Pass.	23	25 B Motor	29 B Pass.	33 B Motor	35 B Pass.	37 K Gds.	39 B Pass.	41 B Motor	43 B Pass.
165|34	Weymouth Junc. dep.	631	A.M. 6 24	A.M. 5 35	A.M. 6 15	A.M. 6 42	A.M. 7 58 U	A.M.	A.M. X7 53	A.M.	A.M. 9 8	A.M. 9 2	A.M.	A.M. 9 13	A.M. 9 55		A.M. X10 45	A.M. 11 35	P.M. X12 45	P.M. 11 0	P.M. 1 12	P.M. 11 57	P.M. 2 25	P.M. 3 1
168|61	Melcombe Regis {arr. / dep.}	679	6 25 / 6 29	5 35 / 5 40	6 16 / 6 20	6 43 / 6 47			7 54 / 7 58		9 23 / 9 30	9 7			9 56 / 10 0		10 46 / 10 50	11 36 / 11 40	12 46 / 12 50	11 1 / 11 5	1	11 58 / 2 2	2 26 / 2 30	3 4 / 3 8
169|2	Westham dep.	680	—	5 43	—	6 50	M	MO	—	—	10 17	—	—	—	10		10 53	11 40	12 50	1 5		2 2	2 30	3 8
169|50	Rodwell {arr. / dep.}	681	6 34	5 46 / 5 51	6 28	6 53 / 6 58	7 44 / 7 46	7 44 / 7 46	8 3	10 23		9 12	8 34 / 8 39	9 22	10 5		10 56 / 11 1	11 45	12 56 / 1 1	1 10	1 21	2 7	2 36	3 13
171|65	Wyke Regis	682	—	—	—	—	—	—	—	—	—	—	—	—	—		—	—	—	—	—	—	—	—
170|69	Torpedo Works	683	—	—	—	—	—	—	—	—	—	—	—	—	—		—	—	—	—	—	—	—	—
172|35	Portland Gds.Jct. arr.	684	—	—	—	—	7 x56	7 x56	—	—	—	—	—	9 x30	—		—	—	—	—	—	—	—	—
172|59	Portland {arr. / dep.}	685	CS 6 44	CS 5 56	CS 6 38	CS 7 3		W	CS 8 13		CXS	CS 9 22	RR	9X30	CXS 10 15		CXS 11 6	CXS 11 55	CS 1 6	CS 1 20	1X30	CS 2 17	CXS 2 46	CS 3 23
172|74	Castleton {dep. / arr.}	686											8 20	Y							W	2 20		
176|36	Easton arr.	691					W	W	8 13			9 40	8 40									2 35		

DOWN TRAINS. — WEEK DAYS. (continued)

	STATIONS.	Station No.	14 B Motor	16 B Pass.	18 K Gds.	20 B Pass.	22 K Gds.	24 M Motor	26 B Pass.	28	30 B Pass.	32 B Motor	34 B Pass.	36	38 K Gds.	40 K Gds.	42 B Pass.	44 B Motor	46 B Pass.
	Weymouth Junc. dep.		A.M.	A.M. 11 10	A.M. CR 11 0	A.M. 11 10	A.M. Z	A.M.	P.M. 12 25		P.M. 1 8	P.M. 1 55	P.M.	P.M. 2 45 CR 3	P.M. W	P.M. 8 10	P.M. 3 65	P.M. 4 27
	Melcombe Regis {arr. / dep.}		10 17	11 20 / 11 32		11 20	12 7	12 25	CS		1 23 / 1 30	CS 2 1	2 25		2X47 / 8 2	8P9 / 3X10		3 25 / 3 33	CS
	Westham dep.		10 23		RR		12 13									3 19			4 1
	Rodwell {arr. / dep.}			11P39 / 11X40		11X20		12 1P / 12 21	12 35		1 40	2 x 8 / 2 10	2X35		1 44 / 1 47		8 47	4 x 7 / 4 9	4X3?
	Portland {arr. / dep.}		CXS 10 2P	11 46	RR	CXS	12 23 / 12 39	CS	CS		CS 1 48	2 13 / 2 15	2 39		1 47 / 1 48	3 24	8 49	CS 4 13	4 13
	Castleton {dep. / arr.}		10 81 / 10 33			11 24 / 11 27		12 24 / 12 26				2 15 / 2 16	2 42 / 2 43				3 50	4 14	4 14
	Easton arr.		10 2P / 10 36			11 28		12 43											

UP TRAINS. — WEEK DAYS.

	STATIONS.	Station No.	1 B Cchs. RR	2 B Motor	4 B Pass.	6 B Motor	8 B Pass.	10 B Motor	14 B Pass.	16	18 K G'ds.	20 B Pass.	22 K Gds.	24 M Motor	26 B Pass.	28	30 B Pass.	32 B Motor	34 B Pass.	36	38 K Gds.	40 K Gds.	42 B Pass.	44 B Motor	46 B Pass.
	Easton ... dep.		A.M.	A.M.	A.M. 7 5	A.M.	A.M. 8 23	A.M. 9 8	A.M.		A.M.	A.M. 11 10	A.M.	A.M.	P.M.		P.M.	Y.M.	P.M.		P.M.	P.M.	P.M.	P.M.	P.M.
	Castleton ... "				7 5																	8 10		3 65	
	Portland ... {arr. / dep.}		CS	CXS 6 13	CXS 7 16	CS 7 33	CS 8 23	9 23 / 9 30	10 17		CR 11 0	11 10	Z	12 7	CS 12 25		1 23 / 1 30	CS 1 55	2 25			8 10		CS	CS
	Portland Goods Yard Jct. "										11 0										8 2				
	Torpedo Works "																								
	Wyke Regis "			6 19	7 39	7 39			10 23					12 13			1 40	2 1							4 1
	Stop Board "																								
	Rodwell {arr. / dep.}		CS	CS 6X25 / 6 27	7X45 / 7 47	8X33	11X20	11X20							12 35			2 x 8 / 2 10	2X35						4 x 7 / 4 9
	Westham "			6 29	7 49	8 37	9 44	9 40				11 24						2 13 / 2 15	2 39						
	Melcombe Regis {arr. / dep.}		6 31	7 51	8 40	9 47	9 48					11 27					1 44 / 1 47	2 15 / 2 42				8 47			4 13
	Weymouth Junc. arr.		6X13	6 32	7X52	X8 41	9 48	9 48	10 36		11 0	11 28	11 61	12 26	12 43		1 48	2 16 / 2 43			3 24	3 50		4 14	4 14

The Passenger Trains and Motors between Weymouth and Portland, and all Trains between Portland and Easton, will be worked by the S.W. Company until December 31st, 1914, and by the G. W. Company for 5 years after that date.

Working timetable 1914.

WEYMOUTH, PORTLAND AND EASTON.—Continued.

DOWN TRAINS.

WEEK DAYS—continued.

STATIONS.	17 Gds.	49 Pass.	61 Motor	63 Pass.	65 Motor	56 Pass.	57 Motor	58 Pass.	59 Motor	60 Motor	61 Pass.	63 Motor	63 Motor R.
	P.M.	P.M.	P.M.	P.M.	P.M.	P.M.	P.M.	P.M.	P.M.	P.M.	P.M.	P.M.	P.M.
Weymouth Junc. dep	3X33	3·58	4·25	6X15	5X35	6X35	6†55	7·25	8†25	9·27		10·35	11†27
Melcombe Regis { arr		3·59	4·28	5† 6	5·36	6†11	6†56	7·26	8·26	9·28		10·36	11†28
Melcombe Regis { dep	—	4· 2	4·30	6·10	5·40	6·20	7· 0	7·30	8·30	9·30		10·40	11·30
Westham			4·33		5·43	6·26	7· 3		8·33	9·33		10·43	11·33
Rodwell { arr	3X39	4·X7	4†37	6X15	5·46	6X30	7X 6	7X35	8·36	9·36		10·46	11·36
Rodwell { dep	3·41	4·11	4·42	6· 7	5·51	6·51	7·11		8·41	9·41		10·51	11·41
Wyke Regis		CS	CxS	CS	5·46	CS	CS	CS	CS	CS		CS	CS
Torpedo Works										9·53			
Portland Gds Jnc. arr	3X51	4·17	4·47	6·25	6·56	6·40	7·16	7·45	8·46	9·46		10·56	11·45
Portland { dep	W			6·28									
Portland { arr				5·43						9·53			
Castleton										10· 8			
Easton arr													

UP TRAINS.

WEEK DAYS—continued.

STATIONS.	48 Goods	50 Motor	62 Pass.	64	66 Motor	68 Gds.	60 Pass.	62 Motor	63 Pass.	64 Motor	66 Motor	68	70 Motor	72 Motor R.
	P.M.	P.M.	P.M.		P.M.	P.M.	P.M.	P.M.	P.M.	P.M.	P.M.	P.M.	P.M.	P.M.
Easton dep	W					P.M.	6·33							11†55
Castleton														
Portland { arr		6· 2	5·35			6· 1	6·48	7·22	7·35	9· 2	9·53	11· 2		
Portland { dep	4X48		CS		CS	6X17	6·55	CS	7·37	CS	CxS	CS		
Portland Gds Jnc dep		6· 9				6· 7		7·28	7·39	9· 8	9·59	11· 8		
Torpedo Works	4P58					6P27								
Wyke Regis						6X29								
Stop Board						8·31	7X 5	7X35		9·14	10· 5	11·14		
Rodwell { arr	CS	6X16	5X45			6·13		7·37	8·10	9·16	10· 7	11·16		
Rodwell { dep		6·17				6·15	7· 9	7·39	8·14	9·18	10· 9	11·18		
Westham			5·49			6·17	7·12	7·41	8·17	9·20	10·11	11·20		
Melcombe Regis { arr	5X21	5·21	5·52			6·18	7·13	7·42	8·18	9·21	10·12	11·21		12†10
Melcombe Regis { dep	5X 4	5·53	X5·53			6†19X	6·36							
Weymouth Junc. arr														

R Wednesday, Thursday and Saturday nights only.
W S.W. Engine and Guard.
Y G.W. Engine and Guard.
U Also runs other days if required, in which case 7||38 does not run.
Z G.W. Engine and Guard.

Working timetable 1914.

London & South Western Railway.

SUPPLEMENTARY PAMPHLET No. 561.

ALTERATIONS in the TRAIN SERVICE commencing 1st OCTOBER, 1917.

The arrangements announced in Pamphlet No. 507, commencing Friday, 20th July, will be cancelled.
The train services will be as shewn in Pamphlet No. 464, dated 18th April, 1917, with the exceptions mentioned hereunder, viz:—

WEEK-DAYS.

The 8.10 a.m. train from Southampton to Portsmouth Harbour will call at Bursledon at 8.34 a.m. and be 2 minutes later at each station, thence to Portsmouth Harbour.

The 8.50 a.m. train from Waterloo to Exeter will not have a breakfast car attached.

The 10.45 a.m. train from Eastleigh to Bournemouth West will run via Hamworthy Junction arriving there at 12.32 p.m. It will leave Hamworthy Junction at 12.38 p.m., Poole 12.45 p.m., Parkstone 12.51 p.m. and Branksome 12.56 p.m., arriving at Bournemouth West at 1.0 p.m.

The 12.43 p.m. train from Basingstoke to Waterloo will leave Esher at 2.13 p.m. and arrive at Surbiton at 2.19 p.m.

The 1.50 p.m. train from Clapham Junction to Kensington will be discontinued.

The 2.36 p.m. train from Kensington to Clapham Junction will be discontinued.

The 6.5 p.m. train from Exeter to Waterloo will not have a dining car attached.

The 6.55 p.m. train from Lyme Regis to Axminster will start at 6.45 p.m, leave Combpyne 7.4 p.m., and arrive Axminster 7.12 p.m.

A train will leave Bulford at 11.35 p.m. for Salisbury, leaving Amesbury 11.41 p.m., Newton Tony, 11.52 p.m., Porton 12.4 a.m., arriving Salisbury at 12.14 a.m.

The train service on the Melcombe Regis (Weymouth), Portland and Easton Lines will be as shewn hereunder:—

WEEK DAYS.

	a.m.	a.m.	a.m.	a.m.	a.m.	a.m.	a.m.	a.m.	a.m.	a.m.	a.m.	a.m.	noon	p.m.	p.m.	p.m.	p.m.	p.m.	p.m.	p.m.	p.m.	p.m.	p.m.
Melcombe Regis ...dep.	5 30	6 20	6 47	7 58	8 28	9 7	10 45	12 4	1 4	2 2	2 57	4 30	5 40	6 10	6 40	7 50		8 30	9 40		10 45		
Westham Halt	5 33	6 23	6 50		8 31		10 48		1 7		3 0	4 33	5 43		6 43			8 33	9 43		10 48		
Rodwell ...	5 42	6 25	6 53	8 3	8 34	9 12	10 51	12 9	1 10	2 7	3 2	4 37	5 46	6 17	6 47	7 55		8 36	9 46		10 51		
Wyke Regis Halt	5 48		6 58		8 39		10 56		1 15		3 8	4 42	5 51		6 51			8 41	9 51		10 56		
Portland ...arr.	5 53	6 33	7 3	8 13	8 44	9 22	11	12 19	1 20	2 17	3 13		4 47	5 56	6 56	8	5	8 46	9 56		11 1		
{dep.					8 47	9 26					3 16			6 30			8 9						
Easton ...arr.					9 2	9 41					3 31			6 45			8 24						

	a.m.	a.m.	a.m.	a.m.	a.m.	a.m.	noon	p.m.	p.m.	p.m.	p.m.	p.m.	p.m.	p.m.	p.m.	p.m.	p.m.	p.m.	p.m.
Easton ...dep.					9 10		12 5			3 36			6 50						
Portland {arr.					9 25		12 20			3 51									
{dep.	6 13	7 5	7 33	8 23	9 30	11 10	12 30	1 30	2 37	3 56	5 2	5 35	6	57	8 7	9	10 10	11 7	
Wyke Regis Halt	6 19		7 39			11 16	12 36		2 33		5 8		6 11		7 28	9	10 16	11 13	
Rodwell	6 25	7 15	7 45	8 33	9 40	11 20	12 42	1 40	2 47	4 8	5 14	5 45	6 18	7 18	7 38	9 18	10 22	11 19	
Westham Halt	6 27		7 47	8 36		11 23	12 44		2 41	4 10	5 16		6 20		7 37	9 16	10 24	11 21	
Melcombe Regis ...arr.	6 29	7 19	7 49	8 38	9 44	11 27	12 46	1 44	2 43	4 12	5 18	5 49	6 22	7 22	7 39	9 18	10 26	11 24	

SUNDAYS.

	a.m.	a.m.	a.m.	a.m.	a.m.	p.m.	p.m.
Melcombe Regis ...dep.	10 0	12 35	2 40	4	5 30	7 0	8 45
Westham Halt	10 3	12 38	2 43	4	5 33	7 3	8 48
Rodwell ...	10 6	12 41	2 46	4 1	5 36	7 6	8 51
Wyke Regis Halt	10 11	12 46	2 51	4	5 41	7 11	8 56
Portland {arr.	10 16	12 51	2 56	4 21	5 46	7 16	9 1
{dep.							
Easton ...arr.		No	Sunday	Service			

	a.m.	p.m.	p.m.	p.m.	p.m.	p.m.
Easton ...dep.		No	Sunday	Service.		
Portland {arr.						
{dep.	10 30	1 50	3 20	4 30	6	8 10
Wyke Regis Halt	10 36	1 56	3 26	4 36	6	8 16
Rodwell	10 42	2 2	3 32	4 42	6 12	8 22
Westham Halt	10 44	2 4	3 34	4 44	6 14	8 24
Melcombe Regis ...arr.	10 46	2 6	3 36	4 46	6 16	8 26

F—1st and 3rd classes only.

Public timetable October Emergency 1917.

Public timetable 1922.

MELCOMBE REGIS (WEYMOUTH). PORTLAND AND EASTON.

	WEEK DAYS.																SUNDAYS.						
	a.m.	a.m.	a.m.	a.m.	a.m.	SE	SO	a.m.	p.m.	p.m.	p.m.	p.m.	p.m.	p.m.	p.m.	p.m.	SO	a.m.	a.m.	p.m.	p.m.	p.m.	p.m.
Melcombe Regis dep.	6 10	7 30	8 5															10 0	12 50	2 30	4 30	6 0	8 10
Westham Halt	6 13	7 34	8 8															10 3	12 53				
Rodwell ...	6 24	7 40	8 18															10 6	12 56				
Wyke Regis Halt																							
Portland {arr.	6 36	7 52	8 23															10 16	1 6	2 46	4 46	6 16	8 26
{dep.																							
Easton ...arr.																		No	Sunday	Service			

	WEEK DAYS.																SUNDAYS.						
	a.m.	a.m.	a.m.	a.m.	a.m.	p.m.	p.m.	p.m.	p.m.	p.m.	p.m.	SO	a.m.	p.m.	p.m.	p.m.	p.m.	p.m.					
Easton ...dep.														No	Sunday	Service.							
Portland {arr.																							
{dep.	6 55													10 30	1 50	3 20	4 30	6 0	8 10				
Wyke Regis Halt																							
Rodwell	7 9													10 42	2 2	3 32	4 42	6 12	8 22				
Westham Halt																							
Melcombe Regis arr.	7 11													10 46	2 6	3 36	4 46	6 16	8 26				

SO—Saturdays only.   SE—Saturdays excepted.

October, 1937 two special trains took the 1st Battalion of the Green Howards to Catterick, the first departing at 6.25 pm. The second at 7.05 pm carried 250 men plus wives and children. The following day Portland station saw the arrival of the 2nd Battalion of the Lincolnshire Regiment.

During the war many troop and Naval specials ran over the branch although for obvious reasons details of them remain scant. However, it is known that many troops arrived by special train following the fall of France.

There were numerous specials and extra workings over the branch, often laid on at short notice. One example occurred following the loss of the paddle steamer *Bournemouth* (1880), which was wrecked near Portland Bill in fog whilst returning from Torquay to Bournemouth on the evening of 27th August, 1886. Miraculously there was no loss of life and just after midnight the 250 passengers, who had been rescued by small boats, assembled at Portland station and returned to Bournemouth in a special train. A 'bonus' from this incident was the vast numbers of people who travelled to Portland by train on the Sunday to view the wreck!

Before the motor coach became popular Sunday school and other organisations used the train for their annual outings. In August 1885, 270 children and teachers from St George's, Fordington, Dorchester travelled to Rodwell by train to spend the day at Sandsfoot Castle. On 31st August, 1904, 113 passengers left Easton at 5.00 am for a trip to Brighton, returning in the early hours of the following day.

On 28th June, 1913 what the local paper described as 'A Monster Excursion' from Portland with over 1,000 passengers departed for London. Organised jointly by the stone masons, the Underhill Conservative Association, and Tophill Liberal Club, it cost 5s. 3d. from Easton, 4s. 9d. from Portland. A number of Whitehead's employees joined the train at Rodwell, after which (apart from an engine change at Weymouth Junction) it ran non-stop to Westbury, Paddington being reached at 8.30 am. It returned from Paddington at 1.00 am the following morning with a breakfast-time arrival back at Portland!

However, although the years up to the Great War were called the 'Golden Age of Railways', changes were already under way. In September 1913 the same paper reported that the employees of one Portland company went on their annual outing, travelling to Wells by char-a-banc. The tide was already on the turn.

A traffic that failed to materialise was passengers for Cunard liners using Portland as an embarkation port. In 1923 discussions took place between the company and the Admiralty, who raised no objections to four liners using the port, the feeling being that the benefits to employment in the area outweighed any disadvantages. However, the scheme was not pursued.

A special train on Tuesday 28th May, 1928 brought nearly 400 Dutch visitors to Easton. Following a conducted walking tour of the Island they rejoined the train at Portland for the return journey to Weymouth where they re-boarded the liner *Ryndan* anchored in Weymouth Bay

Local football matches in years gone by received strong support. In February 1932, when Portland played Kingstonian in the FA Amateur Cup, a special train left Melcombe Regis at 2.10 pm and returned after the match. In those days

WEYMOUTH, PORTLAND, AND EASTON.

Single Line, Weymouth Junction to Portland Goods Yard Junction (crossing place Rodwell), and from Portland Station to Easton, worked by Electric Train Staff.
The passenger trains and autos between Weymouth and Portland and all trains between Portland and Easton, with certain exceptions, will be worked by the S.R. Company until further notice.

DOWN TRAINS.

Mile Post from Padding-ton.	STATIONS.		Ruling Gradient 1 in	WEEK DAYS.													SUNDAYS.							
				B	B	B	B	B	B	B	B	B	B	B		B	B	B	B	B	B	B	B	
				Pass.	Auto.	Pass.	Pass.	Pass.	Pass.	Pass.	Pass.	Pass.	Pass.	Pass.		Pass.	Pass.	Pass.	Pass.	Pass.	Pass.	Pass.	Pass.	
M. C.				a.m.	a.m.	a.m.	a.m.	a.m.	p.m.	p.m.	p.m.	p.m.	p.m.	p.m.		p.m.	p.m.	p.m.	p.m.	p.m.	p.m.	p.m.	p.m.	
168 34	**Weymouth Junction**	dep.	—	6†10	7†14	7†35	8†30	10†45	1†10	2†35	4†32	6†34	7†37	8†50	....	10†55	1† 5	2†10	3†35	5†52	7†37	8†30	11† 0	....
168 61	**Melcombe Regis**	arr.	96 R.	6†11½	7†15½	7†36½	8†31½	10†46½	1†11½	2†36½	4†33½	6†35½	7†38½	8 51½	..	10†56½	1† 6½	2†11½	3†36½	5†53½	7†38½	8†31½	11†1½	..
		dep.	—	6 18	7 17	7 38	8 35	10 50	1 15	2 42	4 35	6 37	7 41	8 53	....	11 0	1 10	2 15	3 38	5 55	7 40	8 35	11 5	....
169 2	**Westham**	,,	98 R.	6 20½	7 19½	7 42½	8 37½	10 52½	1 17½	2 44½	4 37½	6 39½	7 43½	8 55½	..	11 2½	1 12½	2 17½	3 40½	5 57½	7 42½	8 37½	11 7½	..
169 50	**Rodwell**	arr.	58 R.	—	—	—	—	—	—	—	—	—	7 46	—	....	—	—	—	—	—	—	—	—	....
		dep.	66 F.	6 23½	7 22½	7 46	8X40½	10 55½	1 20½	2 47½	4 40½	6 42½	7 48	8 58½	..	—	1 15½	2 20½	3 43½	6 0½	7 45½	8 40½	—	..
170 7½	**Sandsfoot Castle Halt**	,,	—	6 26	7 25	7 48½	8 43	10 58	1 23	2 50	4 43	6 45	7 51	9 1	....	11 8	1 18	2 23	3 46	6 3	7 48	8 43	11 13	....
170 65	**Wyke Regis**	,,	66 F.	6 28½	7 27½	7 52	8 45½	11 0½	1 27½	2 52½	4 45½	6 47½	7 55½	9 3½	..	11 10½	1 20½	2 25½	3 48½	6 5½	7 50½	8 45½	11 15½	..
170 69	**Torpedo Works**	,,	88 F.	—	—	—	—	—	—	—	—	—	—	—	....	—	—	—	—	—	—	—	—	....
172 35	**Portland Goods Jct.**	arr.	205 F.	CS	—	CS	CS	—	CS	—	CS	CS	—	—	..	—	—	—	CS	—	CS	—	—	....
172 59	**Portland**	arr.	216 R.	6 33	7 32	7 57	8 50	11 5	1 32	2 57	4 50½	6 52	8 0	9 8	....	11 15	1 25	2 30	3 53	6 10	7 55	8 50	11 20	....
		dep.		▬	7L35	▬	▬	▬	1L33	▬	4L52	▬	▬	▬	▬	▬	▬	▬	▬	▬	▬	▬	▬	..
172 74	**Castleton**	,,	216 R.	....	—	....	....	....	—	....	—	....	....	....	....	....	....	....	....	....	....	....	....	....
176 36	**Easton**	arr.	40 R.	..	7L47	..	..	..	1L45	..	5L 4	..	..	..	..	..	..	..	..	..	..	..	..	..

UP TRAINS.

STATIONS.		Ruling Gradient 1 in	WEEK DAYS.														SUNDAYS.							
			B	B	B	B	B	B	B	B	B	B	B	B		B	B	B	B	B	B	B	B	
			Pass.	Pass.	Auto.	Pass.	Pass.	Pass.	Pass.	Pass.	Pass	Pass.	Pass.	Pass.		Pass.	Pass.	Pass.	Pass.	Pass.	Pass.	Pass.	Pass.	
			a.m.	a.m.	a.m.	a.m.	p.m.	p.m.	p.m.	p.m.	p.m.	p.m.	p.m.	p.m.		p.m.	p.m.	p.m.	p.m.	p.m.	p.m.	p.m.	p.m.	
Easton	dep.	—	....	....	8L15	....	....	1L53	....	—	5L17	....	....	....	....	....	....	....	....	....	....	....	....	....
Castleton	,,	40 F.	..	..	—	..	..	—	..	SO	—	..	..	..	..	..	..	..	..	..	..	..	..	..
Portland	arr.	216 F.	....	....	8L26	....	....	2L31½	....	—	5L28	....	....	....	....	....	....	....	....	....	....	....	....	....
	dep.	—	6 45	8 7	8 28	10 0	12 27	2 5	3 33	5 5	5 32	7 12	8 25	9 25	..	11 25	1 38	2 40	5 0	6 35	8 5	9 15	11 30	..
Portland Goods Jct.	,,	216 F.	CS	CS	CS	—	CS	CS	—	—	CS	CS	CS	—	....	—	—	CS	—	—	CS	—	—	..
Torpedo Works	,,	205 R.	—	—	—	—	—	—	—	—	—	—	—	—	..	—	—	—	—	—	—	—	—	..
Wyke Regis	,,	88 R.	6 50	8 12	8 33	10 5	12 34	2 10	3 38	5 10	5 37	7 18	8 30	9 30	....	11 30	1 43	2 45	5 5	6 40	8 10	9 20	11 35	....
Sandsfoot Castle Halt	,,	66 R.	6 53	8 15	8 36	10 8	12 38	2 13	3 41	5 13	5 40	7 21	8 33	9 33	..	11 33	1 46	2 48	5 8	6 43	8 13	9 23	11 38	..
Stop Board	,,	66 R.	—	—	—	—	—	—	—	—	—	—	—	—	....	—	—	—	—	—	—	—	—	....
Rodwell	arr.	—	—	—	8 38½	CXS	—	—	—	—	—	—	—	—	..	—	—	—	—	—	—	—	—	..
	dep.	60 F.	6 55½	8 17½	8X41½	10 10½	12 40½	2 15½	3 43½	5 15½	5 42½	7 23½	8 35½	9 35½	....	—	1 48½	2 50½	5 10½	6 45½	8 15½	9 25½	—	..
Westham	,,	58 F.	6 58½	8 20	8 44	10 13	12 44	2 18	3 46	5 18	5 45	7 26	8 38	9 38	..	11 38	1 51	2 53	5 13	6 48	8 18	9 28	11 43	..
Melcombe Regis	arr.	98 F.	6 59½	8 21	8 45	10 14	12 45	2 19	3 47	5 19	5 46	7 27	8 39	9 39	....	11 39	1 52	2 54	5 14	6 49	8 19	9 29	11 44	....
	dep.	—	7† 0	8†22	8†46	10†15	12†47	2†21	3†48	5†20	5†47	7†29	8†40	9†40	..	11†41	1†53	2†55	5†15	6†50	8†20	9†30	11†45	..
Weymouth Junction	arr.	96 F.	7† 1	8†23	8†47	10†16	12†48	2†22	3†49	5†21	5†48	7†30	8†41	9†41	....	11†42	1†54	2†56	5†16	6†51	8†21	9†31	11†46	....

TRAINS WILL CALL AT RODWELL DURING HOURS OF DAYLIGHT ONLY. **L**—Commencing April 5th, 1943.

Working timetable 5th October, 1942.

Portland was considered to be one of the best amateur sides in the Country, and a good crowd always made their way to the Grove Corner ground - many coming by train. Because of the war, a popular local 'Derby', Portland versus Weymouth, did not take place for 10 years, and it was a great day in 1949 when a special train carried many of the 4,000 who watched Portland win 4-1 against Weymouth.

The annual works' outings of the stone companies were usually by train and various other organisations hired trains or reserved a certain amount of accommodation. During 1937 one such group, the Portland Tophill Hospital Collecting Committee, departed from the Island with 366 passengers. All went well on the journey to London, but unfortunately on the return journey a large party from Weymouth boarded the train, resulting in some members of the booked party having to stand in the corridors. This resulted in the organisers complaining to the Southern Railway, and looking at the advantages of road travel for future outings.

Being the year of the Coronation of King George VI, London was the place to visit, and on Friday 21st May a special organised by the South Dorset Conservative Association left Easton at 6 15 am, calling at all stations except Sandsfoot Castle Halt. The fare for this excursion was 11s., an extra 9s. provided a motor coach tour of the decorated City and a lunch. An expensive day out!

The close co-operation between the Southern National and the railway companies produced a variety of combined road and rail facilities, one being a combined Rail-Road Tour, Melcombe Regis to Easton by rail, Easton to Portland Bill and return to Weymouth by road, this being catered for by certain buses calling at Easton station. During the Summer of 1936, 160 passengers took advantage of this facility to bring in gross receipts of £13 18s. 3d. In the period 4th July-26th September, 1937, only 104 passengers were carried, earning £8 8s. 10d., a handwritten note in the bus company minute book blaming poor publicity by the GWR.

Even the regular Summer Sunday half-day excursion to Portsmouth required careful planning. The stock and locomotive, (usually a 'T9' class 4-4-0) would depart from Dorchester at 9.03 am travelling tender first to Portland for the 10.05 am departure, which only called at Rodwell and Melcombe Regis. The return working departing Portsmouth at 7.03 pm arrived at Melcombe Regis at 10.37 pm and Portland at 10.57 pm, the locomotive then running round the stock before returning to Dorchester.

Few special excursions ran from Portland during the final years the line was open to passenger traffic, but one marathon took place on Saturday 16th September, 1950. The special, formed of a 3-coach corridor set and a 5-coach corridor set, left Dorchester South 'empty stock' at 3.08 am arriving at Portland at 4.00 am. There the 5-coach set was detached, the remaining three coaches proceeding to Easton ready for the 5.00 am departure. On return to Portland the 5-coach set was attached next to the engine, and after calling at all stations to Melcombe Regis, Waterloo was reached at 9.51 am. The return journey commenced at 11. 30 pm, Portland being reached at 3.44 am. The first three coaches then proceeded to Easton arriving at 4.02 am on the Sunday, 23 hours 2 minutes after starting off!

MELCOMBE REGIS (WEYMOUTH), PORTLAND AND EASTON.

Week Days.

		a.m.	a.m.	a.m.		a.m.		a.m.	p.m.		p.m.		p.m.	p.m.		p.m.	p.m.		p.m.		p.m.	p.m.	p.m.
Melcombe Regis	dep.	6 18	7 7	7 17		8 35		10 45	1 15		2 35		4 15	4 30		6 7	6 33		7 45		8 50	10 25	11 25
Westham Halt	,,	6 20	7 9	7 19		8 37		10 47	1 17		2 37		4 17	4 32		6 9	6 35		7 47		8 52		
Rodwell	,,	6 23	7 12	7 22		8 40		10 50	1 20		2 40		4 20	4 35		6 14	6 38		7 50		8 55		
Sandsfoot Castle Halt	,,	6 26	7 15	7 25		8 43		10 53	1 23		2 43		4 23	4 38		6 16	6 41		7 53		8 58		11 33
Wyke Regis Halt	,,	6 28	7 17	7 27		8 45		10 55	1 27		2 45		4 25	4 40		6 19	6 43		7 55		9 0		11 35
Portland	arr.	6 33	7 22	7 32		8 50		11 0	1 32		2 50		4 30	4 45		6 24	6 48		8 0		9 5	10 35	11 40
Portland	dep.			7 35				11 5	1 33		2 57			4 48			6 50						
Easton	arr.			7 47				11 17	1 45		3 9			5 0			7 2						

Sundays.

		p.m.		p.m.		p.m.		p.m.		p.m.		p.m.		p.m.
Melcombe Regis	dep.	1 0		2 15		4 15		6 55		7 40		8 35		11 35
Westham Halt	,,	1 2		2 17		4 17		5 57		7 42		8 37		
Rodwell	,,	1 5		2 20		4 20		6 0		7 45		8 40		
Sandsfoot Castle Halt	,,	1 8		2 23		4 23		6 3		7 48		8 43		11 43
Wyke Regis Halt	,,	1 10		2 25		4 25		6 5		7 50		8 45		11 45
Portland	arr.	1 15		2 30		4 30		6 10		7 55		8 50		11 50
Portland	dep.													
Easton	arr.													

F—Stapleton Road.
J—Restaurant Car from Chippenham.
K—Through train to Yeovil (Pen Mill) via Martock, see page 45.
R—Restaurant Car from Reading.
X—Third class only (limited accommodation).
h—Witham arrive 4.28 p.m.

Ⓔ—Third class only.
†—Third class only except on Saturdays.
‡—Langport West Station.
¶—Bradford Peverell and Stratton Halt.
¶¶—Golf Links.
§—For additional trains, see page 56.

EASTON, PORTLAND AND MELCOMBE REGIS (WEYMOUTH).

Week Days.

		a.m.		a.m.	a.m.		a.m.		p.m.		p.m.		p.m.		p.m.	p.m.	p.m.		p.m.		p.m.	p.m.	p.m.	p.m.
Easton	dep.			8 15					12 12		1 53		3 20		5 19			7 10							
Portland	arr.			8 26					12 23		2 4		3 31		5 30			7 21							
Portland	dep.	6 45		8 7	8 28		9 32		12 27		2 5		3 33		4 50	5 32	7 0	7 25		8 10		9 25	10 46	11 50	
Wyke Regis Halt	,,	6 48		8 12	8 33		9 37		12 32		2 10		3 38		4 55	5 37	7 5	7 52		8 15		9 30		11 55	
Sandsfoot Castle Halt	,,	6 53		8 15	8 36		9 40		12 38		2 13		3 41		4 58	5 40	7 8	7 31		8 18		9 33		11 58	
Rodwell	,,	6 55		8 17	8 41		9 42		12 40		2 15		3 43		5 0	5 42	7 10	7 33		8 20		9 35			
Westham Halt	,,	6 58		8 20	8 44		9 45		12 44		2 18		3 46		5 3	5 45	7 13	7 36		8 23		9 38	12 3		
Melcombe Regis	arr.	7 0		8 21	8 45		9 46		12 45		2 19		3 47		5 4	5 46	7 14	7 37		8 26		9 39	11 0	12 4	

Sundays.

		p.m.		p.m.		p.m.		p.m.		p.m.		p.m.		night
Easton	dep.													
Portland	arr.													
Portland	dep.	1 30		2 40		4 50		6 35		8 5		9 15		12 0
Wyke Regis Halt	,,	1 35		2 45		4 55		6 40		8 10		9 20		12 5
Sandsfoot Castle Halt	,,	1 38		2 48		4 58		6 43		8 13		9 23		12 8
Rodwell	,,	1 40		2 50		5 0		6 45		8 15		9 25		
Westham Halt	,,	1 43		2 53		5 3		6 48		8 18		9 28		12 12
Melcombe Regis	arr.	1 44		2 54		5 4		6 49		8 19		9 29		12 14

F—Stapleton Road.
K—Through train to Yeovil (Pen Mill) via Martock, see page 45.
X—Third class only (limited accommodation).
a—Savernake (Low Level) arrive 8.23 p.m.

Ⓔ—Third class only.
‡—Langport West Station.
§—For additional trains, see page 56.
¶—Bradford Peverell and Stratton Halt.
¶¶—Golf Links.

Public timetable 6th October, 1947.

WEYMOUTH JUNCTION, PORTLAND AND EASTON (worked under Western Region Regulations).

Dist.	DOWN WEEKDAYS.		◆ a.m.	〇 a.m.	Dist.	UP WEEKDAYS.			◆ a.m.	★ p.m.
m.c.					m.c.					
0 00	Weymouth Jc. Ⓧ	... dep.	8 58	10 13	0 00	Easton ...	Ⓧ	... dep.		2 25
0 48	Westham Halt ...	,,	...	...	3 57	Portland ...	Ⓧ	{ arr.		2 43
								{ dep.	11 20	3 47
1 16	Rodwell ... Ⓡ	{ dep.	9 8	10 22	5 48	Whitehead Sidings		... dep.	11J43	
		{ dep.	9 17	10 31	6 55	Stop Board		... dep.	11 53	4 2
4 25	Portland ... Ⓧ	{ arr.		11 50	6 66	Rodwell ... Ⓡ		{ arr.	11X55	4X 4
		{ dep.						{ dep.	12 0	4 12
8 02	Easton ... Ⓧ	... arr.		12 10	8 02	Weymouth Jc. Ⓧ		... arr.	12 6	4M18

C—9.19 a.m. Dorchester South.   J—Arr. 11.26 a.m.   M—To Dorchester South.

Working timetable 1953.

Goods Traffic

Stone was the principal goods traffic of the line almost to the end. At Castletown a siding from the Portland Railway ran into the yard of the Weymouth & Portland Railway, where gantry cranes transferred the stone into standard gauge wagons. Some of the quarries and yards were served by private sidings, the first of which opened in 1872 to serve the Portland Stone Company works which was situated alongside Portland station.

During the 1870s an average of 200 wagons of stone were leaving the Island each week, and at one point there was a shortage of railway trucks! The extension of the line to Easton resulted in private sidings being laid into the premises of the various quarry owners. Quarry Tip Siding was already in position, being part of the originally planned Easton and Church Hope Railway, as were sidings into quarries west of Sheepcroft yard.

Messrs Webber & Pangbourne had a siding running directly from Easton goods yard, this coming into operation with the opening of the line to goods traffic. The Bath Stone Company added a siding in 1904 branching off Quarry Tip Siding, and a further siding was added in 1940, whilst the same company added a siding at Bottom Coombe in April 1924.

With the amalgamation of the various quarry companies several sidings fell into disuse following the war, and Webber & Pangbourne's siding into Park Quarry was out of use by the late 1950s. The Victoria Square stone works of F.J. Barnes became disused in the 1930s, but the siding remained until the mid-1950s for stone loading.

Over the years the railways derived a considerable revenue from the transport of stone, usually carried at special rates agreed with the stone merchants which took into account the amount of traffic on offer. To give an example, in 1886 the Association of Portland Stone Quarry Masters issued a set of prices and delivery charges. For instance, a section of stone measuring 3 in. x 1 ft x 1 ft cost 1s. 1d., whilst 1 ft x 1 ft x 4 ft cost 3s., both at Castletown Pier and Portland station. Conveyance to Nine Elms goods depot or Paddington, by sea to Stewards Wharf at Pimlico, cost 1s. 3d. and 3s. 6d. respectively. There followed a table of add-on prices for cartage within London.

The LSWR, and later the Southern Railway, always secured the best of the stone traffic for London, there being a stone yard at its Nine Elms goods depot. The stone for a majority of the City's large buildings travelled by this route. Masonry in its finished form was also handled, much of it packed in straw and loaded in cribs carried in open wagons. Many of the grave stones for the Imperial War Graves Commission cemeteries throughout the World left Portland by rail.

As on most railways coal was an important traffic on the branch. In earlier years the Navy and other industries were vast consumers. In 1899, 150,000 tons of Welsh steam coal were brought to Portland, as a point of interest this costing the Admiralty 19s. a ton! Not all coal required by the Navy arrived by rail, a vast amount arriving by sea in colliers except for periods during both World Wars when the general shortage of ships and U-Boat activities returned much coastal traffic to the railways. Apart from coastal and dockyard vessels, the main fleet had become oil-burning from the early years of the century, and fuel oil was never taken to Portland by rail.

United Stone firm's wagon No. 11 being loaded in the United Stone Company siding at
Perryfield Works during April 1930.   *British Geological Survey*

'57XX' pannier tank No. 7780 heading towards Weymouth with the branch goods during
August 1955.   *C.L. Caddy*

Later there was only coal for the domestic customer, even in the late 1940s most households burning considerable quantities during the winter months. The average house consumed around 2 cwt a week. Not only was this good trade for the Island's coal merchants but also good for the railway, one wagon load providing only about one week's supply for approximately 100 homes. Portland Gasworks received coal by rail, and as the works was situated next to the station it is surprising that a siding into them was never provided. Instead coal had to be hauled from the goods yard. The same applied at Weymouth, where the power station and gasworks were alongside the line near Westham Halt but no sidings were ever constructed, coal being hauled from Weymouth goods yard.

Another regular and important traffic was the conveyance of cattle. The local butcher bought live cattle which, having arrived at the station, was herded through the streets to the slaughterhouses situated near to the butcher's shop. The Navy also received cattle for their slaughterhouse which was situated in the dockyard. The introduction of refrigeration and improved methods of butchery drastically reduced this traffic after the turn of the century, and it virtually disappeared from the branch following the Great War.

Fares and Tickets

When the line opened the single fares between Weymouth and Portland were 3*d*. third class, 4*d*. second class and 6*d*. first class, the respective return fares being 5*d*., 6*d*. and 9*d*. Weymouth being an open station, a ticket platform was situated in the Portland branch loop at Portland Junction, where the tickets of all branch passengers were examined or collected until the opening of Rodwell station.

For many years fares altered very little, at the turn of the century still being 3*d*., 4*d*. and 6*d*. whilst a dog cost 3*d*. and a cycle or pram 6*d*. The fares between Portland and Rodwell were the same as the Weymouth fares! At the opening of the Easton section the fares between Portland and Easton were 3½*d*. third class and 5*d*. second class, the return fares being 7*d*. and 9*d*.; a Weymouth-Easton single cost 6½*d*.

Being a joint line tickets differed from those issued at a normal single-company station, and the style of ticket varied over a period of time. Until just after the turn of the century tickets issued on the branch carried the wording 'Weymouth & Portland Rly', some of these being very colourful. A dog ticket was printed in three colours, red, white and blue. Later tickets were printed 'GWR & LSWR', and certain tickets covering the Easton section were printed 'GWR & LSWR (E&CH Rly)', Weymouth & Portland Rly tickets of the less frequently issued types such as dogs, cycles, etc. continued in use for some considerable time, the situation during the 1930s being that at Melcombe Regis the tickets were generally of the Southern

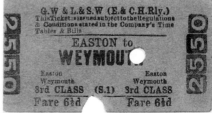

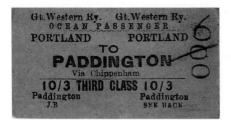

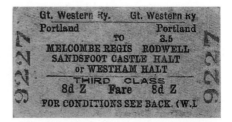

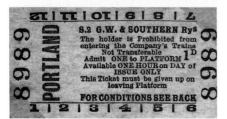

A selection of tickets used on the Portland Branch.

Above left: Forces leave ticket allowing Mr G.H. Jenvey to travel from France to Portland whilst serving with the Royal Engineers during World War I. *Above right:* A child's ticket for the Joint Railway's railmotor service.

Railway type but lettered 'Southern & Gt Western Jt Rly'. At both Rodwell and Portland they were of the Great Western style, and lettered 'Great Western & Southern Jt Rly', whilst at Easton the Southern Railway type of ticket was issued lettered 'Gt Western & Southern Jt Rly (E&CH)'. Three sets of accounts also had to be kept at Easton - Great Western, Southern, and Easton & Church Hope Railway. Tickets purchased at stations on the branch to destinations beyond were either of GWR- or SR-type depending upon the route taken.

Any rise in railway fares has always caused comment, the *Dorset Daily Echo* during December 1927 complaining as follows.

The new railway season ticket rates promise even more hardly on Portland people. Today one can get a season from Easton to Weymouth for £2 12s. 6d., or from Portland for £1 10s. 0d. a sensible reduction on the three months ordinary fares, but on and after 1st January the cost is to be Easton £2 14s. 0d., and Portland £1 10s. 9d. The seasons between Portland and Rodwell will also rise. At present they are very cheap, £1 2s. 6d. for three months. Twenty trains a day, seven days a week.

In November 1933 the fare structure again came in for criticism,

What is the cheapest return fare on the British Railways? It is to be found on the Weymouth and Portland line where one may get a return ticket between Rodwell and Sandsfoot for one penny. The return fare Westham to Melcombe Regis a much shorter distance is twopence.

During the early 1930s inter-available Rail and Road Season Tickets were introduced, the price in January 1935 between Portland station or Victoria Square and Melcombe Regis or the King's Statue being £2 16s. 3d. for three months, or £1 3s. 3d. for 28 days. The railway's proportion of the proceeds was £1 3s. 3d. and 11s. 3d. respectively.

The ever-popular excursions to Portsmouth cost 5s. 9d. in the years just preceding World War II. Also popular were the seven day holiday season tickets, which cost 12s. 6d. third class and 17s. 6d. first class. Area No. 17 covered from Easton to Bournemouth Central, the Abbotsbury branch, up the GWR main line to Maiden Newton and the Bridport branch. Area No. 18 stretched from Easton to Yeovil, the Abbotsbury and Bridport branches, and down the Southern main line from Yeovil to Seaton Junction , including the Seaton, Lyme Regis and Chard branches.

By 1939 fares along the branch had risen by a halfpenny above their 1930 level. By comparison bus fares varied, 1d. dearer to Portland Victoria Square and 1½d. more expensive to Ferrybridge than to Wyke Halt, but 1s. 2d. cheaper to Easton, whilst return fares from Portland and particularly Easton were considerably cheaper.

Tickets were issued at Easton, Portland, Rodwell (until 1941) and Melcombe Regis. From the introduction of the railmotors and the opening of Westham and Wyke Regis Halts guards issued tickets on the trains for passengers joining at unstaffed Halts and other stations when the booking offices were closed. These were carried in ticket racks and cancelled with a bell punch in the same manner as a bus conductor, and guards also carried a cash bag. The tickets issued were a mixture of standard Edmondson card and paper types.

At busy times a second guard joined the train and alighted at either Westham or Wyke Regis Halts to issue tickets for the following or return train. Although the guards endeavoured to collect all fares, during the war the blackout assisted a little fiddle worked by many travellers. A Woodbine cigarette packet was of light green colour, and two pieces cut to size and pasted back to back formed the perfect railway ticket to be handed in on a dark night. The large number of passengers leaving the train at Wyke Halt also gave the ticket collector a problem, as a mass of tickets were quickly gathered; on at least one occasion a miscreant was caught, his 4½d. workman's ticket costing him £1 at the local Court!

Financial Matters

Although a jointly-operated branch, there were certain matters which for obvious reasons had to be the responsibility of one company or the other. The general civil engineering, stations, and signalling equipment were the responsibility of the Great Western. The locomotives, passenger rolling stock, and engine crews were the responsibility of the company operating the service at the time.

Operating expenses were a problem on all branch lines, Portland being no exception. In 1888 thirteen staff were employed at Portland and Rodwell stations. G. Jeans, the Portland station master, received £130 per annum, whilst J. Palmer, the booking porter in charge of Rodwell received £1 7s. 6d. per week. The gateman at Littlefield was paid a mere 18s. The total year's wage bill for the staff was £842 12s., Portland costing £667 and Rodwell £175 12s.

Thirty-four years later the station staff wages for the branch totalled £6,793 7s. 8d., being broken down as follows, Easton £1,033 12s., Portland £3,126 6s., Rodwell £1,133 5s. 8d. and Melcombe Regis £1,500 4s. The Portland station master now received £350 per annum and the gatemen at Littlefield £2 7s., and the number of staff had increased from a mere 13 to 46.

The cost of operating the line had also increased rapidly between 1913 and 1925. The Weymouth-Portland section had working expenses of £10,589 with an income of £10,537 in 1913, but by 1925 the traffic expenses were £23,642 and income only £15,453, both these sums being after paying the annual £4,500 to the Weymouth & Portland Company. The Easton section was in a far worse situation. In 1913 the working expenses had been £2,405 with traffic receipts of £1,801, but by 1925 traffic expenses had risen to £6,171 whilst receipts totalled only £3,670. Here again, an average of £1,435 was paid annually to the Easton company.

The branch came under the close scrutiny of the GWR and LSWR (later SR) Joint Stations Committee, who were ever vigilant to make sure each only paid their share of expenses. The mass of paperwork makes interesting reading and shows that cost-conscious management is nothing new.

Even small items came under their remit right down to the shared profits of station vending machines - albeit in those days just a small bar of chocolate or a small packet of cigarettes. In 1927 it was decided that a Post Office telephone be installed in the office at Easton station, Portland already had a telephone, which was originally in the goods office but was later moved to the booking office. Far more important was the cost of train working. The cost of motive power for passenger trains had been 3s. per mile in 1921, decreasing to 2s. 6d. by 1925, whilst coaching stock was charged at 1½d. per mile per coach.

The Southern company, working the goods trains between Portland and Easton, were credited 2s. 6d. per train mile, whilst the three locomotives provided by the Southern shed at Weymouth required the following resources,

    7 drivers at 15s. per day, one acting as shed foreman.
    2 firemen at 12s. per day, 4 firemen at 11s. per day
    3 cleaners at 7s. per day, 2 coalmen at 52s. per week.

Not only were the joint Committee keen to see each had their share of traffic and revenue, but particularly in the early days, the staff and agents were also keen to look after the company of their own favour. Both passengers and goods would if possible be routed via the line of the favoured company if proceeding beyond Weymouth, and at times the atmosphere in the booking and goods office must have been strained. Even at the top level there were problems. In 1903 it transpired that the LSWR storekeeper was only supplying note paper and forms, but no envelopes! This resulted in the staff sending out the official mail in GWR envelopes which at the time carried adverts for that company's services - a situation that displeased the LSWR superintendent of the line! Needless to say LSWR envelopes soon became available.

WEYMOUTH JUNCTION (1920)

SPARE: 1 : 8 : 41 :

Chapter Nine

Signalling

When first opened the branch was operated on the Train Staff & Ticket system. The points and signals at Portland were under the control of pointsmen, a situation still prevailing in June 1873 when Col Yolland of the Board of Trade inspected a new siding put in for the use of the Portland Stone Company. The facing points were not connected or interlocked with the signals, and the sidings lacked trap points to protect the running line. Added to this there was no run-round loop, passenger trains having to be 'fly shunted' into the platform.

At Weymouth conditions were little better, 'ground signalling', consisting of individual levers situated at the points and on the posts of the signals, being the order of the day. With the building of the Portland branch and Harbour Tramway the Board of Trade Inspector had insisted that a signal box be constructed to control the layout. Because of its early date few details survive of Portland Junction signal box, but it is known to have been equipped with a 'Chambers' frame, one of only four installed on the Great Western Railway.

To allow trains to enter or depart from Weymouth station onto the branch shunting was required, the procedure being for a train from Portland to arrive in the up loop, the locomotive then running forward to the junction points with the main line from where it proceeded to the Portland end of the train via the down loop. The train would then be propelled out onto the main line before being pulled into Weymouth station. A Portland-bound train would be hauled from Weymouth station along the main line to a point just past the junction, it would then be shunted back onto the Portland branch down loop, the locomotive then returning to the junction before running via the up branch loop to gain access to the Portland end of the train before proceeding on its journey. Although this was not the solution sought by the Board of Trade at the opening of the line, it did reduce the reversing of the passenger train to the absolute minimum. Until 1870, whilst the locomotive was running round passengers tickets would be inspected at the ticket platform situated between the up and down branch loops.

These far from ideal arrangements at Portland Junction were a cause of concern to both the Great Western and London & South Western companies, who approached the Board of Trade in 1871 for authority to propel trains in both directions between the junction and Weymouth station, claiming that the signalling was suitable to allow this movement. However Col Yolland would make no concessions. He was not impressed with the existing arrangements, but accepted them in the circumstances.

The junction at Weymouth, 28 chains north of the station, consisted of a normal double junction with a facing connection in the down main line and a trailing connection in the up main line. The Portland branch continued for a short distance as double track, then became single before the point where the Harbour Tramway diverged. About half-way between the main line junction and the end of the double track there was a trailing crossover which facilitated running round a very short train.

Weymouth Junction signal box, a typical Great Western structure of the 1880s viewed from the Weymouth station side. The damage caused by wartime bombing can be seen patched with new brickwork. *Author*

Weymouth Junction signal box, photographed on 20th September, 1956 viewed from the Portland branch side. In the background the new Weymouth signal box that would take over the operation of both Weymouth Junction and Weymouth Station signal boxes the following April is under construction. *J.H. Lucking Collection*

By 1868 the Block System was in operation between Weymouth and Dorchester Junction, although the entire line northwards to Thingley Junction (near Chippenham) was not so equipped until 1873. For reasons unknown both Portland Junction and Upwey signal boxes were excluded from the block scheme. At Weymouth the block instruments were housed in the pointsman's hut, and he had to relay the messages to the signalman by means of a swing bell mounted on a post outside. Trains from Portland were controlled by a double disc-and-crossbar signal, and one of similar type was used to admit down trains directly to the branch.

During 1876 the first Weymouth Station signal box was constructed, at the same time the original Portland Junction signal box was replaced. The Chambers lever frame was put to further use at Kennington Junction (Oxford), whilst the box structure went to Upwey to become the signal box at the original station.

The primitive state at Portland station was rectified in 1877 with various alterations together with the interlocking of all points and signals and the construction of a signal box containing a frame of 23 levers. This was inspected by the Board of Trade on 12th July, 1877, and on 7th March the following year Block Telegraph working, in conjunction with the Train Staff, was introduced on the line.

With the introduction of passenger train working over the Weymouth Harbour Tramway in 1889, a new 43-lever signal box was erected in the 'V' between the main line and the double line section of the branch, this being extended several yards in the Portland direction. The Harbour Tramway then formed an extension of the down branch and ran parallel with the Portland branch for a little way, the two lines being connected by a scissors crossover which allowed direct running to and from both lines. Whilst these improvements were being carried out the last disc-and-crossbar signals vanished from Weymouth. These signals had never been employed at Portland, where signals of conventional semaphore design had been used from the start. The scissors crossover itself was interesting, as it was to survive as the last example of 'baulk road' track at Weymouth until finally replaced in 1910.

The new signal box, the other alterations and extension to the arrival platform were inspected by Major General Hutchinson early in August, who pointed out that as arriving Portland trains used the departure platform (a practice of many years standing), they passed over trailing points which become facing but were not fitted with the necessary locking devices. It was therefore desirable that these trains used the arrival platform. Alterations were quickly carried out, and by mid-October, Portland trains arrived at the arrival platform.

Where the line crossed the Abbotsbury Road on the level a crossing keeper's cottage had existed since the opening of the line. The gates were hand operated and the protecting signals were worked from an outdoor frame, but there was no interlocking between the two. During 1890, in conjunction with alterations carried out at Portland Junction signal box an elevated ground frame was constructed at Littlefield. This was of distinctive design, the lower windows and patterned brickwork being of the same architectural style as Stavordale Villas, two large houses built several years earlier which stood adjacent to the site. The ground frame housed a gate wheel and a 10-lever stud locking frame with 'sweep' segments. This was of course, fully interlocked, and there were to be no more accidents of the kind described in Chapter Four. The original wooden-

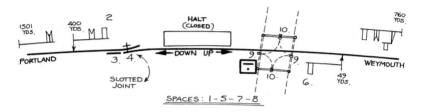

Littlefield Crossing signalling diagram 1957.

Littlefield Crossing signalling diagram 1960. Note the addition of trap points and alterations to signalling.

Littlefield Crossing viewed from Westham Halt, 169 miles from Paddington (via Swindon), across the road the crossing keeper's cottage, and beyond the Backwater viaduct. *C.L. Caddy*

backed nameplate with cast letter reading 'Littlefield Crossing Signal Box' was replaced by a non-standard nameplate of a very small size.

A loop siding to serve the Whitehead's torpedo factory (then under construction) was provided in 1891, this being situated on the Weymouth side of the Fleet viaduct. The points at either end were controlled from a central four-lever ground frame released by the key on the Train Staff, and revolving point discs were provided for movements leaving the sidings, but there were no running signals. This siding was inspected by the Board of Trade in August of the same year.

On 15th December, 1892 the small intermediate station at Rodwell acquired its first signal box. Of timber construction, it stood on the Weymouth end of the platform and contained a stud locking frame of seven levers. No loop or siding was provided so the purpose of this box is a little obscure although there seems to have been a 19th century convention that every station should be signalled, and the 1889 Regulation of Railways Act was very strict on signalling. Rodwell was of very little value for block working purposes, and electrical locking was necessary to prevent the signalman accepting trains from both directions at once! In 1899 Portland Junction signal box was renamed Weymouth Junction.

Easton signal box and signals were supplied by Evans, O'Donnell of Chippenham, a company later to become part of the well known Westinghouse group. The frame consisted of 14 levers, points 7, 10 and 14 being fitted with 'economic' locks - a system that reduced the overall length of the frame by working both points and lock by the same lever. The building itself was of timber on a brick base, and was brought into use on 1st October, 1900, although electric train staff equipment had not yet been installed, and the Easton section was worked by a simple train staff fitted with a key to release the ground frames. On the single line between Portland signal box and Castletown Junction a goods loop was constructed on the station side of Castletown Road Bridge, this being the end of the Easton-Portland section.

Board of Trade requirements for the full opening of the Easton line necessitated considerable alterations to the arrangements at Portland. On the curve giving access to the Easton line a temporary box was provided. This was a timber sectional building of a type much used by the Great Western which had previously seen service at Polperro Tunnel (between Probus and Truro) during the doubling of the main line through Cornwall. It became redundant at its Cornish site on 16th March, 1902, being dismantled and conveyed to Portland for re-erection in the summer of the same year in readiness for the start of passenger services to Easton.

The opening of this box effectively created two separate railways, there being no through working of passenger trains. The single line between Portland main signal box and the down home signal for the temporary station was regarded as a siding only, the only 'through' movements being goods trains, engines and the empty stock to form the Easton service. Bell communication was provided between the two boxes, but there were no instruments.

Construction of the new Portland station included the provision of two new signal boxes. Both of brick with slated hip roofs, they came into use on 7th May, 1905. Portland Station box had a 21-lever frame and occupied a site alongside the temporary edifice described in the preceding paragraph. Portland Goods Junction was situated at the Weymouth end of the station layout at a point where

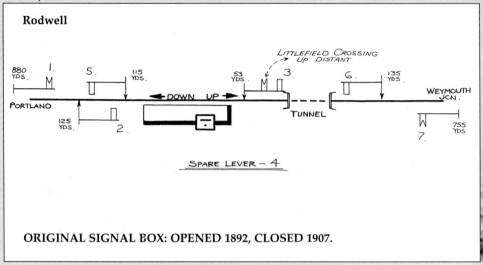

Rodwell station pre-1907 signalling arrangements.

Rodwell station, post-1907 signalling diagram, showing revised layout.

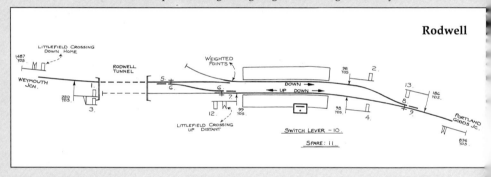

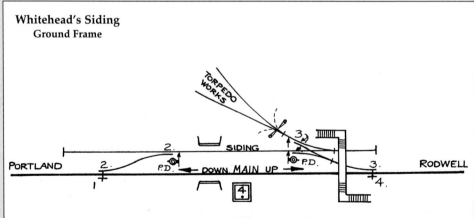

Whitehead's Siding: ground frame arrangements.

the goods yard branched off, and contained a 27-lever frame. With the opening of these boxes both the temporary box and the original Portland box were taken out of use, although the building of the latter survived as a staff room until the 1950s. In the meantime there was a modest expansion of the layout at Easton. A siding was laid into the works of Messrs Webber & Pangbourne, and in connection with this a long loop siding was provided parallel to the running line. A two-lever ground frame was established to control the points furthest away from Easton station, this being brought into use on 25th November, 1903. In the same year an agreement was signed between the GWR and the Postmaster General. It was actually a supplementary agreement to one dating from 1891, at which time it was common practice for GPO telephone wires to be carried on poles owned by a railway company. This new agreement simply clarified the position in the event of alterations becoming necessary. The GPO was to pay for the moving of poles and wires even when this was solely to meet railway needs, but if wires belonging to the Weymouth & Portland Railway were carried on the same poles, the GPO was only to be charged a proportion of the cost dependent on the ratio of Post Office to railway company wires.

Reconstruction of the viaduct over the Backwater at Weymouth was facilitated by the provision of temporary sidings at each end of the work, by which means spoil wagons and other equipment gained direct access to the site. On 16th December, 1907 the two ground frames controlling these sidings were brought into use. The one at the Weymouth end consisted of two levers locked by a key on the train staff, whilst at the Littlefield Crossing end a single ground lever was provided, locked by a key kept in the crossing box and released by the key on the staff. At the same time work was under way at Rodwell. A passing loop was installed, and a new brick-built signal box containing 13 levers constructed on the up platform. This new box came into use on 8th December, 1907, the old box being closed at the same time.

World War I brought much additional traffic to the branch, and to enable Portland goods yard to accept longer trains, the access points were moved further up the shunting neck towards Weymouth. This placed them well beyond the limit of rod working from Portland Goods Junction box, but this connection was apparently too important and heavily used to be entrusted to ground frame operation. A small signal box known as Portland Siding was therefore provided , this being completed on 22nd March, 1916. Like so many wartime boxes it was a short-lived affair. Once hostilities were over and traffic reverted to more normal proportions the goods yard points were moved back to their original position, and Portland Siding box closed on 11th June, 1919. Around the same period the electric train staff equipment in use between Weymouth Junction and Rodwell was replaced by the smaller electric key token equipment. On 24th April, 1924 a new ground frame and siding serving Bottom Coombe stone yard at Easton was opened.

Falls of stone from the high cliffs along parts of the Easton section of the branch had caused problems for years, a flagman having to be employed to check this section of line. To eliminate this problem a wire screen was erected alongside the most vulnerable section. It consisted of wires stretched zig-zag fashion between poles over a length of 211 yds and set back 6ft from the running

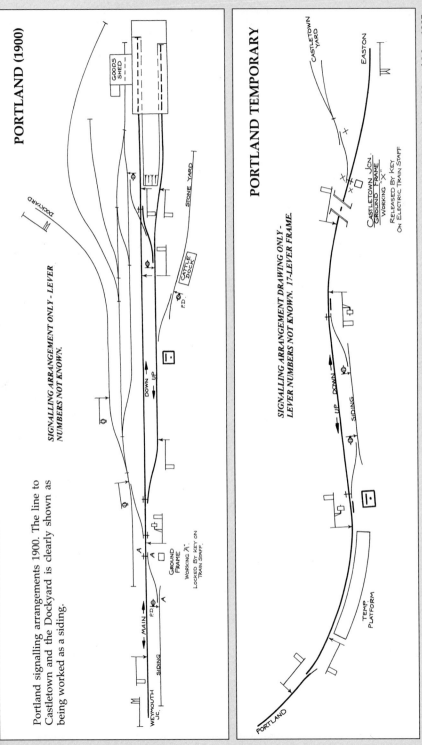

PORTLAND (1900)

Portland signalling arrangements 1900. The line to Castletown and the Dockyard is clearly shown as being worked as a siding.

SIGNALLING ARRANGEMENT ONLY - LEVER NUMBERS NOT KNOWN.

PORTLAND TEMPORARY

SIGNALLING ARRANGEMENT DRAWING ONLY - LEVER NUMBERS NOT KNOWN. 17-LEVER FRAME

Portland temporary signal box. This diagram shows the position of the temporary signal box and platform used between September 1902 and May 1905, for the independent train operating the Easton section. The siding was used to allow the engine to run round its stock. The section of line towards Portland station was only operated as a siding to allow the transfer of stock and locomotives, but not the through running of passenger trains.

PORTLAND GOODS JN

PORTLAND STATION

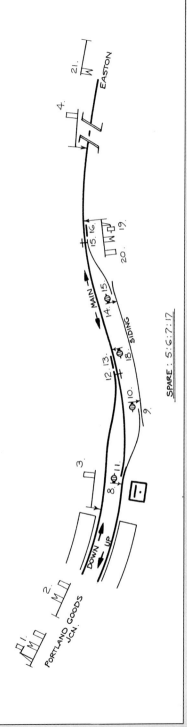

RODWELL

1299 YDS.

381 YDS.

162 YDS.

62 YDS.

73 YDS.

10 YDS.

155 YDS.

271 YDS.

384 YDS.

GOODS SIDINGS

MAIN

SIDING

UP   DOWN

DOCK SIDING

PORTLAND STATION

SPACES : 1 – 6

EASTON

MAIN

SIDING

DOWN   UP

PORTLAND GOODS JCN.

SPARE : 5:6:7:17

Four signal boxes at Portland. In this view commencing from the left we see: Portland Goods Junction signal box of 1905 (*a*), Portland signal box of 1877 (*b*), Portland signal box of 1935 (*c*), Portland Station signal box of 1905 (*d*). The photograph was taken around the time of the opening of Portland signal box in 1935. Portland Goods Junction and Portland Station signal boxes were demolished shortly after. *Author's Collection*

PORTLAND SIDING

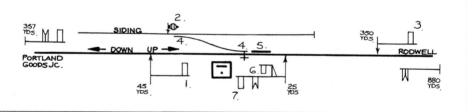

PORTLAND

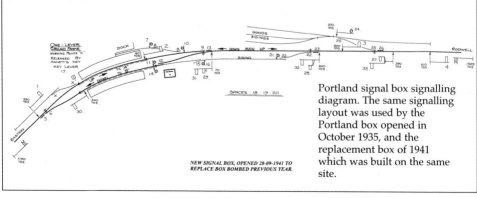

NEW SIGNAL BOX, OPENED 28-09-1941 TO REPLACE BOX BOMBED PREVIOUS YEAR.

Portland signal box signalling diagram. The same signalling layout was used by the Portland box opened in October 1935, and the replacement box of 1941 which was built on the same site.

rail. Situated at each end of the screen was a signal held in the 'off' position by the wire of the screen, and in the event of a rock falling and breaking the wire the signals returned to the danger position and tremulous bells rang in both Portland and Easton signal boxes. This equipment was brought into use in December 1928. Although fairly common in the Highlands of Scotland, such provision is almost unique on an English branch line.

On 19th March, 1931 a switch lever was provided in Rodwell box to enable it to close at times of light traffic, and to allow for this the up loop was signalled for running in both directions. The switching out of block posts on single lines calls for a little explanation. With 'short section' working in operation the sections were Weymouth Junction - Rodwell and Rodwell - Portland Goods Junction, a separate staff controlling each section, but with Rodwell switched out the whole line between Weymouth and Portland became a single unit. Two sets of instruments were therefore necessary- for 'long' and 'short' working respectively - and electrical locking was provided between the two to ensure that only one set was in use at any one time. Before Rodwell could close the sections on either side had to be clear of traffic. The points would be set for the up loop, then having requested the signalmen at Portland and Weymouth to hold in the plungers of their staff instruments, the switch lever (No. 10) was pulled to the halfway position. This freed the mechanical locking to permit the signals to be lowered for trains to pass over the up loop in both directions. Once the signals had been pulled, the signalmen on either side released their plungers, the Rodwell signalman pulled the switch lever to the full reverse position, and direct communication then existed between Weymouth and Portland. At the time of conversion the electric train staff in use between Rodwell and Portland Goods Junction was replaced by the smaller electric key token instrument.

As a further act of cost cutting, to avoid the opening of Portland Station signal box for trains terminating at Portland, a connection was provided to form a run-round loop from a siding near the Goods Junction signal box, saving an estimated £46 per year on Sunday duty and overtime. The cost of this alteration was just over £400, and in the event proved to be a short term measure. During the weekend 20th-22nd October, 1935 both Portland Goods Junction and Portland Station signal boxes were taken out of use and replaced by one box about halfway between the two. Many parts of the lever frame for this new box came from frames salvaged from the Bradford Junction (near Trowbridge) rationalisation scheme, under which three signal boxes had been replaced by one several years previously. The life of this new box was unexpectedly short, for it became the victim of an air raid on Sunday 11th August, 1940, in which it received a direct hit. For just over a year a temporary outdoor frame of eight levers was used to operate the main points and a hut 10 ft square erected to house the instruments. A new box of typical wartime design and containing a 33-lever frame was brought into use on 29th September, 1941.

The emergency road laid over the Fleet viaduct required special signalling arrangements to ensure safe working. This was achieved by having the entrance gates at either end locked with Annett's keys, the instruments for which were located in groundsmen's huts. Upon a request from the Military to open the road the groundsman at the Portland end would telephone the signalman at Portland

Portland station master Mr G.H. Jenvey stands next to checker Roy Pullen and two other members of the station staff outside the original 1877 signal box in Portland yard.

Author's Collection

Portland signal box, shortly before the closure of the line. A typical wartime structure, the nameplate was unusual as only the word 'Portland' appeared instead of the usual full title including the words 'signal box' as was standard with most GWR boxes. Standing alongside is Mr J. Vatcher the Weymouth station master.

M. Thresh

who would then consult with the Rodwell signalman. Once the line was clear of trains and all tokens were in their machines, the Portland signalman would release the Annett's keys which were then used to unlock the gates. Whilst the keys were out of their machines the signalmen at Portland or Rodwell could not draw out a token to allow a train into the section. Before this could take place the gates had to be locked against road traffic and the Annett's keys replaced in their machines, the groundsman informing the signalman accordingly. The movement of road traffic was under the control of the Military Police. Fortunately the Fleet road bridge was never damaged, and apart from a trial run, the emergency road was never required. If it had been, the success of a large section of the invasion forces could have depended on one railway viaduct on the Portland branch.

In October 1946 the gates at Littlefield Crossing were renewed, the new ones on the box side being set back to the inside edge of the pavement. The corner of the box had to be cut back to allow the gate at the box end to lie parallel to the inside edge of the pavement when open to road traffic. The previous arrangement had included wickets on the pavement side for pedestrian use. On 23rd December of the same year the gates at Ferrybridge, protecting the wartime emergency road across the railway bridge, were removed.

Apart from minor signalling alterations, which included the erection of a banner repeater signal on the Marsh embankment to give advance warning of the home signal at Littlefield Crossing, few other alterations took place during the years of passenger working. When the passenger service was withdrawn in March 1952 the signalling was still complete, with boxes at Rodwell, Portland and Easton and an elevated ground frame at Littlefield Crossing, but the management were quick to seek more economical methods of working. One suggestion involved dividing the branch into two 'One Engine in Steam' sections - Weymouth Junction box to Melcombe Regis station and Melcombe Regis to Easton. The wooden train staff for the latter section would have been housed in a locked box at the Portland end of Melcombe Regis platform, and trap points installed to protect the platform from the branch - an essential precaution at this location, as trains from Portland approached on a steep falling gradient. This seemingly rather unwieldy idea was suggested because plans were afoot to rebuild Weymouth station, and it was intended to use Melcombe Regis as a relief platform during the work. On 18th February, 1952 the Yeovil district inspector wrote to the divisional superintendent in Bristol to explain that the scheme was impracticable, as trap points could not be provided on the Backwater viaduct and it was only two yards between the end of that structure and the bottom of Melcombe Regis platform ramp. To site the points at the other end of the viaduct would bring them into close proximity of Littlefield Crossing so that a train derailed thereon would block the public highway. At a meeting held in Bristol on 6th March that year it was decided to upgrade Littlefield Crossing to a block post, retaining electric token working between there and Weymouth Junction, the remainder of the branch to be operated under One Engine in Steam regulations. This had the desired effect of offering flexible working into Melcombe Regis whilst allowing most of the branch signalling to be removed. The same meeting agreed that the rock fall screen between Portland and Easton could be taken away (because of the heavy cost of maintenance) in view of the fact that the line would now carry only freight trains during the hours of daylight. This economy was never made.

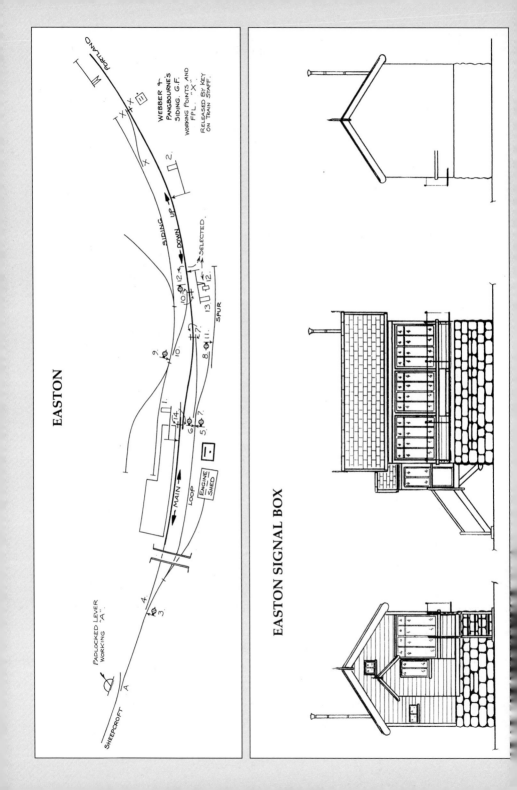

EASTON

EASTON SIGNAL BOX

Despite the positive tone of the correspondence nothing much happened. It was another two years before any action whatsoever was taken, Rodwell box closing on 1st March, 1954. The points were clipped out of use to allow all trains to pass over the former down loop, and all signals were removed except the post that had carried the up starting signal which was retained to carry the up fixed distant for Littlefield Crossing. A 'Stop' board and telephone were provided a few yards on the Portland side of Rodwell station, from which the guards of up freight trains were to advise the Littlefield Crossing keeper of the position of the train. This was done so that the crossing gates would be across the road for the shortest possible time. Some preparatory work was done in connection with raising Littlefield to block post status. One of the key token instruments from Rodwell was transferred to the crossing box, where it was destined to remain until closure of the line without being wired up, a couple of SR 'rail-built' signal posts were erected on the Marsh embankment and the rodding laid down for the proposed catch points, but the realisation that Naval leave specials would also have to work over the branch brought about a halt to the alterations.

At Easton Naval leave trains were not a consideration, so the signal box at that station was replaced by a ground frame on 24th April, 1955 and One Engine in Steam working instituted between there and Portland. At the same time some rationalisation of the Portland layout was carried out, the down loop through the station and 'The Mere' siding being taken out of use.

On 5th January, 1956 a meeting was held at Weymouth station to discuss the possibility of converting the Littlefield-Portland section to 'No Signalman' Token working with Electric Token between Weymouth Junction and Littlefield. Mr Scale, Bristol district operating superintendent, declared himself against the proposal on the grounds that the heavy gradient between Portland and Easton presented difficulties in the event of a runaway, and in his opinion 'a suitable unit should be on duty at Portland when an up train left Easton, readily accessible by telephone' to take quick and decisive action. After much discussion it was decided to leave matters as they stood, with Electric Token working between Weymouth Junction and Portland and One Engine in Steam from Portland to Easton. The only other alterations to the signalling on the Portland branch took place at Littlefield Crossing on 26th April, 1959, when the signal posts erected some years earlier were at last fitted with arms and brought into use, together with the long awaited trap points. The banner repeater was removed at the same time.

By 1960 the salt air had caused serious corrosion of the point rodding at Portland, but in view of the light usage of the line it was decided not to incur the considerable expense of renewing it. Early in 1961 the points leading from the single line into the goods yard were disconnected and worked on the ground, the signalman walking from the signal box to bar them into the correct position and secure them with clip and plugs. This effectively put the down home signals out of use and also the up main and 'from goods sidings' starting signals, leaving only six levers in use - a state of affairs that lasted until final closure.

This arrangement gave rise to an incident that could have been serious but, luckily, was simply amusing. The instructions were for the signalman to bar the goods yard points over to set them for the main line after departure of the last train each day, but as the walk from the box to the points and back again was nearly half a mile there was a distinct lack of enthusiasm for doing so. The practice developed of leaving the points set for the yard overnight, and one night a box van on which the handbrake had not been firmly applied was blown out by a southerly gale which was strong enough to propel it a considerable distance along the Chesil Beach section. The signalman knew nothing of the escaped wagon when he took duty the following morning, and when Weymouth offered the goods he accepted it without hesitation.

Fortunately for all concerned the driver spotted the wagon from some distance away and was able to stop, but the signalman was most surprised to see the train approaching his home signal propelling a 'vanfit'. Had the morning been foggy the result might have been quite serious, but there was no evidence to suggest that this rather slack method of working was brought to an end by this incident, and it is likely that news of it never spread beyond the confines of the branch!

Both Weymouth Junction and Weymouth Station signal boxes closed in April 1957, being replaced by a new 'Weymouth' box containing a 116-lever Westinghouse 'A3' frame. It was the last large mechanical box to be installed on the Southern. Following the complete closure of the Portland branch in 1965 everything was left more or less intact for a while, but the gates and frame were removed from Littlefield on 30th April, 1969 and the box demolished on 8th July, whilst the signals and fittings were removed from Portland the following year. Now with the age of power signalling, Weymouth box closed in September 1986, movements at Weymouth being controlled from a newly installed panel at Dorchester South signal box.

It is interesting to note that although the Portland branch was a 'joint' line the GWR had always assumed responsibility for signalling matters, and all the equipment bore the unmistakable hallmark of that company into BR days. Regional boundary changes in April 1950 brought the whole area under Southern Region control. Within a year a Southern rail-built down starting signal had appeared at Rodwell, and by 1956 a scattering of upper quadrant arms were appearing. At Portland, the up outer home, up starting, up advanced starting and 'from goods siding' starting became upper quadrant, although the new fittings were attached to the square section wooden posts of GWR origin. The up inner home was totally renewed as an SR rail-built signal. The new signals erected at Littlefield in 1959 were also of the rail-built type, so when the line closed the only Great Western signals surviving were Portland down homes (tubular bracket), Littlefield Crossing down home (tubular straight post), and some truly antique wooden signals applying to the branch at Weymouth.

The single line staff used on the Portland-Easton section during the last years of the branch.   *D.M. Habgood*

Chapter Ten

The Joint Railway
1939-1948

It was a glorious summer in 1939, but in Europe an almighty storm was gathering. As the holidaymakers enjoyed the sunshine on the beaches of Weymouth and Portland, a crisis point was reached. The European situation deteriorated rapidly, and on 24th August, 1939 the Emergency Powers (Defence) Act received the Royal Assent, Britain's railways being taken under the control of the Ministry of Transport.

On Sunday 3rd September at 11.00 am war was declared against Germany. It was to be a different kind of war to that of 1914-18 which was fought hand to hand on the battlefields of France; this time the civilian population at home would become involved. The aeroplane had become a sophisticated machine capable of travelling great distances, and armed with the right weapons, became the source of tremendous damage and loss of life.

Fearing a mass attack on the large cities, children were evacuated to country areas and many London children were sent to Weymouth and Portland. Although 774 of these evacuees arrived at Portland, they were not allowed to stay long as it was quickly realised that the Admiralty premises on the Island represented a prime target, and they were subsequently moved to other West Country towns.

Although the Weymouth and Portland area did not suffer the privations of many large cities or the ports of Portsmouth, Southampton and Plymouth the war took its toll. In Weymouth there were 787 alerts, 481 high explosive bombs, two land mines, and 4,300 incendiaries which fell in 51 raids with the loss of 83 lives. On neighbouring Portland in 784 alerts, 244 high explosive bombs and 19 oil bombs caused 34 fatalities. Portland, with its Naval harbour, Dockyard and other military installations was a prime target, whilst Weymouth with its commercial harbour, ship repair yards, Whitehead's torpedo factory, and the railway at Weymouth and the Portland branch received attention from the Luftwaffe. Despite this and the build up to D-Day in which Weymouth and Portland played a vital role, the rail service kept going under the difficult conditions.

The Portland branch soon became a vital link in the war effort. Gone were the holidaymakers, sightseers and tourists who had crowded the line during that unforgettable summer of 1939. The principal traffic on the line was now goods, naval stores and personnel, and troops. Many Portland men said 'farewell' to the Island and their families, and took the branch train on the first stage of their journey to join service units throughout the Country.

Within weeks all train services were reduced to the extent that on the Portland branch only the 1.15 pm ex-Melcombe Regis divided the interval between the 8.35 am and 4.38 pm departures. Some other trains had been augmented to meet the needs of Portland Dockyard and Whitehead's torpedo factory. By January 1940 the service had been restored to 21 trains each way daily, seven of which were extended to Easton. Eleven trains ran on Sunday but all terminated at Portland. Later the main service was reduced by a third!

SR 'T9' class locomotive No. 284 leaves the Backwater viaduct just before World War II hauling a 'B' set. This was probably the unusual working refered to on page 161.

W. Newman

Early 1940 also opened with the discovery of the body of an 18-year-old local girl who had been missing from her home for eight days. She was found alongside the track at the foot of a cutting on the Easton line. Coastal defences were quickly built, and early in the year several 6 inch ack-ack guns were unloaded at Sheepcroft and transported to Portland Bill by road.

The evacuation of Dunkirk during June brought more traffic to the branch, returning men being billeted at The Verne before rejoining their units. Later in the month ships from Portland helped in the evacuation of the Channel Islands prior to German occupation. By July both Weymouth and Portland had become a 'War Zone', and restrictions were placed upon visitors to the area. A section of Chesil Beach was put out of bounds.

The war was now taking a grim turn. From occupied airfields in Cherbourg a Junkers 88A could reach Weymouth in just over 15 minutes with its deadly load of bombs, and much damage was caused throughout the area. The vulnerability of the Portland railway soon became apparent, the first air raid on the railway taking place on Sunday 11th August, 1940 when Goering unleashed the full might of the Luftwaffe against Britain. High above the coast the Battle of Britain began as the small but gallant Royal Air Force valiantly held back large numbers of German bombers who had Weymouth and Portland as their objective. Further up the Channel a similar battle was going on over Portsmouth. It was a key part of Hitler's plan to immobilise the ports of the south coast as a prelude to an invasion.

On Portland the wail of the air raid siren was heard at 10.20 am and at 10.25 am Portland signal box received a direct hit, killing the signalman on duty, William John Small. Small was actually signalman at Rodwell, but owing to the shortage

Portland station looking towards Weymouth following the air raid damage of 11th August, 1940. In the foreground bomb craters and damage to the end of the up platform. In the background the original signal box of 1877 still stands! To the right of the line of wagons had stood 'Portland Signal Box' until completely obliterated in the raid.   *National Railway Museum*

The remains of Portland signal box following a direct hit by a bomb on Sunday 11th August, 1940.   *National Railway Museum*

Bomb damage near the junction of the Easton line and the Dockyard entrance *(visible in the background)* looking towards Portland station. Just inside the Dockyard boundary fence can be seen Andrew Barclay No. 1570. (The full details of this locomotive and the Dockyard railway system are covered in Volume One.) Although the Dockyard sidings had been restored to use, the Easton line in the foreground had to wait until more important damage had been attended to. The photograph was taken on 23rd August, 1940. *National Raillway Museum*

The temporary lever frame and hut installed following the bombing of the signal box at Portland, with, from left to right, Arnold Doel, Bernard Lee, signalmen, G.H. Jenvey station master. Behind is the temporary hut erected to house the instruments and telephones. *Author's Collection*

of staff he was working an overtime turn at Portland. The raid also caused a vast amount of other damage at Portland and Weymouth, 463 houses and two breweries being affected. Following the bombing of the signal box at Portland trains were suspended for several days and then a revised service was put into operation. The passenger service to Easton was withdrawn temporarily owing to closure of the line near the Dockyard, a section of track being destroyed by bomb damage which not only made a crater but also a small landslide.

Changes in staff were now taking place, Mr L.N. Hanger, who had been clerk at Easton for 16 years was promoted to senior clerk in the goods office at Portland to replace Mr G.H. Jenvey who had been appointed station master at Easton - a vacancy caused through the removal of Mr A.J. Pike to Badminton. Shortly after this Ernest James Neate Carter retired as station master at Portland. He had been due to retire in September 1939, but due to the war had agreed to stay on. Mr Carter had been at Portland since November 1927, arriving there from Bewdley (on the Severn Valley Line) where he had been station master for 13 years. He started his career in September 1894 as a clerk at Gloucester, and in 1928 was decorated by King Amanullah of Afghanistan for his part in the railway arrangements during the King's visit to Portland. Mr Carter's place was taken by Mr Jenvey who now also had control of Easton, Portland and Rodwell stations.

The Portland branch remained a vital supply link in the war effort, and being so close to military establishments it was very vulnerable to enemy attack. Apart from invasion, the landing of parachutists and saboteurs were considered a serious threat, and soon pill boxes, tank traps, and other reinforcements appeared along the branch including a 40 mm Bofers gun on the Marsh embankment and two Orlekon guns at Ferrybridge to protect both the railway and Whitehead's torpedo factory. Home Guard units from Whitehead's also patrolled the Wyke Regis section of the line and guarded the Fleet viaduct. Other guns were placed in position near the railway to protect both it and other places of importance, and more 6 in. guns were brought by rail and unloaded at Sheepcroft Yard to bolster coastal defences.

Owing to a combination of air raid damage and its low potential as a passenger carrying line, the Easton section was closed to passenger traffic from 11th November, 1940, although the service was restored during the Summer months from 1941 to 1944. This put additional strain on an already over-crowded bus service, and combined road and rail season tickets had to be issued and charged on a proportional basis.

Unusual events for 1941 commenced on 31st January with the discovery of the mutilated body of a 60-year-old Portland man on the line between Wyke Halt and Rylands Lane bridge. He had been struck in the dark by the 6.49 am Portland-Weymouth train. The year also brought more air raids to the Weymouth and Portland area and at 9.45 pm on Tuesday 15th April a high explosive bomb demolished the main building of Rodwell station, killing the only member of the staff on duty, Mr Arthur Percy Long, aged 55 years. There were 10 heavy air-raids during May; during one on Saturday 3rd at 10.30 pm four high-explosive bombs were dropped close to the railway south of Ferrybridge causing sufficient damage to put the railway out of action until the early hours of Monday. Repair work was hampered that Sunday when the track was further damaged during another air raid, and later that evening bombs fell on Weymouth goods yard causing severe damage to coaches and wagons including the Portland branch stock. Several buildings in the yard were also damaged, but Weymouth Junction signal box, although somewhat battered, survived.

Traffic over the branch was delayed on Wednesday 7th May when an unexploded bomb (which had fallen the previous night, in the cutting between Rodwell station and Buxton Road Bridge) had to be removed. Damage had also occurred further along the line near Southlands Estate. Part of the line which ran past Whitehead's torpedo factory was damaged during a raid shortly before midnight on Sunday 11th May, when 13 high-explosive bombs were dropped. Twelve of the bombs exploded, but the 13th failed to detonate. It had fallen just inside the north-east side of the factory, about 10 yards from the railway. The removal of this bomb, plus repairs to the track together with the damage that had occurred between Buxton Road and Sandsfoot Castle Halt, caused the railway to be closed until the following Tuesday morning. On 31st May a bomb fell on a siding at Easton, this causing some problems although the running line was not damaged.

Having had the line blocked by enemy action three times during the year, the slight delay caused to traffic by the derailment of the branch engine at Weymouth Junction during August was only a minor mishap. During August passenger traffic to Easton was restored, a landslip overlooking the Dockyard and a rock fall at East Weares caused by bombing having been cleared. At the end of September Portland's replacement signal box came into operation, and to end the year a small landslip occurred on the embankment near Sandsfoot Castle Halt on 22nd November.

The damage caused at Rodwell on 15th April resulted in trains calling at the station only during the hours of daylight until 1945. Although there were several air raids on Weymouth and Portland during 1942 the railway escaped damage except for one incident on 2nd July, when an unexploded bomb lodged in the side of the cutting just south of Rodwell station, causing delays to trains until it was removed. There were also delays at Wyke Regis following a raid on 11th July, when slight damage was done to the line.

Passenger traffic during 1942 was heavy, and in October there were 12 passenger trains daily each way between Weymouth and Portland, the Easton section being closed for the winter period. Seven trains ran on Sundays, although the first departure from Weymouth was not until 1.05 pm, returning at 1.38 pm.

Ironically, it was not the war but nature that caused the greatest problem at Portland station. On Sunday 13th December the weather took a turn for the worse, a severe south-west gale pounding high seas against Chesil Beach. As high tide was reached, winds were estimated to be gusting at 80 mph causing the water to pour over into Victoria Square to a depth of 6 ft. By noon 150 houses in the Chesil area had been damaged and the railway was cut off. The water could not escape, as a concrete apron had been erected over the oil pipe line from the Dockyard to the oil tanks, and this acted as a dam. The gas works was also put out of action, and the railway was not finally cleared until Wednesday 23rd. During this time a shuttle service was provided between Melcombe Regis and Wyke Halt.

On Thursday 5th April, 1943 Colonel Sir Robert Williams died at the age of 94 at his home 'Bridehead', near Dorchester. He had been the Chairman of the Easton and Church Hope Company, and its Joint Receiver following its financial problems in 1901. Colonel Sir Robert had been Conservative MP for West Dorset since 1895 - a position he held for 27 years. Amongst his many business interests was a directorship of the LSWR and its successor, the Southern Railway, and he was also Chairman of the Axminster & Lyme Regis Light Railway which had opened in 1903. He also served on the Board of William Deacons Bank, as well as actively serving his Country, State, and Church. He was laid to rest in the churchyard at Littlebredy, near Dorchester, on Monday 19th April, 1943.

Further tragedy took place during the year with two deaths on the line. On 17th April Leonard Priest (whose brother had been a conductor on the GWR buses) was struck by a train from Easton, whilst employed by Messrs Monk who were carrying out work close to the line above the Dockyard. On Sunday 3rd October, CPO Sonley RN was fatally injured late at night on the track near the platform ramp of Melcombe Regis station. Towards the end of the year the tide of war turned, and after being on the defensive for so long Britain now took the offensive. The Americans had become actively involved, and the build-up for the invasion of Europe was about to take place. It was not realised at that time, but Weymouth and Portland were to be two of the main departure points for the invasion when the time was right. Late in 1943 work started on the building of a single lane concrete road at 170 miles 51 chains, on the south side of the line, which ran from a point on the Weymouth side of Wyke Regis Halt to a point south of Ferrybridge. As previously mentioned, the bridge itself was fitted with timber decking to allow road vehicles to use it in the event of the adjacent road bridge being put out of action. This facility was ready for use on 30th May, 1944.

On 20th January, 1944 Mr Leonard Mortimer, Chairman of the Weymouth and Portland Company, died, Lord Bradbury being elected to take his place. By mid-March the branch was open 24 hours a day; the build up for D-Day had begun. A large area between the Portland Road and the Chesil Beach had been levelled to form an assembly area for the Americans, and a level crossing over the railway provided at the Weymouth end of the oil tanks to give access to loading ramps constructed on The Mere in Portland Harbour.

By May the passenger service had increased to 13 trains each way daily with an extra on Friday and Saturday, the latter departing from Melcombe Regis at 9.55 pm and running non stop to Portland. The return working at 10.13 pm was also non-stop. The daily 10.35 pm from Melcombe Regis and return were also non-stop, but the last outward train, the 11.25 pm, stopped at Sandsfoot Castle and Wyke Regis Halts, and the return at 11.50 pm at all stations except Rodwell.

As the build-up of forces transported by both road and rail gained momentum, the harbour became the focal point for embarkation on D-Day, 6th June, 1944. Exactly how much of the invasion traffic the railway carried we shall never know, but 418,585 American troops and 144,093 vehicles were embarked from Portland for the Normandy Beaches.

The preparations for D-Day had caused much extra work on the branch. On top of the extra rail traffic, there was the disruption and difficulties caused by

Rodwell station photographed on 28th July, 1945, looking towards Weymouth, a concrete hut on the down platform replaces the station building destroyed during the war.

J.H. Lucking Collection

No. 233 stands at Easton with a former LSWR 3-coach non-corridor set during 1947. The signal box and other equipment supplied by Evans O'Donnell of Chippenham is clearly visible.

Author's Collection

engineering such as the temporary roadway at Fleet viaduct which required lookout men and speed restrictions during its construction, and other works took place across the beach section, American Forces operated smoke generators to hide the activities taking place within the harbour. The Mere crossing was also up-graded, and had to be attended by flagmen, whilst many of the vehicles involved in the invasion were assembled at that point to reach the landing hards and load onto the tank landing craft.

On 16th July engine No. 221 became derailed at Weymouth Junction causing a slight delay to branch traffic. After D-Day the traffic started to flow in reverse, a transit camp for prisoners-of-war being set up on the Royal Naval sports ground alongside Portland station. From there they were taken to Devizes by special trains.

Every station has its own particular war story, but perhaps one of the most unusual belonged to Rodwell where the breeding of rabbits became big business. Shortly before war was declared it became apparent that fresh meat was going to be in short supply, so signalman Fred Fowler and leading porter George Barter decided to breed rabbits. To get the best results they obtained a Belgian Hare and crossed it with a Flemish Giant in order to obtain large animals. George Barter left Rodwell in 1940, but the 100-strong rabbit farm still flourished in an enclosure behind the signal box. Although the box was damaged during the bombing of the station, the rabbits survived to provide a valuable meat supply to the local butcher. 'Dig for victory' was the slogan of the time, and to further the cause the famous flower beds at Rodwell were dug up and transformed into vegetable patches.

Lady guards were employed during the war years and worked on many of the branch trains. This gave the line some very close family ties. George Penny was signalman at Weymouth Junction, his son Alex was a relief signalman covering boxes on the branch, whilst his daughter Phillis was employed as a guard and was married to fireman Leslie Miller, whose brother Eddie was also fireman on the branch. Another lady guard, Lilly Summers, married fireman Norman Allan. They worked the first train to Easton on D-Day together, and saw the great armada on its way across the Channel.

The lifting of certain blackout restrictions late in 1944 allowed trains to call at Rodwell station again during the hours of darkness. From 1st January, 1945 passenger services were restarted on the Easton section with three trains each way daily; Portland-Easton at 7.35 am, 1.33 pm and 4.52 pm, and Easton-Portland at 8.15 am, 1.53 pm and 5.17 pm, these services being extensions of Weymouth trains; shortly after this the 6.55 pm from Weymouth was also extended to Easton. This was a clear signal that a return to normality was within sight. The end of the war took a great deal of the pressure off the branch, although it was still very busy and was to remain so for several years.

Vandalism is nothing new, although in those days it was often described as 'drunken high spirits'. In December 1945 a Portland-based sailor was fined £6 for stealing six window blinds from a coach. The Portland station master told the Court that damage on the 9.55 pm and 10.40 pm trains to Portland was a nightly occurrence. In the following February four Wyke Regis boys of 10 and 11 years of age turned a facing point lock cover plate on edge at Whitehead's Siding, resulting in its destruction and damage to the engine of a Weymouth-bound train, a relief engine having to be obtained to complete the journey. Needless to say, the Weymouth Juvenile Court took a very serious view of the matter.

Maintenance and repair work still needed to be carried out, and in July 1946 part of the platform at Westham Halt was rebuilt with a stone face, and new gates were installed at the crossing in the November. The platform at Wyke Regis Halt was likewise reconstructed that September, and in January 1947 the gates protecting the temporary wartime road entrances at Wyke were removed.

Although the war was over the railways still remained under Government control, and remained so until the Transport Act of July 1947 nationalised them, together with various other transport undertakings, under the British Transport Commission. From 1st January, 1948 the Great Western and Southern railways ceased to exist, becoming British Railways Western Region and Southern Region respectively. In 1921 the Weymouth & Portland Company had been omitted from the Railway Grouping Act as the leasing companies were constituted into two of the groups. Now it really was the end for this private company, and as it approached a Board meeting held on Thursday 7th August, 1947 announced that the general account held £1,873 5s. 2d., but as the Transport Act of 1947 had received the Royal Assent the previous day the Board were precluded from applying the dividend. The Secretary was instructed to approach the Ministry of Transport to obtain the consent of the Minister under section 18 of the Act, for declaration of a dividend at the rate of £4 9s. 0d., less tax as prescribed in the Act. A year later, in August 1948, the last meeting of the Weymouth & Portland Company was held in London.

A commercial postcard view of Portland taken from Ferrybridge just after the end of World War II. To the extreme right the gates protect the entrance to the wartime road along the railway. *William Dean Collection*

Chapter Eleven

The Final Years

The sea - always an enemy of the Portland line - again caused the disruption to services on Wednesday 26th October, 1949. It had come over Chesil Beach the previous evening, and the crew of the last train to Weymouth had reported a 'bump'. The track was awash so it was decided to send a light engine and some permanent way staff out to investigate. Pannier tank No. 3765, with driver Tom Woods in charge, duly set out from Weymouth and just before the Mere crossing at the Weymouth end of the oil tanks) their journey was brought to an abrupt end when the engine plunged down a hole torn out of the trackbed by the sea. Although it was not severely damaged, it took several days to recover the engine, fill the hole, and relay the track.

The incident also brought to light a serious case of failing to apply the basic rules of signalling which resulted in the downgrading of several persons concerned. It had become the practice for a certain Portland signalman who resided in Weymouth to travel home on the last train. He was, of course in contravention of the regulations which required him to remain on duty until 'Train out of Section' was received from Weymouth Junction, which he should have acknowledged. Furthermore the token was left out of the machine overnight, the first train being 'talked by' the relevant signal at Weymouth Junction. Needless to say, the area signalling inspector had a field day! The irony was that the principal participant was one of the old school who could be described as 'a company's man', and a regular church-goer, for whom the great day of judgement came earlier than expected.

In April 1950 the Bath & Portland Stone Company obtained the contract to supply stone for the United Nations Building in New York. The first consignment was sent by rail to Avonmouth Docks for shipment the following month, 1,750 cubic feet of slabs and blocks being sent from Portland on 11th May for shipment from the Royal Victoria Docks, London, but unfortunately it was delayed *en route* and missed the sailing of the ship on the 14th.

On 6th March, 1951 driver George Budd arrived at Portland with the 8.45 pm train from Weymouth hauled by locomotive No. 30229, and reported that he thought that the engine had struck something near Ferrybridge. Returning at 9.25 pm the crew stopped the train to investigate, and after a short while discovered the body of a sailor. It later transpired at the inquest that he had been walking the line to Portland, this being considerably shorter than walking the main roads. Over the years many sailors had done the same thing, some paying the cost of trespass with their lives, but Robert George Smart will go down in history as the last to do so. At the subsequent inquest a railway police inspector stated that since 1947 he had conducted 27 prosecutions for trespassing on the Portland Railway!

The afternoon Southern goods came to a sudden halt on Thursday 24th May, 1951. Upon approaching Rodwell it entered the up loop, where it was expected to stop, but the weight of the wagon loads of stone pushed the engine on. As the

The scene at the Mere crossing following the wash out of the track after the floods of 26th October, 1949, '57XX' pannier tank No. 3765 awaits recovery and the return of her dignity.

Author's Collection

Above: 'O2' class No. 30229, fitted with a Drummond boiler, heads towards Weymouth across Chesil Beach on 14th July, 1951. The stock consists of one of the former Isle of Sheppey Artic Sets. The luggage van was required as there was limited space in these unpopular sets!

R.H. Tunstall

Right: An 'O2' with former GWR coaching stock departs from Sandsfoot Castle Halt for Portland during 1950. In the background can be seen the footbridge linking the Halt with Southlands estate. *J. Smith*

points had not been set for the line to Weymouth the '02' carried on along the spur siding and into Rodwell tunnel, finally demolishing the buffer stops and becoming derailed at the Weymouth end of the tunnel.

The Portland branch had for many years been vulnerable to competition from buses, the only two stations on the Island being at Victoria Square, at the bottom of the hill, and at 'Tophill' near the centre at Easton. From Weston and Southwell, the other main centres of population, there was over a mile to walk. At Weymouth one either alighted at Westham Halt, ideal for the Grammar School but quite a walk into town, or at Melcombe Regis which involved a longer walk into the town centre. The buses operated from the town centre and served the centres of population and business premises *en route*. The fears expressed by the railway companies just after the turn of the century concerning competition from proposed tramways were now to manifest themselves in the form of an efficient bus service which the railways had no means of matching.

By early 1951 a situation had developed whereby the buses to Portland were heavily patronised at the expense of the railway. Wyke Regis was served by both, but the Halt was not in a convenient position. For people living in the Fortuneswell district of Portland, travelling home by rail involved a long uphill walk from the station, whereas travelling by bus they could be carried almost to their doors. At that time buses were running every 10 minutes between the King's Statue, Weymouth, and Portland Victoria Square, and every 20 minutes to Tophill. There was an understandable preference on the part of a majority of travellers to go by bus on this very frequent service, even though there was little difference in the fares. In fact, at 8*d.* the cheap day return between Weymouth and Portland was 2*d.* less on the railway! Easton to Weymouth was 1*s.* 5*d.* return by both forms of transport. Many of the regular passengers on the train were children going to Weymouth Grammar School, mothers with prams, and service personnel who were going beyond Weymouth on their train journey. At that time there were 18 passenger trains each day, the first leaving Weymouth at 6.18 am, the last returning from Portland at midnight.

Many people associate rail closures with the Beeching Plan of the 1960s, but a considerable number of branch lines were closed during the early and mid-1950s. As early as September 1950 the closure of the Portland branch to passenger traffic was being considered, and in March 1951 the rumours gained some substance when a letter to the Town Clerk of Weymouth Borough Council from the district traffic superintendent of British Railways brought the matter into the open:

> Having regard to the general financial position of the railways, attention is being given to the withdrawal of unremunerative services and in this connection investigations into the working of the Melcombe Regis-Portland-Easton train service have led to consideration being given to its withdrawal. Alternative facilities for passengers already exist in the Southern National Omnibus Services covering the same ground as the branch line. There will be no interference with the freight train services.

Councillor Tudor Griffith argued that the Council must take a broad view. He said that the idea of nationalisation was to close branch lines which did not pay. and he had seen trains on the Weymouth-Portland line carrying only two

'02' class No. 30177 arrives with the 4.05 pm Melcombe Regis to Portland on 1st March, 1952.
S.C. Nash

The scene at Melcombe Regis on Saturday 1st March, 1952, as the local population gather to take a final ride on railway to Easton. The children standing on the platform are now over 50 years of age!   *Author's Collection*

people. He moved that the council should make no protest. Councillor C. Price pointed out that women would be unable to take perambulators on buses if the train service was discontinued. The railway should be asked to experiment in reducing fares. A deputation from both Weymouth and Portland Councils appeared before the Transport Users' Consultative Committee early in November, but by the end of the month it was announced that the Committee were of the opinion that the proposals of the Railway Executive were reasonable, having regard to the alternative facilities which were already available or could be provided.

Although by 1951 the station staff employed on the branch numbered just under 30, a considerable reduction on the 46 employed 29 years earlier, British Railways stated that in 1950 they had lost £14,000 on the passenger services but had made a profit on the freight trains. Despite an appeal by both Councils the closure was to go ahead, the *Dorset Daily Echo* for 12th January, 1952 carrying the headline, 'Last Portland Trains on March 3rd'.

As the day of closure drew near many local people took an opportunity to travel over the line for the last time; during the last six days of operation 2,884 people travelled from Melcombe Regis. On Saturday 1st March, 858 tickets were sold at Melcombe Regis, and on that day the usual two-coach sets were replaced by main line stock. The 2.35 pm Melcombe Regis to Easton consisted of six coaches double-headed by two '02' class tank engines, Nos. 30179 and 30197, and the train was packed to capacity. It was not only local people who travelled this day, many had come great distances to pay their last respects to what was arguably one of the most scenic lines in the Country. Owing to the crowds travelling, the 4.30 pm from Melcombe Regis did not depart until 4.55, and consisted of four well-filled coaches hauled by No. 30179. As there was no Sunday service to Easton, Saturday was the last day over that section. The final regular passenger train from Portland was just before midnight on Sunday 2nd March. There was no ceremony and no delegation of Portlanders (official or otherwise) to see the last train depart. The sole occupants of the train were about half a dozen passengers singing 'Now is the Hour' and a goose wearing a vivid American necktie! Driver George Drake opened the regulator and locomotive No. 30177 steamed into history. Just recently repainted in British Railways' lined black livery, she had been polished to perfection and deserved the honour.

The passengers had gone and the Halts and stations were deserted, but the goods traffic was still heavy. Within less than a year a passenger train was seen on the branch. On the afternoon of Wednesday 28th January, 1953 an eight-coach special train travelled to Portland conveying 230 Naval airmen from Ford, Sussex. Upon arrival at Portland station they marched to the Dockyard where they joined the aircraft carrier HMS *Eagle* to commence exercises. Later in the year a special ran from Portland conveyed stone workers on an outing to London.

No doubt these activities encouraged Weymouth Borough Council to request in February 1954 that a deputation be received by the Transport Users' Consultative Committee to discuss the possibility of reopening the branch to passenger traffic. At that time workmen were removing the huts from the halts and other items from the line, and by the end of April Portland station was being demolished.

Nos. 30179 and 30197 await to depart from Easton with a six-coach train during the afternoon of Saturday 1st March, 1952, the last day of passenger operation on the Easton section.   *G. White*

Nos. 30179 and 30197 ready to depart from Easton during the afternoon of Saturday 1st March, 1952. To the left stands station master Jenvey.   *Author's Collection*

Mr G.H. Jenvey retired from the position of station master at Portland in December 1954. Fifty years earlier he had commenced his career at Eastleigh, moving on to Romsey where he had helped unload the wreaths for the funeral of Florence Nightingale. Further moves to Andover, Oakley, Sherborne, Fordingbridge and Templecombe eventually brought him to Portland in 1914. He then saw war service in France with the Royal Engineers before returning to Portland to complete his career. He was awarded the BEM in October 1944 for meritorious service in connection with the railway, and was one of the six station masters chosen nationwide to march in the victory parade at the end of the war. Although Portland was now only a goods branch it remained busy enough to warrant a station master, and Mr Michael Pitman from Weymouth was appointed to succeed Mr Jenvey.

July 1955 saw several special passenger trains over the branch to convey Naval personnel going on leave. On Sunday 8th July, 1956 an enthusiast special worked over the line to Easton hauled by pannier tank No. 4624 with a three-coach non-corridor set of LSWR vintage. This set was only used for the branch part of the journey, the main train running to Weymouth Quay. The train had arrived at Weymouth behind 'T9' class 4-4-0 No. 30287 and was worked between Weymouth Junction and the Quay by pannier tank No. 1370. The return journey to London was via Westbury, Savernake and Andover with '43XX' class 2-6-0 No. 6372 as the motive power.

During this time the station at Melcombe Regis had not been without activity. At various times when traffic was heavy several arriving main line trains used it owing to a platform shortage at Weymouth, and from the summer of 1955 until October 1956 the approach road to Melcombe Regis was used to park Southern National buses whilst their war-damaged garage was rebuilt. Around that time the plans to rebuild Weymouth station were resurrected, and it was the intention to use Melcombe Regis as a relief platform while the work was in progress. In anticipation of this the buildings were repainted and the gas lighting reinstated late in 1956.

Bridge renewals formed an important item in 1957. On 14th April a concrete bridge was put into place at Rylands Lane, between Sandsfoot Castle and Wyke Regis Halt, the salt air having caused the failure of the previous steel structure. In July, Park Road bridge at Easton was also replaced by a concrete structure. On the other hand the clock was turned back by the visit of a former LSWR 'M7' class 0-4-4T No. 30107 with a two-coach push-pull unit to the branch on Saturday 7th June, 1958. The Railway Enthusiasts Club of Farnborough had hired the special to tour from Poole, visiting the Hamworthy Goods branch, Portland, and the Bridport branch, the fare for the whole trip being 26s.

On Wednesday 29th April, 1959 Her Majesty The Queen visited HMS *Eagle*. Arriving at Weymouth station in the Royal Train, she travelled by road to Weymouth Harbour, thence by launch out to the aircraft carrier at anchor in Weymouth Bay. Accompanied by Prince Charles, she went for a short trip to sea before returning to Portland Dockyard. After servicing at Weymouth the Royal Train was taken empty to Portland, travelling between Portland station and the Dockyard entrance with an engine at both ends. At the Dockyard gate the leading engine was uncoupled and went ahead onto the Easton line whilst the rear

Pannier tank No. 4624 at Easton station with RCTS 'Wessex Wyvern' railtour on 8th July, 1956, by which date the engine shed and signal box had been reduced to a pile of rubble.

Lens of Sutton

'M7' class No. 30107 stands amongst the remains of Portland station,whilst hauling the Railway Enthusiasts Special on 7th June, 1957.   *C.L. Caddy*

The Royal Train heads past Sandsfoot Castle Halt returning from Portland on 29th April, 1959, headed by '57XX' class pannier tanks Nos. 3737 and 4624.   *The late J.D. Blackburn*

The remains of Sandsfoot Castle Halt in 1960, looking towards Weymouth.   *G.A. Pryer*

locomotive pushed the train inside the gate. The leading engine then came onto the front of the train. The train consisted of power brake No. 31209, dining saloon No. 77, saloon No. 806, sleeping saloon No. 495, saloon No. 2901, dining saloon No. 499, saloon No. 799, saloon No. 2900, and first brake No. 5155. The leading engine was pannier tank No. 3737 with driver A.G. Drake and fireman G. Brewer, and the train engine was No. 4689 with driver J. Barnes and fireman E. Murphy.

At 3.00 pm the train departed, climbing the stiff gradient out of the Dockyard. It was to be the last Royal Train to travel on the branch, and the last passenger train to leave the Dockyard. At Weymouth Junction 'West Country' class locomotives Nos. 34048 and 34046 took the train forward to Southampton.

A little drama was added to the otherwise routine life of the branch on Thursday 5th May, 1960, when fire broke out in a wagon on a train from Portland to Weymouth. As it passed Sandsfoot Castle Halt the driver, John Bonney, noticed smoke pouring from the tarpaulin covering the fifth wagon from the engine. He promptly stopped the train, and with his fireman, Henry Petty, uncoupled the wagon and isolated it from the rest of the train. Fireman Petty attempted to put the fire out with buckets of water from the engine. Upon arrival of the fire brigade the train was recoupled and drawn forward under Buxton Road bridge where it was properly extinguished, but as a safeguard firemen with a pump rode in the wagon to Weymouth goods yard.

On Tuesday 5th July, when returning to Weymouth in the evening with Channel Islands traffic, a '57XX' pannier tank ran by the Littlefield Crossing up home signal and was derailed on the catch points at the down end of Westham Halt. Being single line it caused a little difficulty! The Weymouth breakdown vans were propelled from Weymouth Junction by a '41XX' class tank, but in order to clear the train from the engine the guard's van had to be man-handled back up the steep rising gradient, followed by each individual wagon in turn, before work on jacking the engine back on the line could commence. It gave the local inhabitants a summer evening's entertainment to watch the Weymouth breakdown gang push a goods train uphill and rerail the engine.

On Sunday 14th August, 1960 the RCTS ran 'The Greyhound Railtour' from Waterloo to Weymouth, via Yeovil Junction, returning via West Moors and Salisbury. The Waterloo-Salisbury sections were handled by former SECR 'L' class 4-4-0 No. 31768, and from Salisbury to Weymouth and return by former LSWR 'T9' class 4-4-0 No. 30718. For the trip over the Portland branch pannier tank No. 3737 and three coaches was provided, into which over 240 enthusiasts crowded for the trip to Easton. On the return journey the train was halted at the Mere Crossing and searched by the police who were looking for two escaped Borstal boys, but it was eventually allowed to continue to Melcombe Regis, its compliment of passengers undiminished!

Although over the years the various plans to establish a cross-Channel port in Portland Harbour had failed, a small amount of Channel Islands traffic had used the Portland branch. During the late 1950s, owing to the amount of goods sent to Weymouth Quay for the Channel Islands and the lack of space to handle this traffic, a vast amount of it was taken to Portland, where it was checked and sorted in the goods shed before being reloaded and returned to Weymouth for shipping. Customs Regulations required a cargo manifest of all goods loaded aboard a ship, and this documentation was carried out at Portland so that when the goods were brought back to Weymouth and taken down the Tramway they could be loaded straight into the ship - thus saving time and valuable space on the quay. To cover this work an additional journey was made to Portland at around tea time, returning in the early evening.

Also at this time owing to a shortage of space at Weymouth empty passenger stock used for 'Saturday only' specials was stored at Portland during the week, being worked to and from Weymouth as required. Sidings at both Portland and Castletown yard were also used to store 'Palvans'. A large fleet of these had been constructed to handle the Channel Islands tomato trade, but were found to be unsuitable as the loaded pallets would not fit through the sliding doors! Portland was one of the many places that gave them a home until they were converted for other purposes.

Congestion at Weymouth Quay, or flooding under the Town Bridge, on occasions caused boat trains to depart from Melcombe Regis station, passengers being transferred from the quay by bus. Saturday 15th July, 1961 was one such occasion when the 'Channel Islands Boat Express' departed from Melcombe Regis hauled appropriately by No. 30852 *Sir Walter Raleigh*!

In August 1962 Portland lost its station master, Michael Pitman being transferred to the relief staff. The branch then became the responsibility of the Weymouth station master, and goods traffic business was dealt with by Mr W.H. Davis, the Weymouth goods agent. By this time traffic on the branch was decreasing. During 1962 11,445 tons of goods were dispatched from Portland, out of which total 9,800 tons was stone, whilst of the 8,721 tons received at Portland. 6,177 was coal and coke. Very little traffic was now handled at Whitehead's private siding.

The forecourt of Melcombe Regis station was chosen as the site of the new provedore Store to supply the railway cross-Channel boats at Weymouth. Work started on the construction of the pre-cast concrete building in the February of 1963, and it was completed for the Summer season.

On Sunday 25th August another enthusiasts' special travelled over the branch, this time organised by the Southern Counties Touring Society. It was hauled from Waterloo by former LNER 'A3' class No. 60112 *St Simon*, and the train first visited the Hamworthy goods branch, arriving at Weymouth Junction at 1.45 pm. The Pacific locomotive was exchanged at that point for two '57XX' pannier tanks - No. 4689 (driver M. Kent) hauling, and No. 7782 (driver C. Bown) pushing - for the journey to Easton. A stop was made at the remains of Portland station before the seven-coach train climbed to Easton on what must have been the wettest, most gloomy, day of the Summer. This train included a buffet car, and it is the only known occasion that one of these vehicles passed over the line. Upon return to Weymouth both pannier tanks were coupled to the front for the journey to Maiden Newton, and a visit to the Bridport branch.

During the evening of Thursday 26th September, 1963 a section of track approximately 50 feet in length was left suspended about 200 yards south of Sandsfoot Castle Halt when a slip occurred on the landward side of the embankment. It took from Friday morning until late on the Sunday to fill the gap, wagons loaded with spoil being propelled to the site from Weymouth

On Sunday 25th August, 1963 mist and fine rain shroud the Island as pannier tank No. 7780 stands at Easton with the special train organised by the Southern Counties Touring Society. This was probably the only time a train containing a restaurant car ever reached Easton. The tin hut in the foreground contains the lever frame which replaced the signal box.   *Author*

BR class '4 MT' 2-6-0 No. 76057 with ballast train at the scene of the subsidence near Sandsfoot Castle Halt, 29th September, 1963.   *C.L. Caddy*

Junction by pannier tanks and Ivatt Type '2', 2-6-2 tanks. On the Saturday a British Railways Standard class '4' 2-6-0, No. 76057, was used to propel the wagons, but on the first trip she stalled on the Marsh embankment and had to retreat to Weymouth Junction for a second attempt! After this it was considered more prudent to take fewer wagons per journey. Freight train services were restarted on the Monday and following a period of settling, more spoil was added on Sunday 13th October, by the end of which 180 wagon loads had been consumed. This slip had occurred very close to a similar one in January 1907.

Slipping to a standstill on the Marsh embankment was not a one-off affair either, it had doubtless happened quite a few times during the life of the branch! However, the last time this occurred was on 10th November, 1964, when engine 41305, heading towards Portland with the morning goods, came to grief on the wet rails at the approach to Rodwell tunnel. The fireman shovelled small grit onto the crown of the rails, but it still failed to provide adequate adhesion. Eventually help was requested from Weymouth, and No. 41374 was sent to assist the stranded train.

Time was now running out for the Portland branch. During November 1964 a staff consultation memorandum was circulated concerning the proposed closure of the line. It revealed that during 1963, 2,917 loaded wagons (excluding Channel Islands traffic) had been forwarded and received at Portland, stone being the principal outward traffic, whilst coal and Admiralty consignments were the main traffic received. The annual earnings of the branch amounted to £6,300, but operating expenses totalled £12,500. Added to this, major expenditure on the line amounting to £92,450 was deemed necessary within the next five years, including the renewal of Fleet viaduct at a cost of over £50,000.

Alternative facilities were available at Weymouth goods yard, and in any case the Beeching Plan then being implemented favoured large goods depots delivering by road to the surrounding area. Early in 1965 a freight concentration scheme for Weymouth was announced, the area taken in extending to Bridport in the West, Wool in the East and Maiden Newton to the North. Tied in with this was a plan for the complete closure of the Portland branch, scheduled for 1st February. However this was delayed, as work had not then started on the alterations required at Weymouth goods depot to accommodate the extra traffic, and 1st March became the revised target date. On Friday 28th February, 1965 the Chief Civil Engineer's inspection train was propelled over the branch to Easton. It was now only a question of time, and a small local society, the South & West Railway Society of Weymouth, quickly arranged three special trains to make the final passenger journeys over the line. These journeys took place on Saturday 27th March, leaving Melcombe Regis at 11.30 am, 2.15 pm and 4.15 pm. The train was made up of six main line coaches with an Ivatt class '2' tank at each end. At the Portland end was No. 41324 with driver Leslie Moore and fireman Dennis Turner, and at the Weymouth end was No. 41284 with driver David Pointer and fireman Tony Bush, the guard being Frederick Hooper. A total of 1,056 specially printed souvenir tickets were sold for the occasion, and a small brochure giving a brief history of the line was on sale at 2s. This now was the end, and the trains were packed as both local people and enthusiasts from far afield made their final journeys over the line.

Class '2', 2-6-2 tank No. 41298 climbs the Marsh Embankment towards Rodwell tunnel with a goods for Portland on 18th February, 1965. To the right of the guard's van can be seen the remains of the anti-aircraft gun position built on the bank during World War II.   *Author*

The final passenger train waits to leave Easton station on Saturday 27th March, 1965 behind class '2' 2-6-2 tank No. 41284.   *C.L. Caddy*

Class '2' 2-6-2 tank No. 41324 heads into Red Bridge cutting heading one of the last passenger trains to Easton on 27th March, 1965. *M.R. Thresh*

Driver Leslie Moor and fireman Dennis Turner await departure from Melcombe Regis with the last passenger train to Portland on Saturday 27th March, 1965. *Dorset Evening Echo*

The final freight from Portland, class '2MT' 2-6-2 tank No. 41294 hauls the last wagons out of Whitehead's siding to make up the final freight train to use the branch. In the left foreground is part of the concrete road constructed alongside the Halt during World War II.
J.H. Lucking

However, there were still several goods trains yet to run, as the final facilities at Weymouth were still not quite ready. The line eventually closed on and from Monday 5th April, but as there were still wagons to be cleared the last run of all did not take place until Friday 9th April, when Ivatt Type '2' No. 41284 went to Portland to clear the remaining wagons. Just after 9.30 am the train, consisting of a solitary open wagon (for loading tools and other equipment) and a brake van, headed for Easton. At Portland yard the wagon was detached to be loaded with gear belonging to the Permanent Way Department, then following the traditional cup of tea in the signal box, the engine and brake van proceeded on the climb towards Easton. There was no reason to stop at Easton station, so the last train proceeded to the end of the line at Sheepcroft Yard, where two empty coal wagons awaited collection. Having shunted to marshall up the train, the final departure drifted back to Easton where the engine took on water at the water tank for the last time. It was then back through the cutting and around the East side of the Island for the final journey down one of the most scenic lines in Britain, past the Dockyard and over the remains of the 'Merchants' Railway' - one of the earliest railways in the Country. At Portland some shunting was carried out to attach the wagon left on the outward journey and two empty coal trucks. As the train moved off towards Weymouth its departure was marked by exploding detonators.

The return trip stopped at each ganger's hut to collect tools, and also made a final shunt at Whitehead's siding to pick up four wagons - two of which were empty, whilst the other two provided the Portland branch's last revenue.

Following a stop at Rodwell to telephone Littlefield Crossing, the final train of nine trucks and guard's van ran back to Weymouth yard, thus bringing to a close the life of what was once the busiest branch line in Dorset just six months short of its centenary.

After this final goods train the line lay disused, although the viaduct over the Backwater was used to stable stock. By late 1965 a long line of condemned wagons stood thereon awaiting their fate. Demolition of the buildings at Melcombe Regis station took place during the February, making way for the construction of workshops to repair and maintain railway delivery lorries - a project that had been in the pipeline since the closure of the branch to passenger traffic in 1952.

On 10th January, 1966 the last of the condemned wagons were removed, and on 26th February a stop block was erected at the Weymouth goods yard end of the line, marking the complete closure of the branch. By August 1966 contractors had started to remove track from the top end of the branch and Easton station, and early in 1967 the entire Easton line was lifted from Sheepcroft to the junction at the Dockyard - together with all the sidings in Portland yard - leaving just a single line between Weymouth and Portland Dockyard. To enable work to start on a new roundabout in Victoria Square the original Portland station was demolished in February 1969. In the same month it was reported that the Ministry of Transport was withholding consent for the disposal of the railway between the Dockyard and Weymouth pending possible development on the Island, but the following year it was decided that the branch was no longer required by the Admiralty, and by the end of the year T.W. Ward of Sheffield had removed all the track from Portland to Westham Halt. Ferrybridge was removed by Messrs Arthur Aldridge of Bloxwich at the end of 1971.

On 31st May, 1972 the land at the Easton end of the line was purchased by Portland Urban District Council, and in that December the station site and footbridge were cleared to make way for the building of Ladymead Hall, a residential home for the elderly. The section between Ferrybridge and Melcombe Regis station was purchased by the newly-formed Weymouth & Portland Borough Council on 19th November, 1974, and the same month work started on demolishing the viaduct over the Backwater. The first two spans at the Melcombe Regis end were lifted out by crane, one side-frame at a time, but the removal of the other sections was more difficult. Some were dropped in the lake and dragged ashore.

By mid-March 1975 the Council told the contractors to be off the site by Easter so as not to interfere with the holiday trade on the boating lake and the car park. Consequently for the summer of 1975 the south span remained in position, whilst boating types had to navigate around a submerged section marked off with buoys.

The trackbed between Westham Halt and Ferrybridge was converted into a footpath which has proved to be a very popular walk with many people. During 1980 plans for the construction of a miniature railway along this section were put forward. Had it been built, this line would have attempted to provide an alternative form of public transport along the former railway route, similar to the miniature trams running on the trackbed of the former Seaton branch in Devon. The Weymouth plan was soon withdrawn, and a revised one later rejected by the Borough Council.

In the meantime the Dorset County Council proposed that this section of the route be used for a relief road, but in March 1978 Weymouth & Portland Borough Council's Policy and Resources Committee recommended that a stand be taken against this plan - a position they have maintained ever since. A scheme for a bypass along the west side of Radipole Lake linking Weymouth with the north end of Radipole had been planned and discussed since the 1930s. Eventually work commenced in 1985 with the construction of a roundabout at the end of Kings Street which took in part of the former Melcombe Regis station approach road. During its construction timber sections of the original Backwater viaduct were uncovered from the infilled ground.

In 1986 a five-span concrete road bridge was constructed across the Backwater just a few feet north of the site of the former railway viaduct. Linked into the first part of the bypass from Radipole, it opened to traffic during April 1987. To enable this work to take place the embankment and archway between the west end of the former viaduct and Littlefield crossing was removed, and the few feet of former trackbed from the bypass to Abbotsbury Road is the only part of the former railway converted into a road. On 27th January, 1987 demolition started on Newstead Road arch under the Marsh embankment, this being part of a road widening scheme for the redevelopment of the football ground site.

The local Council policy of keeping the route as a footpath has enabled many features of the former branch to survive. At the time of writing the platform of Melcombe Regis station still stands overlooking a car park, the 'provedore' store and road motor repair workshop having been demolished at the time of the roundabout construction. The platform of Westham Halt still stands, and one can still walk through the 58 yds-long Rodwell tunnel. The platforms at Rodwell are intact, although trees have encroached from the sides of the cutting. A few rotten pieces of timber are all that remain of Sandsfoot Castle Halt, but the concrete face of Wyke Regis Halt and the wartime concrete road survive. The footbridge crossing the line at this point has long gone. The course of the trackbed can still be traced across the causeway, but from Mere Crossing (at the end of the oil tanks) to the gunnery range on the Easton section the land has reverted to the Ministry of Defence and has been redeveloped for the use of the Navy. Only the bridge carrying the Castletown Road over the line remains.

When viewed from Grove Point, the faint outline of the Easton branch trackbed can be seen climbing around the cliffs. Further along quarry working has taken place, Yeolands Bridge demolished, and part of the trackbed forms an internal road between quarries. The road bridges at the Mermaid Inn, Park Road, and Reforne still carry traffic over the earthworks, but otherwise little remains.

But the railway is not alone in being a thing of the past; other once familiar landmarks such as the the power station, gas works and football ground have all disappeared in the name of 'progress'! During 1996 the former Whitehead's factory closed and has since been demolished whilst on Portland the unthinkable has happened with the closure of the Naval Base and other defence establishments. Like the Weymouth & Portland Railway, they have served their purpose in an ever-changing world.

Appendix One

Chronology

1845	Wilts, Somerset & Weymouth Rly Act of Parliament passed.
1845	Southampton & Dorchester Rly Act of Parliament passed.
1st June, 1847	Southampton & Dorchester Rly opened.
20th January, 1857	Wilts, Somerset & Weymouth Railway opened.
1865	First signal box at Weymouth, Portland Junction.
5th July, 1867	Easton & Church Hope Rly Act of Parliament passed.
1st June, 1870	Rodwell station opened.
1870	Ticket platform taken out of use at Portland Junction.
January 1872	Severe earth slip to line near Sandsfoot Castle.
December 1872	Easton & Church Hope Rly only six furlongs laid.
12th March, 1873	Fatal accident involving horse-drawn wagons at Rodwell.
18th June, 1874	Last broad gauge train, conversion of gauge.
1876	Portland Junction signal box replaced,
1876	First signal box at Weymouth station.
13th September, 1876	Passenger train collision at Portland station.
July 1877	First signal box opened at Portland.
23rd December, 1877	Passenger train collision at Portland station.
August 1884	Easton & Church Hope Rly extension of time Act.
3rd August, 1885	Train smashed through gates at Littlefield Crossing.
August 1887	Easton & Church Hope Rly revised Act of Parliament.
1890	Littlefield Crossing ground frame opened.
1891	Whitehead's Factory built at Wyke Regis, siding added.
6th November, 1892	Train derailed on Backwater viaduct.
December 1892	Signal box opened at Rodwell.
January 1894	Rodwell station platform extended.
July 1894	Easton & Church Hope Rly extension of time Act.
August 1896	Easton & Church Hope Rly extension of time Act.
1896	Improvements to accommodation at Portland station.
August 1898	Easton & Church Hope Rly extension of time Act.
January 1899	Easton & Church Hope Rly joined to Admiralty line.
July 1899	New signal box replaced Portland Junction.
1899	GWR/LSWR sell share of Admiralty line to Admiralty.
1st October, 1900	Easton & Church Hope Rly open to goods traffic.
May 1901	Easton & Church Hope Rly into Receivership.
August 1901	Easton & Church Hope Rly additional Act of Parliament.
1902	Temporary signal box at Portland for Easton trains.
May 1902	Temporary station built at Portland for Easton trains.
1st September, 1902	Easton & Church Hope Rly opened to passenger traffic.
1902	Replacement viaduct constructed across the Fleet.
28th November, 1903	Severe fire at Easton station.
September 1904	Completion of rebuilding of Easton station.
5th February, 1905	Easton engine shed into use.
March 1905	Trials carried out over branch with steam railmotor.
7th May, 1905	New Portland station and new signal boxes into use.
1st July, 1905	GWR commence bus service between Radipole and Wyke Regis.
September 1907	Construction started on new Backwater viaduct at Weymouth.
27th November, 1907	Severe landslip on Easton & Church Hope Rly.

July 1908	Rodwell station improvement works taking place.
7th February, 1909	New Backwater viaduct open to traffic.
April 1909	Melcombe Regis station opened for traffic.
1st July, 1909	Halts at Westham and Wyke Regis open to traffic.
September 1909	LSWR railmotors commenced work on branch.
September 1909	GWR bus service withdrawn.
22nd July, 1912	GWR bus service reinstated.
March 1916	Portland Siding signal box opened.
11th June, 1919	Portland Siding signal box closed.
1921	Both Weymouth & Portland and Easton & Church Hope Rlys omitted from Railway Act.
3rd April, 1928	Royal special for King of Afghanistan.
1st August, 1932	Sandsfoot Castle Halt opened to traffic.
31st December, 1933	Last GWR bus run, service to Southern National
12th November, 1936	Royal Train trapped in flood water at Portland station.
January 1939	Southern Railway engine shed at Weymouth closed.
11th June, 1940	Portland signal box destroyed by bombing.
15th April, 1941	Rodwell station building destroyed by bomb.
29th September, 1941	Replacement Portland signal box opened
July 1946	New platform constructed at Westham Halt.
September 1946	New platform constructed at Wyke Regis Halt.
October 1946	Littlefield Crossing gates replaced, new layout.
1st January, 1948	British Railways created.
April 1950	Weymouth area under control of Southern Region.
1st March, 1952	Last regular passenger trains Portland-Easton section.
2nd March, 1952	Last day of passenger service Weymouth-Portland.
1st March, 1954	Rodwell signal box closed.
24th April, 1955	Easton signal box closed.
April 1957	Weymouth Station and Weymouth Junction signal boxes closed.
April 1957	New Weymouth signal box opened.
29th April, 1959	Royal train ran over branch for last time.
27th March, 1965	Last three passenger trains over branch (Specials).
9th April, 1965	Last goods train clears branch, complete closure.
August 1966	Track removal commenced Easton-Dockyard Junction.
February 1969	Original Portland station demolished.
1970	Track removed Dockyard Junction-Weymouth.
December 1971	Ferrybridge demolished
November 1974	Trackbed between Ferrybridge-Weymouth sold to Council.
November 1974	Demolition of Backwater viaduct commenced.

Saturday 1st March, 1952, '02' class tanks Nos. 30179 and 30197 having just arrived at Melcombe Regis with one of the six-coach trains fully-loaded on the last day of services to Easton.   *G.White*

Appendix Two

Staff

Originally vacancies on the branch were filled in turn by the operating companies, and this arrangement lasted until 1911 when it was decided to appoint all uniformed staff from the Great Western. However, appointments of station masters and clerical staff continued with the old system of alternate nominations.

The situation at Weymouth station was complicated. Although owned by the GWR it was for practical purposes a joint station, both the GWR and LSWR appointed their own station master and staff, this practice ceasing in 1914 when the GWR took over responsibility for the entire working.

The uniform worn by Portland branch staff was also distinctive. Supplied by the Great Western, it was to their style except for having red piping and the woven letters 'W&PR', and these initials were repeated on the brass buttons. Guards uniform had gold piping and lettering. Guards on the branch were based at Melcombe Regis, and were completely separate from the main line men. Transfer porters were also employed at Melcombe Regis to wheel parcels and luggage to and from the main station, a petrol driven 'Lister Auto Truck' being used in later years. The station came under the control of the Weymouth station master.

Many staff worked on the branch over the years, some being content to remain there, other seeking promotion moved away. W.H. Davis, one-time goods clerk at Portland became Weymouth goods agent. Melcombe Regis foreman Mabbett progressed to become chief inspector at Weymouth station, as did Rodwell signalman Fred Fowler. Portland chief booking clerk since 1931, L. Head became chief at Weymouth after closure of the branch, whilst booking clerk Alfred White-Bower moved to a similar post at Dorchester South.

Service to the public outside of work was also given by branch staff. As previously mentioned H.G. Day, the Rodwell station master, had served on Weymouth Town Council for a short while. Portland station master George Jenvey served on Portland Urban District Council as an independent from 1940, becoming Chairman of the Council in 1954. He also served 30 years as treasurer of Portland British Legion, and was Vice President of both Portland Football and Swimming Clubs.

Before his move to Badminton, Easton station master A.J. Pike had also served on Portland Council for five years from 1934 as Chairman of the Electricity Committee, and a prominent member of the local St John Ambulance Brigade. Before leaving the Island Mr Pike donated most of his fossil collection to Portland Museum. Upon retirement from railway service he returned to Portland, enjoying his retirement on the Island he had such an interest in.

Weymouth-based Southern driver on the branch, Mr A.C. Billett, served both the Dorset County Council and Weymouth Town Council. Born on Portland in 1882 he commenced his railway career at Dorchester LSWR engine shed in 1898. Moving to the London area in 1900, he returned as a driver on the Portland branch in 1922, a position he held until retirement in 1947. Having a lifelong interest in local government and trade unionism, he was first elected to Weymouth Town Council in 1932 and become Mayor during 1954, that being the year when both Weymouth and Portland had railwaymen as their Number One citizens.

Station masters at Portland	From	To
Edwin T. Targett	October 1865	1870
George Francis Parsons	1871	May 1885
George Jeans	1885	February 1892
James Laver	1892	June 1914
Charles Bartlett	June 1914	November 1927
Ernest J. Neate Carter	November 1927	August 1940
George Henry Jenvey	August 1940	1954
Michael Pitman	1954	1963

Station masters at Rodwell		
John Palmer	May 1870	October 1905
Edwin John Smart	October 1905	November 1907
Thomas C. Loosemore	December 1907	May 1915
Henry George Day	May 1915	November 1925

Station masters at Easton		
Frank Tett	1902	1904
Percival H. Brayley	1905	1915
Sidney Dunn	1915	August 1926
Alfred James Pike	August 1926	1939
George Henry Jenvey	1939	August 1940

LSWR station masters at Weymouth		
William Mears	1858	
J. Arnold	by 1865	
E.T. Target	1871	October 1904
John Alex Richardson	October 1904	October 1912

GWR/BR station masters at Weymouth		
Thomas Smith	by 1859	
Samuel Martin	by 1865	
William Reynolds	by 1867	
John Pearson Collett	by 1880	November 1888
Jonathan Hogg	November 1888	August 1892
Elliot Gardner	August 1892	1896
Frederick George Davis	1896	June 1909
H.G. Cotterell	July 1909	February 1915
A.J. Humphrey	December 1915	1926
W. Best	1926	September 1930
J.N. Roberts	1931	1932
T.F.E. Jakeman	1932	1945
Frederick Joacham Colls	1946	1952
W. Flew	1952	1962
J. Vatcher	1962	1965
W.R. Westhead	1965	1979
J. Smith	1979	1985